DATE DUE

MAR - 4 2004		
GAYLORD		PRINTED IN U.S.A.

STUDIES OF WAR
Nuclear and Conventional

STUDIES OF WAR
Nuclear and Conventional

P. M. S. BLACKETT

HILL AND WANG • NEW YORK

FIRST AMERICAN EDITION SEPTEMBER 1962

Manufactured in the United States of America

PREFACE

In Part I of this book are reproduced all my substantial articles and lectures on general aspects of nuclear war, arranged in order of their first publication. The first of these is nearly contemporary with my first book *Military and Political Consequences of Atomic Energy*, published in 1948 in the United Kingdom and in 1949 in the U.S.A. under the title *Fear War and the Bomb*. This short article gives an account of some of the main theses of the book. The various articles from the period 1954 to 1957 cover essentially most of the same field as my second book *Atomic Weapons and East West Relations*, published in 1956.

All the articles are reproduced as first published except for some minor verbal clarifications and the deletion of some paragraphs which are essentially repetitive. However, a number of repetitions are deliberately left in since this repeated occurrence in my writings is evidence for the continued importance I attached to the points under discussion. It will be noticed that many of the problems of Western nuclear defence policy, discussed in my first article in 1948, are still with us and are the subject of much of the argument of my latest article in 1962. Though vast technological changes have taken place in the intervening fourteen years, leading to different practical conclusions, I do not find that I have had to change basically my mental attitude and analytic approach to these complex problems.

This attitude arose in great part from the detailed studies of various aspects of the Second World War carried out by the Operational Research Groups at Anti-Aircraft Command, Coastal Command, and at the Admiralty, for which I was successively responsible. In Part II of this book are collected various articles and memoranda from this period dealing with many detailed problems of conventional war-

fare and of the methods for handling them. Clearly
one of the most vital and difficult tasks is the extent
to which one can transfer some of the lessons of pre-
nuclear war into the nuclear age. Much of my later
writings are essentially concerned with this problem. Great
emphasis is also laid repeatedly on the necessity of discussing the problem of nuclear war against a realistic international and political background, which takes into account
the behaviour of real nations. To do this it is often
necessary to consider those internal economic and social
factors which may influence national defence problems—not
the least in importance are inter-service rivalries. Since
nuclear war involves whole nations, even the more purely
military aspects cannot be usefully discussed without taking
into account essentially non-military facts.

If the republication of these articles can help others to
clarify some of those vital but complex problems where
weapon performance, military tactics and strategy, international and social politics all meet, I will be well rewarded.

I am indebted to many journals and institutions for
permission to reproduce these articles, in particular to the
following: *The New Statesman, Encounter, Nature, Brassey's
Annual,* British Association for the Advancement of Science,
The Royal Society, *The Scientific American,* Royal United
Services Institution, Royal Institute of International Affairs,
Allen and Unwin Ltd., *The Listener.*

P. M. S. B.

CONTENTS

Part I

Nuclear and Conventional Warfare

Part 1

Nuclear and Conventional Warfare

One

The Military Consequences of Atomic Energy[1]
1948

However much disagreement there may be as to the history of the first use of atomic bombs or of the subsequent efforts to set up an international system for the control of atomic energy, there can be none as to the fact that the American stockpile of bombs is now playing an important role in present-day power politics. Since the centre of the power-political struggle in the world today is the threat of war between East and West, it is necessary to analyse in some detail the likely military effects of atomic bombs if a third world war breaks out within a few years, with Russia and America as the major contestants. In particular we must examine the popular thesis that such a war could be quickly and cheaply won with the aid of atomic bombs.

But before we enter into what must be a somewhat technical discussion of the effect of atomic bombs on modern warfare, it may be fitting to remind ourselves that the present epoch is not by any means the first in which the belief has been widespread that the invention of a new weapon has completely changed the character of war and rendered most previous arms obsolete. History must have seen this happen a number of times. The early sixteenth century was one of these.

In 1494, Charles VIII of France crossed the Alps and rapidly destroyed, by means of artillery and Swiss infantry, the military organisation of medieval Italy which was based

[1] No. I of the Sir Halley Stewart Lectures, 1948. First published in M. L. Oliphant *et al.*, *The Atomic Age*, London 1949.

on fortified castles and the valour of the armoured knight.[2] When Machiavelli wrote his famous treatise *The Art of War*, he was much concerned to estimate the effect of firearms on warfare and to study realistically how their devastating effects could be minimised. He argued forcibly the incorrectness of the view " that hereafter all wars will be made altogether with artillery." Machiavelli's contemporary, the poet Ariosto, dramatised this threat to the contemporary order in a poem in which his hero Orlando, embodiment of all the knightly virtues, meets an enemy with a firearm. When finally Orlando had triumphed over his opponent he took the offending weapon, sailed out into the ocean, and plunged it into the sea exclaiming:

> " O! curs'd device! base implement of death!
> Fram'd in the black Tartarean realms beneath!
> By Beelzebub's malicious art design'd
> To ruin all the race of human kind . . .
> That ne'er again a knight by thee may dare,
> Or dastard cowards, by thy help in war,
> With vantage base, assault a nobler foe,
> Here lie for ever in th' abyss below! "[3]

It might not be inappropriate to utter again these 400-years-old words on the hoped-for future occasion when the United Nations finally decides to consign the world's store of atomic bombs to the depth of the ocean.

Let us now jump forward in history some 400 years to the invention of aircraft in the early twentieth century. Already in 1912, not many years after the Wright brothers first flew, air experts were writing of the devastating results to be expected of air attacks on cities.

A military expert of high repute, speaking of the havoc that a hostile air fleet might work by an attack upon the Thames valley between Hammersmith and Gravesend, has observed: " This whole 50 miles of concentrated essence of Empire lies at the absolute mercy of an aerial machine, which could plant a dozen incendiary missiles in certain pre-selected spots." It was only the

---

[2] This account of the early history of firearms is taken from an article by Felix Gilbert entitled: " Machiavelli: The Renaissance of the Art of War," which appears in *Makers of Modern Strategy*, Princeton 1944, an invaluable collection of studies of warfare, edited by Edward Mead Earle.
[3] *Orlando Furioso*, IX, 83-4, Eng. trans. by John Hoole.

other day that a famous constructor showed how . . . it would be possible for an enemy to drop a couple of hundred tons of explosive matter upon London. . . . What such an aerial attack as this would mean has been pictured by Lord Montagu of Beaulieu. Suppose London was thus assailed from the air, at the beginning of a war, he says: " What would the results be? Imagine the Stock Exchange, the chief banks, the great railway stations, and our means of communication destroyed." Such a blow at the very heart of the Empire, declares Lord Montagu: " Would be like paralysing the nerves of a strong man with a soporific before he had to fight for his life; the muscular force would remain but the brains would be powerless to direct."[4]

Such anticipations were not, in fact, fulfilled in the First World War. Aircraft played a most important, but almost exclusively a tactical role. Their main use was in reconnaissance and spotting for artillery, together with some light tactical bombing. The intense and costly fighter battles that developed were directed to securing the air supremacy over the battle fronts without which these tactical operations could not be carried out. German airships operated very ineffectively over England in the early years of the war, and later on a few raids were made on London by German bombing aircraft. Britain planned a heavy attack on Berlin towards the end of 1918 but the German Armies were defeated in the field before it could be carried out.

Out of these plans, however, there arose in the Royal Air Force in the early post-war years the conception of the independent use of air power against the cities and communications of the enemy, unrelated to the operation of land armies. Foremost theoretical exponent of this view was the Italian General, Giulio Douhet, whose fundamental theses have been summed up thus: [5]

(1) Aircraft are instruments of offence of incomparable potentialities, against which no effective defence can be foreseen.
(2) Civilian morale will be shattered by bombardment of centres of population.
(3) The primary objectives of aerial attack should not be the military installations, but industries and centres of population remote from the contact of the surface armies.

[4] C. Graham-White and H. Harper, *The Aeroplane in War*, London 1912, cited in *Makers of Modern Strategy*, ed. Earle, p. 487.
[5] *Makers of Modern Strategy*, p. 489.

(4) The role of surface forces should be a defensive one, designed to hold a front and to prevent an enemy advance along the surface and in particular an enemy seizure by surface action of one's own communications, industries, and air force establishments, while the development of one's own aerial offensive is proceeding with its paralysis of the enemy's capacity to maintain an army and the enemy people's will to endure.

Referring to such attacks, Douhet writes: [6]

And if on the second day another ten, twenty or fifty cities were bombed, who could keep all those lost, panic-stricken people from fleeing to the open countryside to escape this terror from the air?

A complete breakdown of the social structure cannot but take place in a country subjected to this kind of merciless pounding from the air. The time would soon come when, to put an end to horror and suffering, the people themselves, driven by the instinct of self-preservation, would rise up and demand an end to the war—this before their army and navy had time to mobilise at all!

Such an effect was to be achieved in a few days by a force of 1,500 bombers, of which only 100 were to be heavy bombers of the type used in the Second World War.

At least as influential was the American General, William Mitchell, who shared with Douhet the belief that civilian morale would break quickly under air attack. "It is unnecessary that these cities be destroyed, in the sense that every house be levelled to the ground. It will be sufficient to have the civilian population driven out so that they cannot carry on their usual vocation. A few gas bombs will do that."

In future the mere threat of bombing a town by an air force will cause it to be evacuated, and all work in factories to be stopped. To gain a lasting victory in war, the hostile nation's power to make war must be destroyed,—this means the factories, the means of communication, the food producers, even the farms, the fuel and oil supplies, and the places where people live and carry on their daily lives. Aircraft operating in the heart of an enemy's country will accomplish this object in an incredibly short space of time. [7]

[6] G. Douhet, *The Command of the Air*, trans. D. Ferrari, New York 1942, pp. 57-8, cited in *Makers of Modern Strategy*, p. 491.

[7] W. Mitchell, *Winged Defense*, New York and London 1925, pp. 126-7, cited in *Makers of Modern Strategy*, p. 498.

One of the chief British supporters of such a strategy was General Groves. His views have been summed up as follows: [8]

Enemy air forces would, in the future, make naval and military movements practically impossible.

Our towns would be quickly destroyed from the air and there would be no defence against that form of attack. All we could do would be in our turn to try and destroy the enemy's towns and people.

So long as our Navy and Army exist, they must be considered as being secondary to the Royal Air Force and be reduced as and when necessary to meet the requirements of the latter.

The story of the attempt of the British, German and American Air Forces to put these theories to the test in the Second World War has been often told—in particular by the writer in a recent book. [9] It will suffice here to remark that the inhabitants of London learnt to carry on the business of a great city, from which a world war was being directed and supported, under a weight of bombardment vastly greater than the followers of Douhet, Mitchell and Groves had thought would bring immediate collapse. In four years 60,000 tons of bombs and rocket weapons fell on England; 40,000 people were killed, but neither production nor civilian morale collapsed.

When the Anglo-American bombing offensive got into its stride, that is from 1943 to 1945, Germany took a still higher punishment from the air. In these two and a half years sixty German cities received 600,000 tons of bombs, but German civilian morale never broke, and war production rose steadily till August 1944, by which time the German Armies had been decisively defeated on two vast land fronts.

The Anglo-American bombing offensive was neither decisive nor cheap. The number of air personnel lost was 160,000—some of the best of the youth of the two countries; the loss in planes was 20,000 bombers and 18,000 fighters.

Those who remembered the senseless slaughter in the mud of Passchendaele in the First World War vowed that never would this country tolerate a repetition. In an endeavour to

---

[8] Sir G. C. Dickens, *Bombing and Strategy*, London 1946.
[9] Blackett, *Military and Political Consequences of Atomic Energy*, London 1948.

avoid one, we came near to staging an aerial Passchendaele in the night skies of Germany, and bolstered up our morale by a new set of self-deceptions. Where General Haig ordered all able-bodied prisoners to be removed from the cages so as to impress the visiting politicians with the desperate straits to which he believed the Allied offensive had reduced the German Army,[10] so did the British High Command delude itself and the public by bad intelligence and misleading propaganda into believing that the bombing offensive had reduced German morale and civilian economy to desperation.

Heavy aerial bombing of cities was also carried out in the war against Japan, but only in the last five months of a struggle that had already lasted forty months. In these first forty months Japan had first captured and then lost an empire —both by combined air-sea-land war not involving the attack on the civilian populations of cities. When the devastating air raids on Japan started in March 1945, they fell on a nation already essentially defeated by conventional methods of warfare. The two atomic bombs used in early August provided a way out for the ruling clique which had long known that defeat was inevitable.

A detailed study of the immediate world press reactions to the dropping of the atomic bombs would be of great historical interest, but does not appear to have yet been made. However, the main lines of the "atomic age," which were ushered in by screaming headlines, stand vividly in one's memory. All other weapons can be relegated to the scrap heap; a small nation with atomic bombs can defeat an unsuspecting great nation in a few days; Russia has been reduced to a second-class power overnight; such were the widespread beliefs of those scared August days. Though time has brought signs of returning sanity, these themes still persist and have slipped from the newspaper headlines into State documents. America, hitherto inviolable between its oceans, might now be destroyed in a few days by atomic bomb attacks; conversely, Russia, hitherto undefeatable by the vastness of its territory, could be defeated in a few weeks.

[10] B. H. Liddell Hart, *Why Don't We Learn from History?*, London 1944, p. 14.

" It is we who hold the overwhelming trump cards. It is our side, not Russia, which holds atomic and post-atomic weapons and could if sufficiently provoked, literally wipe Russia's power and threat to the world's peace from the face of the earth.[11] To those who remember the prophecies of the Douhets of the early 1930's, these prophecies of the neo-Douhets of the late 1940's have a familiar ring.

Leaving aside such extreme estimates of the efficacy of atomic bombs in major wars as unrealistic, the problem remains as to how to estimate as reliably as possible the likely effect of the use of atomic bombs in a third world war between America and Russia. The only reliable method available to use at present is to base our predictions on the actual experiences of the bombing offensives of the Second World War, taking into account the greatly increased destructive power of atomic bombs and making every possible allowance for the various other ways in which a third world war is likely to differ from the second.

Official American figures show that the early types of atomic bombs produced about the same destruction as some 2,000 tons of ordinary bombs evenly spread over the same area. Now some 1,200,000 tons of ordinary bombs were dropped by the Anglo-American Air Forces on Germany in the thirty months from January 1943 to the end of the war. The number of atomic bombs required to do the same damage to buildings would thus be about 600. From this we can deduce at once that many hundreds of atomic bombs would have to be dropped on Russia in order to have the slightest chance of forcing a decision by air attacks alone.

If one compares such a hypothetical future atomic bomb offensive against Russia with the actual normal bombing offensive against Germany, one finds a number of different conditions which must be taken into account.

The first relates to the duration of an attack and is favourable to the atomic bomb. An atomic bomb attack could be delivered in a shorter time than it would take to drop the equivalent weight of ordinary bombs. Consequently it is often held that the total effect on morale and on production

[11] *Observer*, 27 June 1948.

2

might be much greater. This is possibly so if large armies were previously poised to follow up the atomic bomb attack by immediate invasion by land. In this case a high concentration of atomic bombing in time—assuming this to be technically practicable—might be the best method to adopt. If, however, land armies were not immediately available for invasion, then clearly it would be most unwise to use the bombs at once. It would be preferable militarily to plan for a preliminary period of low intensity atomic bombing, designed to disorganise production as much as possible, lasting till the time when land armies were ready to invade, and then only greatly to increase the intensity. It is seen, therefore, that the markedly increased *intensity* of attack possible with atomic bombs is likely only to be of decisive significance in a third world war as a concomitant of invasion of Russia by land forces. If, however, the atomic bomb attack was not offensive in character, that is, if it had not the objective of forcing the defeat of Russia, but was essentially defensive in character, perhaps to attempt to stop an expansive move by Russia, then the time factor would not have such a great significance. For under these circumstances the tempo of the war would be in Russian initiative and so the advantage to the Western Powers of staging an attack, which was highly concentrated in time, would probably be small.

Another factor favourable to atomic bombing compared with the equivalent weight of ordinary bombs is the fewer sorties required and so probably the higher degree of training that can be expected of the operational crews.

The other main differences between our hypothetical third world war and the real second one are on the whole adverse to the atomic bomb. Some of these factors are as follows. Russia is much larger than Germany, European Russia alone being over eight times larger, and the flying distance to most of the important targets is much greater. The population of Russia is over three times as large as that of Germany. The German High Command was compelled to improvise air defence measures, both active and passive, in the midst of a major land war, while now Russia has already had over three years in which to prepare measures against atomic bombing and, unless the Western Powers force the issue, may have many more. The heavy air attacks on Germany did not take place till she was engaged in a desperate land battle on the Eastern front in which she had already lost some 3,000,000 killed, wounded and missing.

The most effective parts of the Anglo-American bombing offensive were only made possible by almost complete command of the air over Germany. It is unlikely that this could be achieved over Russia.

Taking these arguments into account it is clear that a few hundred atomic bombs could not possibly bring quick victory in a hypothetical third world war against Russia. These arguments cannot, of course, prove that many thousands of atomic bombs might not be decisive, for there is no experience available to gauge the reactions of a nation to such a vastly destructive attack.

It is, of course, only to be expected that the American Chiefs of Staff should have prepared in some detail plans for the waging of an atomic bomb war against Russia. It is, however, somewhat surprising that General George C. Kenney, Commander of the American Strategic Air Force, should have described such plans publicly. This appears, however, to have been the case, according to a report in the American periodical *Newsweek* of 17 May 1948, from which the following extracts are taken.

General Kenney assumes that Russia will attack America as soon as she thinks she can win, and that the United States will reply to such an attack primarily by an atomic bomb attack. What would be likely then to happen is described as follows:

Although only the most extreme air-power enthusiasts still argued that planes alone could bring victory, even the Army and Navy long ago agreed that, if the Russians suddenly went berserk and swept into Western Europe, the Air Force would have to bear the brunt of the war for the first months at least.

In those initial months, the United States would have little to fight back with except the Air Force. Against the 208 divisions in the Red Army itself and the 75 additional divisions in Russia's satellite armies, the American, British, and French troops now in Europe could do little more than offer token resistance and run. Slow and ponderous as the Red Army might be, the most optimistic estimate was that it would reach the Channel Ports within two or three months. Theoretically, the Western Powers might be able to stop the Reds at the Pyrenees in Southern France or Northern Spain, and in Turkey if all the breaks went their way. The probability, however, was that within six months at the most the Hammer and Sickle would be flying over Gibraltar and on the shores of the Persian Gulf.

In the Far East the story would be the same. A few days would find all Korea in Russian hands. In three months the Red Army would be standing at the Yellow River.

What the Russians would do then, only the Russians themselves could know. They might decide to by-pass Japan and grab the Aleutians if only for the nuisance value; by landing 5,000 troops on the chain in 1942, Japan managed to keep 120,000 Americans occupied in that part of the world for months. They might decide to invade Alaska, and from it bomb the Pacific coast. They might decide to invade Greenland to strike at the east coast.

In any event American strategy called for securing bases around the perimeter of Russia and then striking back from the air.

The Joint Chiefs of Staff had already decided what these bases would be and, while their decision was necessarily top secret, it could only be assumed that North Africa, Japan, England and Iceland were high on their list.

Once in possession of the Channel ports the Russians would, of course, attempt to knock out England with the German V-2's which they are known to have, and with the improved rockets they are believed to have. In all probability, they would eventually succeed in making England untenable for Air Force operations. Meanwhile the Air Force would be making life extremely unpleasant for them.

This statement is of exceptional interest. Europeans will note that Western Europe is treated as undefendable, or, as it is often expressed, as " expendable." England is expected to become eventually " untenable for Air Force operations," and so presumably also for Englishmen to live in. But before this happens it will be a useful base.

The planes would go out from England in very small groups —perhaps in twos or threes. Flying at more than 35,000 feet, they would seek to slip into Russia unnoticed. Their targets: first Moscow—Moscow above all. Then the other large cities of European Russia—Kiev, Leningrad, Kharkov, Odessa.

General Kenney states that the American heavy bomber group are still equipped with B-29 aircraft, but that the first operational squadrons of the improved types B-36s and B-50s will be ready towards the end of 1948 or the beginning of 1949. No mention is even made of when jet bombers will come into operation, so presumably this is far in the future.

On the other hand, much emphasis is put on the large number of jet fighters in use both by America and Russia. Russian jet fighters are stated to be the equal of any in the world; the Russian Air Force is said to have 14,000 operational planes, with the emphasis on fighters.

Russian radar is extremely bad, and the country's radar defences are spotty. It would be relatively easy for American planes to get across the border undetected. But in view of the excellence of the Russian fighters and fighter pilots they would face hot and heavy going once they were detected.

The likely nature of the development of such a war—after Europe had been expended—is described thus:

The United States has no intention of landing mass armies in Europe and slugging it out with the Red Army—manpower against manpower. Napoleon and Hitler both made that mistake; and Russia, with its huge population to draw on, swallowed them up. American strategists are thinking, rather, in terms of closing the circle of air bases around Russia, making it smaller and smaller, tighter and tighter, until the Russians are throttled. This means getting bases through combined air, sea and ground operations ever closer to Russia's heartland, then using the bases for sustained bombing and guided-missile attacks. The closer the bases are, the more sustained the attacks can be. Meanwhile, the Air Force will also be dropping weapons to occupied peoples behind the Red Army lines and paratroopers to help them attack the Russians from the rear.

It would be technical superiority in the air against Russian superiority in manpower. How long it would take for air-technical superiority to win is anybody's guess.

What is particularly striking about this statement is the emphasis that, even in the period before Russia acquires any atomic bombs, there is no possibility of a cheap and quick victory over Russia. This represents a distinct change from the wild hopes of the atomic Douhets of the last three years. If General Kenney has been correctly reported and if what he is reported to have said does represent roughly the pattern

of contemporary American military thinking, we may conclude that there is very little likelihood of the Western
Powers deliberately forcing the present clash between East
and West to the point of war.

Some further light on American strategic thinking is provided by two articles in *Life* by General Spaatz, Commander
during the war of the United States Strategic Air Force in
Europe and in the Pacific. In the last post he commanded
the air forces which dropped the atomic bombs. In main
outlines these articles resemble that of Kenney but still more
emphasis is placed on the necessity of acquiring suitable
advanced bases.

The first question is: is it possible to reach the vulnerable
industrial system of Russia? The controlling factor now is the
radius of the B-29, which with postwar improvements is more than
2,000 miles. Russia's industrial system has four centers of
gravity: Moscow (chiefly light industry), the Urals and the
Ukraine-Volga (predominantly heavy) and the Caucasus (oil and
metal).

Take a globe and a string scaled to 2,000 miles, pin one end
down at Moscow and swing the free end westward. It will take
in the British Isles and part of Iceland. Swing it south and it
will take in part of North Africa. Now do the same thing from
the Urals, fixing one end of the string on Magnitogorsk and
swinging the other south. The free end in its sweep will take in
Iraq, Iran and Pakistan as far south as Karachi. From the
Ukraine-Volga center the string will pass through Britain, France
and North Africa. From Baku in the Caucasus the sweep will
encompass part of India, Saudi Arabia and part of Europe. There
is additionally in Siberia a fast-growing center of industry, not to
mention the double-track Trans-Siberian railroad. This region
could be reached by B-29 from China and Japan.

General Spaatz evidently reckons the effectiveness of
atomic attacks on Russia higher than General Kenney, for he
is reported to have written: " . . . the attackers do not have
to plod laboriously and bloodily along the Minsk-Smolensk-
Moscow road in order to strike at Russia's vitals. Hence the
war may be concluded within weeks and perhaps days."

Discounting these slight tendencies to revert to atomic
Douhetism, the two Generals effectively agree that while
atomic bombs do not now make a quick preventive war
against Russia possible, they do constitute a deterrent against

Russian expansion. If this conclusion is accepted, many extremely important conclusions follow.

If the American stockpiles of atomic bombs are looked on as the main deterrent to Russian expansion, rather than as a means of forcing her to contract her sphere of influence, then the diplomatic and strategic initiative is in an important sense handed over to Russia. For suppose that no Russian aggression, say by expansion over the Yalta line, does take place in the next few years, and suppose further that this lack of aggression is widely held in the West as due to the threat of atomic bombing, then the West will, in its own view, have saved the world from a third world war at any rate for some years.

The dilemma comes later. For this policy inevitably implies leaving Russia time to make at least some atomic bombs, and when this has happened there are only three possibilities open to the West: to wage preventive war before Russia has acquired a large number of bombs, that is under less favourable military conditions than at present; to initiate a new approach to control of atomic energy on terms much more favourable to Russia; or finally to continue the atomic arms race, with a devastating atomic war with bombs available to both sides as a possible final outcome.

It is this real dilemma that exercises such a hold over many logically-minded people as to lead them to become open advocates of preventive atomic war. The logic is sound, given the premiss that a clash between East and West is inevitable, or that the Soviet system and Capitalism cannot exist side by side for a long time. The only escape from this dilemma is to base policy on the opposite premiss, that is that a clash between East and West is not inevitable. On this view, the building up of defensive armaments by the West remains a reasonable objective, whereas the attempt to build up an offensive armament for preventive war is highly unreasonable, and is as likely as not to lead eventually to the destruction of much that is characteristic of the Western world without achieving its advertised end.

A strictly defensive policy in the West for the immediate future, to be followed as soon as possible by an attempt to negotiate an agreement with Russia while the West still holds a relatively strong bargaining position, would seem the policy most likely to achieve the objective of stopping the advance of Communism. This is not, however, the policy of Mr Churchill, who recently said: [12] "We ought to bring matters to a head and make a final settlement." "The Western nations will be far more likely to reach a lasting settlement without bloodshed, if they formulate their just demands while they have the atomic bomb and before the Russians have it too." The leading article in the London *Observer* has several times advocated a similar view. Having laid down the conditions of peace with Russia, which, following Churchill, include withdrawal to her own borders, abandonment of political subversion and economic sabotage, and acceptance of the full Atomic Energy Commission plan for the control of atomic energy, the *Observer* discusses how this is to be achieved.[13] "The only chance is to build up overwhelming strength to back our just and moderate terms of peace. Faced with overwhelming, instantly available strength, Russia might without going to war, resign herself to the position which today among all the nations of the world, she alone refuses—as a chess player resigns when it is clear that any exchange of pieces would lose him the game." The only possible interpretation of such statements as these is that the authors either have not read, or do not agree with the views of General Kenney, Commander of the United States Strategic Air Force, that atomic bombs do not now at any rate provide the quick and decisive weapon by which such a policy could be successfully achieved. It appears that atomic Douhetism, already waning in influence in some realistic military circles in Washington, still survives in some political circles in London. Military realism is usually a desirable objective for any nation and at any time; it is a condition of survival for the countries of Western Europe which have already twice this century been the battlefield of the world wars and are now threatened with playing the role again in a still more devastating third one.

[12] At the Conservative Party Conference, 9 Oct. 1948.
[13] *Observer*, 21 Nov. 1948.

Two

America's Atomic Dilemma[1]
1954

A great debate is in progress in the United States on the implication of the new situation which has arisen from the belief that the Soviet stockpile of atomic bombs is already of a substantial size and that operational Soviet hydrogen bombs may not be far off. It is not easy to keep track of the form the debate is taking; but the appearance in this country of a book[2] by Gordon Dean, lately Chairman of the Atomic Energy Commission, provides an opportunity to try to piece together some account of what the debate is really about. Mr Dean has given an extremely readable account of most of the important aspects of the United States atomic energy programme. He was Chairman of the Atomic Energy Commission from February 1950 to June 1953, when he resigned. Many details are given of the U.S. atomic energy programme, and its vastness is well conveyed. Incidentally, he gives figures which show that this industry for making atomic weapons consumes more electricity than the whole of Great Britain.

To a European, much the most important parts of the book, to my mind, are those relating to the military role of atomic bombs and of their influence on tactics, strategy and international affairs. For these are matters which decisively affect the defence requirements and so the domestic and foreign policies of individual European nations. What Mr Dean says about these military questions has special interest because he is not a military man. The fact that he is an academic lawyer by profession makes it probable that what he writes reflects the atmosphere of Washington military

---

[1] *The New Statesman and Nation*, 13 Feb. 1954.
[2] *Report on the Atom*, New York 1953, London 1954.

circles at the time when he was Chairman of the Atomic Energy Commission rather than his own personal views. Indeed, any doubt that Mr Dean's duties as Chairman lay solely in the civilian field and that he was not in close touch with military and diplomatic affairs is set aside by the emphasis he gives to his membership of a special committee of the National Security Council, together with the Secretary of State and the Secretary of Defense.

His most important conclusions seem to be somewhat as follows. The United States stockpile of bombs is already sufficiently large to make it possible that an all-out attack on the U.S.S.R. would destroy all her main cities and a large part of her industry. A broad hint is given that the American stockpile now amounts at least to a few thousand atomic bombs: perhaps about 5,000 would be a fair guess. This is certainly large enough to inflict a major blow against the U.S.S.R., assuming an appreciable fraction of the bombs reach their target. For it will be remembered that rather more than 1,000 atomic bombs of the Hiroshima type would have been required to inflict on Germany and the occupied territories the same material damage as was done by the 2·7 million tons of chemical bombs actually dropped on them.

Mr Dean reminds us that quite a different conclusion was popular at one time. Referring to the summer of 1945, Mr Dean writes: "The Japanese surrender, then, found the United States in the uniquely favourable position of being the sole possessor of a weapon that was almost universally credited with a capacity to destroy cities on a ratio of one bomb per city, and to end wars on a ratio of two bombs per war." Seldom can an arithmetical misapprehension have had such disastrous consequences!

Mr Dean's next conclusion relates to the effects of Soviet atomic progress.

An enormously important new factor was introduced into this world situation in 1949, when the first atomic explosion took place in the Soviet Union. This may not have been too important in itself, for it is a long way from a first test bomb to a significant stockpile. But it was of the utmost importance so far as the future was concerned, for it meant that one day the Russians would undoubtedly have enough bombs to deliver an atomic attack on the U.S. and the other countries of the free world, if they chose to do so. Thus, since 1949, we have been watching the value of the main ingredient in our national defence arsenal gradually diminish as the Russians build towards a stockpile of atomic bombs which they will feel, no matter how crude their design, will some day reach sufficient proportions *to cancel out the atom as an instrument of warfare.* If such an impasse occurs, the United States would appear to be left in a rather unenviable position. The most useful product of our technological competence would appear to be lost to us, except as a deterrent to the use of A-bombs by the enemy, and the Russians would appear to be free to take full advantage, in world, military and diplomatic affairs, of their vast superiority in man-power and their highly favourable strategic position dominating the Eurasian land mass.

No specific figure is given for the probable Soviet stockpile today, but by implication it can hardly be believed to be less than a hundred or so. One other writer puts it at 300, and yet another at 3 per cent. of that of America. Mr Dean in his chapter " Behind the Iron Curtain " emphasises that it is most unwise to assume that the Soviet rate of technological development is appreciably behind that of the United States, and emphasises that it is now four years since the first Soviet trial bomb was exploded. A few hundred Soviet bombs might well be adequate to inflict serious damage to the United States, assuming that a reasonable fraction " got home."

As a remedy for this impasse, which Mr Dean often refers to as existing now rather than as something to come about in the future, great emphasis is laid on the successful develop-ment in the United States of atomic tactical weapons. It is evident that some very brilliant scientific work has enabled atomic bombs to be made which are certainly much cheaper and smaller than the earlier models, and possibly also, though Mr Dean is not explicit on this point, smaller in explosive power. Their smaller size allows them to be delivered as atomic shells from a 280 mm. cannon or by small and fast aircraft. One report suggests that the cost of an atomic bomb has been brought down to about £100,000, roughly that of a heavy tank.

The further argument is best left to Mr Dean.

What effect does the introduction of this new factor have on the impasse we appear to be drifting towards in the strategic use of atomic bombs? Briefly, it could mean that, while we might be unwilling to use our bombs strategically against Russia for fear of retaliation, and Russia might be unwilling to use hers against us for the same reason, we would nevertheless be in a position to use our tactical weapons in the field, thus so increasing the fire-power of our forces that Russian man-power superiority would be virtually cancelled out. Under this line of reasoning, our atomic stockpile once again becomes a deterrent, not only to an atomic attack against us, but also to an act of major aggression against us or our allies with conventional arms.

The last sentence seems to me very important, for it implies clearly that an act of aggression with conventional arms against the U.S. or her allies would not necessarily be countered by a strategic atomic attack on the U.S.S.R., for fear, of course, of provoking a similar attack on the U.S. This is the essence of the impasse. In regard to long-range strategic bombing of centres of civilian population, a hundred or so Soviet bombs have cancelled out a few thousand U.S. bombs. The argument continues:

In answer to this, one might of course say: " But if we used atomic weapons in any form at all—even tactically in the field— shouldn't we expect the Russians to retaliate with a strategic attack against the United States interior, or against our allies, assuming they were in a position to do so?" I can only reply that, if I were a Russian, I would certainly think twice before I did so. Our retaliation against the Russian heart-land in such an event would be terrifying.

One might also ask: " But isn't it possible for the Russians to make these tactical weapons and use them against our troops in the field?" Of course, it is possible. But the important thing to remember here is that, even in that event, we will have succeeded in getting the competition back on a basis where the premium is no longer on man-power, where we are at our weakest, but rather on technological competence and production capacity, where we are at our best.

The gist of all this is that U.S. military opinion, if we are right in assuming that this is what Mr Dean is reflecting, considers that the huge United States stockpile and the fleet of long-range strategic bombers to deliver it are still the essential deterrent to a Soviet strategic atomic attack on America. However, the opinion is clearly gaining ground that the great American atomic retaliatory power can no longer be considered as an effective deterrent against aggression even on a massive scale by conventional arms. This would have to be met by conventional arms supported by a large number of atomic bombs and shells for tactical use.

In view of this argument, it is not altogether surprising that Mr Dean does not lay any very clear stress on the role of the H-bomb. In fact, he says, " There has been some controversy among experts about the real significance of the H-bomb." No doubt there has! Of its explosive power, he only tells us that it can be made " many times more powerful than the most powerful A-bomb." (President Eisenhower has told us that ordinary atomic bombs 25 times stronger than the early types have been made.) Mr Dean then shows that if an H-bomb were a thousand times as powerful as the first A-bomb, its radius of destruction would be only ten times as big. This fact he calls " a small ray of hope," and adds: " I believe there is a law of diminishing returns working on the side of humanity."

Looking further into the future, Mr Dean envisages a situation in which the United States no longer attempts to keep ahead of the U.S.S.R.

It does not follow, however, that we need match them twenty to one, or ten to one, or even one to one, in atomic bombs for ever—certainly not if deterrence is our primary objective, as indeed it should be. Simply staying " ahead " of the Russians, or even " far ahead " of them, is not the goal. The weapons goal for the United States should be a sizeable stockpile, no matter what the Russian stockpile may be. Deterrence is accomplished when a sizeable number is reached, for " sizeable " means that point where an enemy, calculating the risk of retaliation, says to himself, " No matter how many atomic bombs I may be able to deliver on the cities and on the industrial and military targets of the United States and its allies, I simply cannot afford to take the punishment which retaliation by the United States would bring."

The essence, then, of the impasse described by Mr Dean is that Soviet atomic bombs, believed to amount to more than perhaps 3 per cent. of those of the United States, have already partially neutralised the diplomatic and military value of the American stockpile. An important factor in this situation is the relatively low level of the active and passive defence measures of America and her allies. Mr Dean does not give many details of these. They were presumably outside his brief as Chairman of the Atomic Energy Commission. It is therefore necessary to consult other and possibly less reliable sources. Among the embarrassingly large number of articles in the American press one has to choose by internal evidence of reliability. Of special interest are a series in *Fortune* during 1953 by Charles J. V. Murphy and another series by J. and S. Alsop in *The New York Herald Tribune*. These, together with a number of articles in the *American Bulletin of Atomic Scientists,* allow one to fill in some of the background.

The essential element in the situation is the far greater development of the offensive power of atomic warfare than of the counter-measures against it. This is partly a matter of technology; that is, the technological problem of producing atomic bombs and their carriers has proved easier than the production of an effective active and passive defence system. However true this is, it is evident that a greatly improved active and passive defence system could exist today if enough of the national resources had been devoted to producing it. Recently two major investigations, under the names Project East River and Project Lincoln, have been made of the feasibility and problems of attaining an adequate defence of the United States against strategic bombing attack. Some of the findings of these investigations have been made public. An important conclusion is that the civil defence problem can only be reduced to manageable proportions if the active defence is able to reduce the number of bombers which find their target to a relatively small number. Very great emphasis is placed on the importance of a long warning time in order to take advantage of shelters, etc.

Several commentators implore the President to tell the American public the full danger of their situation and urge him to embark on a huge civil defence programme. Actually, the very small appropriations for civil defence are apparently being cut. Clearly the American public in general take relatively little interest in achieving an adequate civil

defence programme. Anyway, even if such a defence programme as envisaged in these projects were adopted, it would
take many years to complete, and in the intervening period
the civil defencelessness would remain—with all its consequences in the international field. Moreover, it is clearly
understood by Americans that their European allies, so much
more in the danger zone, are even less interested in doing
anything serious about civil defence.

As regards active defence, a wealth of important detail
about the existing state of American air defence and of the
possible improvements have been given in Mr Murphy's
articles in *Fortune.*

Today, in the event of a surprise attack on the continental
U.S., it is calculated that U.S. interceptors and anti-aircraft
artillery could bring down between 15 and 20 per cent. of the
bombers—if the bombers came over in daylight. If they came
at night, the kill ratio would be a fraction of 1 per cent. The
existing continental defense system, though steadily improving,
is a jerry-built affair. Its radar coverage is sketchy and the equipment mostly of World War II design. Some sixty battalions of
World War II anti-aircraft cannon, only part of them radar-
sighted, have been optimistically positioned around major cities.

Mr Murphy suggests that a kill ratio of up to 50 per cent.
may be reached by 1957, but by then the weight of possible
Soviet attack will have greatly increased.

Given enough time and money, a defense system capable of a
90 per cent. kill ratio could probably be built. According to
Major General Frederic H. Smith, Jr., a deputy commander of
the Air Defense Command and one of the Air Force's most
thoughtful officers, the curve of the dollar cost *versus* kill capability rises fairly steadily. " The amount of air defense you get,
assuming you choose the right weapons systems at the start, is in
direct proportion to what you are prepared to pay for it."
But how much is the U.S. prepared to pay? How much
punishment, as an alternative to a colossal continental defense
investment, is the nation prepared to risk? The most elaborate
defense schemes might cost as much as $100 billion; there are
modest ones available—at $50 billion, $40 billion, $30 billion.
Would the U.S. be willing to *add* the cost of a superdefense
system to present military outlays, or would it want to buy the
high kill ratio at the expense of other defense programmes,
including the retaliatory power that is represented by the pro-

grams of the Strategic Air Force and the Atomic Energy Commission?

This is a crude argument between Maginot-minded exponents of the defensive and the fire-eating bombardiers who want to stake everything on a frightful counter-blow at Russia, and never mind what is happening to the American civilians.

A closely similar argument has been developed by the Alsop brothers in *The New York Herald Tribune*. They remark: " We have no air defence today. In two years' time we shall be nakedly exposed to air-atomic destruction by the Kremlin." They emphasise that American concentration on atomic striking power has led to air defence being consistently given low priority. We are told by the Alsops that President Eisenhower and the National Security Council in the spring of 1953 seriously considered recommending an expenditure of well over 20 billion dollars to develop an effective active defence system. This sum would have supplemented the normal defence budget. ˊ

Mr Murphy gives great prominence to various trends of thought, some sponsored especially by a group of scientists led by Dr Robert Oppenheimer, as to what ought to be done now that the United States is in this " very tough fix." One such trend is that the United States should first develop a more effective air defence as a " disincentive " to a possible Soviet atomic attack, and when this has been done, that the problem of reaching some kind of accommodation with the U.S.S.R. in relation to atomic bombs should be studied. Murphy expresses Oppenheimer's reputed view as follows:

Implicit in his reasoning is the idea that, if the U.S. Government should show itself ready to modify " the very great rigidity " of its existing atomic strategy, particularly as regards the stockpiling of super-atomic weapons and the building of long-range bombing fleets, the Soviet Union *might* respond by intimating that it was prepared to modify its own forces of the same type. That is, while it might not be possible, at this stage of world conflict, to secure an absolute abolition of atomic armaments, nevertheless there *might* arise a situation in which each of the main adversaries would agree to reduce its stockpile and its long-range striking force to a point where neither need thereafter fear a knockout blow launched in surprise by the other. Such a settlement would be based on a mutual understanding that atomic stockpiles would stop short of catastrophic quantities.

On the whole, Mr Dean, Mr Murphy, the Alsop brothers and the group of scientists around Oppenheimer seem to agree on many aspects of the impasse.

In the light of this situation, how are we to estimate the significance of the recent announcement by the President and by Mr Dulles of a change of fundamental strategy? Mr Dulles said on 12 January: " But before military planning could be changed, the President and his advisers, as represented by the National Security Council, had to take some basic policy decisions. This has now been done. The basic decision was to depend primarily upon a great capacity to retaliate, instantly, by means and at places of our choosing." This policy is reflected in the new Budget figures, which show a drastic cut in the Army vote but a small increase in those for the Air Force and Atomic Energy. A marked strengthening of the active and passive defence systems of America seems to have been abandoned in favour of strengthening the offensive power.

There is a marked contrast between the apprehensive caution of Mr Dean and the confidence of Mr Dulles in the virtues of the big atomic threat. What has happened since last summer when, according to the evidence provided by Mr Dean's book, the atmosphere of Washington was different? Has the President decided that, after all, the defencelessness of the American population, and still more that of their allies, is of no significance? Has some new technical advance altered the basic situation? Probably the explanation of the change is quite simple. The views that Mr Dean absorbed and conveyed to the world in his book must have been in the main those of the last months of the Truman regime, when General Bradley, a noted exponent of the balanced-force view of war, was Chief of Staff. When the Eisenhower Government came into effective action, it was pledged by electoral promises to toughness abroad and economy at home. The second pledge led to the rejection of any great strengthening of active or passive defence, and the first to the rejection of any move towards limiting the use of atomic weapons against civilian populations.

3

In the light of the two pledges, what else could they have done? The lack of any other politically possible action open to the Administration does not, however, imply that the action that was taken has much direct relevance either to the problem of avoiding a major war or of winning it if it came. Still less has it any relation at all to the ending of minor wars such as that in Indo-China. Is it possible that the much-advertised New Look of American strategy has something to do with winning the November elections? Evidently the great debate is not over, and the fundamental dilemma of American atomic policy persists and, moreover, is likely to get more acute with time. Assuming the U.S.S.R. does not make a major aggression and that America does not precipitate a preventive war, nor spend huge sums on a defence system, a day will come when the Soviet stockpile will be large enough—to quote Mr Dean again—" to cancel out the atom as an instrument of war." Perhaps this day has not arrived. Yet, for all their different views, there is one proposition which probably Mr Dulles and Mr Dean may agree: whatever the role of the atom as an instrument of future war, it has already been cancelled out as an instrument of present diplomacy.

Three

British Policy and the H-Bomb[1]
1954

At 4.30 p.m. on 31 May 1916, on the bridge of H.M.S. *Lion,* Vice-Admiral Beatty turned to his Flag Captain and said: "Chatfield! There seems to be something wrong with our damned ships today." He was commenting on the fact that two of his six battle-cruisers had blown up during the first forty minutes of the battle with five German battle-cruisers off Jutland. Half an hour later, the Fifth Battle Squadron passed the spot where the *Queen Mary* had disappeared. That patch of oily water, where a dozen survivors of the crew of 1,200 were clinging to pieces of wreckage, as I saw it through the periscope of the front turret of the *Barham,* gave me a strong awareness of the danger of assuming superiority over the enemy in military technique; and this youthful memory came vividly into my mind when I found that the defence planning of this country, as set out in the recent White Paper,[2] explicitly assumes an important degree of technical superiority over the U.S.S.R.

In the first decade of this century, belief in the technical superiority of the British Navy was almost an article of national faith. This faith was shaken at Jutland, with the loss of three British battle-cruisers by explosions caused by enemy gun-fire. No major German ship blew up—in fact, none was sunk during the action, though one was so badly damaged that it was later sunk by the crew. What was wrong with the British battle-cruisers? The answer is simple. They had not been designed structurally to survive hits by enemy projectiles of the same type as they themselves were designed to fire. Their defensive strength had been unduly sacrificed

[1] *The New Statesman and Nation,* 14, 21 and 28 Aug. 1954.
[2] Defence White Paper 1954, *Statement on Defence.*

to offensive power. Luckily, this defect was confined to the battle-cruisers: the battleships did not suffer from it to the same extent. The Battle of Jutland was won strategically by the weight of numbers. Ship for ship, the Germans were at least equally good at gunnery and markedly better in the amount of punishment they could take.

Looking back over the history of military weapons and techniques during the first two World Wars, one can watch the prize of technical military superiority going at one time in one field to the Allies, and at another time in another field to Germany. In the 1914-18 War, Britain invented the tank and made decisive use of it in the field. But in the general techniques and tactics of land warfare, Germany held the decisive superiority throughout, as judged by the relative casualties, which were in the ratio of 1·6 British killed to 1·0 Germans. In the 1939-45 War, Britain led in radar from the start, and with our American allies held the lead to the end. Our fighters had just sufficient edge over their German opposite numbers to win the Battle of Britain in 1940. But there was little to spare, then or later, in quality. In armoured warfare and the associated ground attack aircraft, Germany started with a high technical superiority. In long-range bombers, Great Britain started with some inferiority but, with America, ended in the enjoyment of a big superiority. Weighing one factor against another, one can fairly say that, in both the first and second World Wars, the winning side won mainly by numbers rather than by any overall technical superiority.

To be sure, conventional military planning has not normally assumed technical superiority. When military planners count up relative numbers of armoured divisions, aircraft, ships, etc., they are tacitly assuming their approximate equality in quality with those of the enemy. They plan, in the ordinary way, to win wars by making sure that they have a marked superiority in numbers. Technical superiority in this field of weapons in the past has been something to strive for and to hope for, but not often to rely on for planning purposes. Has the situation changed with the advent of atomic weapons, long-range jet aircraft and guided missiles, together with the virtual division of the industrialised world into two power blocks?

In the comprehensive survey of our defence strategy given in *Statement on Defence 1954,* future British policy is broadly outlined in the following passages:

The primary deterrent, however, remains the atomic bomb and the ability of the highly organised and trained United States strategic air power to use it. From our past experience and current knowledge we have a significant contribution to make, both to the technical and to the tactical development of strategic air power. We intend as soon as possible to build up in the Royal Air Force a force of modern bombers capable of using the atomic weapon to the fullest effect. . . .

With all these considerations in mind, the Government have concluded that a gradual change should be brought about in the direction and balance of our defence effort. Still greater emphasis will have to be placed on the Royal Air Force because of the need to build up a strategic bomber force and because of the importance of guided missiles in air defence.

The technical assumptions behind this policy are clearly stated: " It also makes clear the need to keep the lead which we now hold in technical development, on which we must rely to offset the preponderance of the Communist States in manpower."

The arguments in the White Paper make it plain that the new trend in British defence policy, which appears closely related to the contemporary shift in American policy, and to the policy argued very cogently in Sir John Slessor's recent book *Strategy for the West,*[3] is directly based on the assumption of technical military superiority, particularly in atomic weapons and their carriers. More emphasis seems to be placed on the *prevention* of war by the possession of massive atomic offensive power than on the ability to fight a war, if one cannot be prevented. This is often called the Policy of the Great Deterrent; and, in implementing it, there are four major technical aspects:

1. The number and power of the atomic bombs available.

2. The method of delivering them (I shall only at present consider long-range, manned bombers), and their power to penetrate the enemy defences.

[3] London and New York 1954.

Active defence against possible counter-attacks in kind. is comprises radar, fighters and guided missiles. It is on new types of guided missiles as anti-bomber weapons that the main hope of an effective active defence is usually based.)

4. Passive defence, both material and organisational. (The main ingredients are adequate shelters, evacuation arrangements and fire fighting, etc.)

In the field of atomic weapons America, until recently, clearly had a big lead. However, evidence from the American press makes it clear that Soviet progress in making H-bombs has been unexpectedly rapid and that, in certain respects, Russia has outstripped America. Moreover, it now appears that an ordinary atomic bomb of uranium 235 or plutonium can fairly easily and cheaply be up-graded into an H-bomb with up to a thousand times or so the explosive power. Thus we may be entering a period when H-bombs are relatively cheap and plentiful—on both sides.

This rather surprising technical development has still further increased the power of offence compared with that of defence, and consequently has made the precise relative numbers of atomic bombs available to each side for strategic bombing of less significance. For each side will soon have enough to destroy many of the cities of the other. This situation will exist unless some revolutionary advance is made in air defence methods, so as to intercept and destroy nearly 100 per cent. of the attacking bombers.

Thus we arrive at the problem of active defence. I can find no firm ground on which to assume that the British active defence system is markedly superior to that of the U.S.S.R. The evidence from Korea suggests that it would not be safe to rely on any superiority of Allied over Soviet day fighters. American military commentators seem to assess the Soviet MIG.15 as superior aerodynamically to the American Sabre. The fact that the American fighters claimed a 10 to 1 kill ratio in their favour is explained by Americans as due to the inferior training of the North Korean and Chinese pilots and to a superior American gyro gun-sight. There is no reason to suppose that the Soviet pilots in a future war would not be as well trained as those of the Allies, or that their fighters would not by then be fitted with an efficient gun-sight.

I know of no published evidence on which to base a comparison of the likely relative efficiency of the two main ingredients of an active defence system, guided anti-aircraft missiles and all-weather and night fighters with airborne radar. The West certainly had a big lead in night fighters at the end of the war, but that was nine years ago. The art of guided missiles is a new and experimental one, and I doubt if one can safely assume that the West will always keep well ahead in this field. In the case of long-range ground radar it is almost certainly wise to assume technical equality. For this is a matter nowadays of fairly straightforward electrical engineering. In some apparently very well informed articles in *Fortune* magazine last year, it was suggested that the actual state a year ago of the American long-range warning system may have been inferior to that of the Soviets. This view is based on the report that American planes flying near the Siberian coast seem to be more quickly picked up and intercepted by Soviet fighters than are Soviet planes flying near Alaska by the American defence system.

As for long-range manned bombers, many assertions of decisive Western superiority have been made. General Gruenther has recently claimed that the new B-47 can easily penetrate the Soviet defences; he adds that in some years' time this superiority may vanish. It seems to me, however, that the evidence provided by the MIG.15 of Soviet competence in aerodynamic and engine design is strong enough to make it dangerous to assume the U.S.S.R. will not soon produce numbers of atomic bombers of long range and high performance. I conclude, therefore, that in numbers of hydrogen bombs, in long-range bombers, in fighters, guided missiles and radar, realistic military planning should not assume any marked superiority over the U.S.S.R. Any superiority that may now exist cannot be assumed to last. Thus, unless preventive war is envisaged soon, long-range planning should be on the basis of an assumed technical equality.

We now have to deal with the problem of civil defence. I consider that its importance is grossly under-estimated, both in the White Paper and in Sir John Slessor's recent book. In the former we read:

In the development of a policy which gives first priority to preparations designed to deter a would-be aggressor, the role of Civil Defence is necessarily a secondary one, and its contribution to that policy must inevitably be through the indirect support which it can give to increasing the efficiency of the armed forces.

This seems to me just false. For if it came to a point at which the U.S.S.R. had to be deterred from some hostile action by threat of atomic bombardment of her cities—this, after all, is the very essence of what Sir John Slessor has called " the wielding of true air power "—the Government of the day would find the weak state of the active and passive defence system of our cities a major factor in inhibiting the use of atomic air power as a deterrent. Neither the authors of the White Paper nor Sir John Slessor in his book have, in my view, fully faced the political implications of a situation where both main contestants have both A-bombs and H-bombs, and a greater power to deliver them on their opponents' cities than to defend their own.

Some years ago I remember asking a friend, a distinguished airman: " Suppose the U.S.S.R. invaded Yugoslavia by land and you, as A.O.C. Bomber Command, were instructed to dispatch immediately atomic bombers to Moscow. Suppose, further, that your wife and family were in London and that you expected that the U.S.S.R. would retaliate with the bombing of London. How would you feel?" "Well," he said, " I was brought up in an Armed Service and taught to believe that in certain circumstances it was my duty to die for my country. I suppose "—here a long pause ensued—" in some circumstances this holds also for my wife and children." Sir John Slessor indulges in similar heroics when he suggests that all civilians but those working in essential installations " must steel themselves to risks and take what may come to them, proving that thereby they are playing as essential a part as the pilot in the fighter or the man behind the gun."

It is my view that the efficacy of the Great Deterrent as the main basis of British and American military policy became extremely doubtful as soon as the U.S.S.R. started to acquire a sizeable stockpile of ordinary A-bombs. Now that we have to assume approximate H-bomb equality, I believe the theory and practice of the Great Deterrent is in fair way to becoming the theory and practice of the Great Bluff. Even if we had a far better active defence system than we have in sight, it would still seem to me to be exceedingly hazardous to base our policy on the assumption that we could stop the great majority of enemy bombers. A really effective defence system—even if we knew how to set about building one—would be a vast undertaking and one of enormous technical and scientific complexity. We have good electronic and aeronautical engineers and scientists, but have we enough to design, build, man and maintain a vast system of electronically-controlled fighters and guided missiles? And are we prepared to pay the huge price in money and in man-power? If we had a really effective active and passive defence system, the deterrent effect of our atomic bombers might be effective: without such a defence system, the deterrent fails, and at a critical moment will be found to be a sham. Common sense would seem to point to the wisdom of basing our foreign policies on the facts of our defensive strength rather than, as the White Paper and Sir John Slessor's book seem to suggest, on our assumed greater offensive power. The most dangerous course would be to base our defence strategy, as we seem to be doing at present, on an exaggerated estimate of our defensive military strength. If we make this mistake, there is a chance that some future A.O.C. Air Defence Command, gazing down on the smoking patch where London had been, may have to turn to his Chief of Staff and say: " There seems to be something wrong with our damned electronics today."

II

The first American H-bomb was exploded at Eniwetok in November 1952; the first Soviet H-bomb explosion took place in August 1953; the second and third American H-bombs were tested in March 1954. Shortly afterwards, a number of articles began to appear in the American press purporting to tell something of the scientific and technical story behind the development of the American and Soviet hydrogen bombs. These reports have been widely quoted in the European press, but, as far as I know, no connected account has appeared in Great Britain. Since the story, if true, has important implications in the field of defence planning and of foreign politics, it may be useful to put together as coherent a picture as possible of what seems to have taken place. One difficulty is to know what reliance to put on the various articles; but, failing an official version, they are all we have, and we can only apply the obvious criteria—that the articles must have appeared in journals of high standing, that the technical facts quoted must be consistent with accepted scientific data, and that the facts in them must not have been subsequently denied officially. Indeed the articles in question seem to deserve the name of " inspired leaks." One would need a very detailed knowledge of American politics to attempt to understand why and how the information should be allowed to leak, rather than be officially released. Most of it can only have come from official sources.

To appreciate the story told, it is necessary to bear in mind the distinction between hydrogen (or fusion) bombs and atomic (or fission) bombs. Two fission bombs were dropped at Hiroshima and Nagasaki in August 1945. The first was made of uranium 235 and the second of plutonium. Uranium 235 is separated from natural uranium by an expensive diffusion method, while plutonium is manufactured out of uranium in an atomic pile, and then separated chemically. Both types of bomb derive their energy from the break-down, or fission, of heavy elements.

The 1945 bombs had an explosive force equivalent to 20,000 tons of T.N.T. exploded in one place, and they produced fairly complete destruction on the ground up to a radius of nearly a mile. Fission bombs have recently been developed with up to fifty times the explosive force of a 1945 bomb. Since the radius of destruction varies as the cube root of the explosive force, such a super-fission bomb will have a radius of destruction of rather less than four miles.

A fission bomb itself consists of some arrangement of pieces of fissile material which are rapidly brought together by means of an ordinary chemical explosive such as T.N.T., so as very suddenly to produce a lump of fissile material of larger size. If this size is more than a certain critical size, a chain reaction starts, and it blows up with much-publicised results. The minimum mass of fissile material to make a fission bomb go off probably lies between a few pounds and a few tens of pounds. Unofficial estimates of the stockpile of American bombs accumulated in the nine years since 1945 suggest some 5,000 to 10,000 bombs, many of which would be much bigger than the 1945 bombs. The present annual rate of production would seem likely to be of the order of 1,000.

The U.S.S.R. exploded the first fission bomb in September 1949—that is, four years after the first American bomb. There has been speculation as to the present Russian stockpile and rate of production. Figures of a stockpile of a few hundred are often suggested in the American press. If, however, the Soviet rate of production in the five years since 1949 has been as fast as that of the first five years of American production, one would expect a Soviet stockpile of nearer 1,000 by the end of this year.

The general principle underlying the possibility of making a so-called hydrogen (or fusion) bomb has been public knowledge for many years.[4] If two light nuclei are made to fuse with each other to form a heavier nucleus, a large amount of energy is emitted. This is the process which goes

---

[4] The account here of the mechanism of fusion bombs has not been revised in the light of recent information, but has been left as giving the state of public knowledge in 1954.

on in the centre of the sun and which keeps the sun hot. However, the fusion process requires a very high temperature to initiate it, generally considered to be some tens of millions of degrees. The only way known so far of producing such a high temperature is to use the explosion of a fission bomb made from uranium 235 or plutonium. Thus a fusion bomb in its simplest form consists of a fission bomb surrounded by a ton or so of some mixture of light elements. When the fission bomb detonates, the temperature of the light elements is raised sufficiently to start the fusion process, and so releases an immense amount of energy—perhaps a thousand times that of the fission bomb itself.

To go on from such simple general principles to a practical bomb is, however, not at all straightforward. For there are many possible combinations of light elements, and different selections will give quite different results and require different temperatures for ignition. Then, when ignition does take place, numerous side-reactions will occur which must make reliable calculations of the expected effects very difficult. Nature herself pointed the only two obvious ways to make simple fission bombs, leaving little scope for man's judgment; but she left open several possible paths to make fusion bombs.

The early part of the story of the H-bomb is told in great detail by William L. Laurence, the distinguished science reporter of the *New York Times,* in a book called *The Hell Bomb,* published in 1951. Mr Laurence has a very high reputation among scientists for his deep understanding of scientific matters. The book, the author tells us, was submitted to the Atomic Energy Commission and no objection was found to its publication on security grounds, though the Commission did not, of course, vouch for its correctness. Writing in 1950, Mr Laurence gives more details of the possible mechanism of fusion bombs than were, as far as I know, available elsewhere at the time. He discusses—in a way which suggests a detailed knowledge of nuclear physics —the various possible reactions between light nuclei which might be employed to make a fusion bomb. He gives estimates of the ignition temperature of elements and of their probable speed of explosion. He concludes that the most likely method to work would be a mixture of deuterium and tritium, detonated by a plutonium or uranium 235 bomb.

Now deuterium, or doubly heavy hydrogen, can be separated from ordinary hydrogen in various ways, particularly by electrolysis of water. It is a relatively cheap substance costing not more than a million dollars a ton. On the other hand, tritium, or trebly heavy hydrogen, does not occur at all in nature, and has to be made at immense expense in uranium piles. The Savannah River plant was built to make tritium by bombarding lithium 6 (the light isotope of the common metal lithium) in the pile, with an intense flux of neutrons. When a lithium 6 nucleus captures a neutron, an alpha particle and a nucleus of tritium are produced. The tritium is then extracted from the pile. The great expense of producing tritium can be understood from the fact that a neutron which could be used to make a tritium nucleus could alternatively be used to make a plutonium nucleus. Since plutonium is 80 times as heavy as tritium, one needs effectively to sacrifice 80 kilos of plutonium to make 1 kilo of tritium. Thus tritium must be about the most expensive material in the world—Laurence mentioned the figure of 1,000 million dollars a kilo, but this is probably exaggerated.

Not only is tritium expensive, but it is radioactively unstable, so that half of it disappears every 12 years. Thus if it has to be stored for many years before use its effective cost is still bigger. In addition, tritium emits heat when it decays so making it necessary to remove heat continuously from the bomb. I have not been able to find any statement telling how much tritium is required to make a tritium-deuterium bomb. It might be only a small fraction of the deuterium.

To follow the later course of events we have to turn to the stream of " inspired leaks " which started to appear in the press at the end of March of this year. From these articles we are informed that the first American H-bomb in November 1952 was indeed a deuterium-tritium bomb, detonated by either a plutonium or uranium 235 bomb. Now, owing to the fact that deuterium and tritium are gases under ordinary conditions, they had to be stored under high pressures and at very low temperatures. Thus the bomb had to include complicated pressure vessels and refrigeration plants. In a detailed account in the science section of *Time* (12 April 1954) it is suggested that the 1952 hydrogen bomb weighed 65 tons, and was thus much too big and heavy to carry in an aircraft. It was not so much a bomb as a whole laboratory! An official statement put its explosive power as 200 times that of a 1945 atomic bomb.

Then came a surprise development. When the Soviet H-bomb exploded in August 1953 special investigation showed that there was a lot of lithium 6 in the upper atmosphere. This was unexpected, as the 1952 American bomb did not contain any lithium 6. American scientists concluded that the Soviet bomb was essentially a lithium 6 deuterium bomb, not a tritium-deuterium bomb. This information was given in considerable detail in an article in *Time* and in articles by William L. Laurence in the *New York Times,* especially that of 11 April, in the *Christian Science Monitor* of 3 April, and in many other papers. It was, of course, common knowledge that the light element lithium has two isotopes of mass 6 and 7. By separating out the lighter constituent, which amounts to 8 per cent. of natural lithium, and making a chemical compound of it with deuterium, one obtains a stable chemical compound, lithium 6 deuteride. This compound appears to have been the main constituent of the Soviet bomb, apart from the detonator, which was probably an ordinary A-bomb.

Since little or no tritium is required, and since deuterium is not used in a liquid form, this type of " dry " hydrogen bomb is much smaller and lighter and vastly cheaper than the original American " wet " bomb. The Soviet bomb is held to have been small enough to be dropped from an aircraft. American reports quote Soviet publications which suggest that its explosive power was comparable to the effect of the Siberian meteor of 1908, which destroyed trees up to a radius of 15 miles. This would give this bomb an explosive

power of the order of 1,000 times or more that of a 1945
bomb. Of the two American bombs exploded on 1 and 26
March 1954, one or both were probably lithium 6 deuteride
bombs, and one or both were dropped from an aircraft. One
was stated to have about 700 times the explosive power of a
1945 atomic bomb. Probably the actual functioning of this
type of bomb is fairly complex, but an important role, at
any rate in the initial stages, is that in which a neutron from
the initiating fission bomb is captured by Li6 to give an
alpha particle and tritium; this latter then combines with
deuterium to give an alpha particle and a neutron. Complex
side reactions probably also occur. Thus tritium plays an
essential part in the lithium 6 deuteride bomb as it does in
the tritium-deuterium bomb. But the tritium is made *in situ*
during the explosion instead of previously at vast expense.

The invention of the lithium 6 deuteride bomb has made
the H-bomb cheap.

The discovery means that any nation with a small supply of
A-bombs may soon be able to use each A-bomb as a trigger for a
thermo-nuclear bomb, thus easily and inexpensively multiplying
the power of each A-bomb a thousand-fold.[5]

Some public controversy has broken out as to whether
America copied the U.S.S.R. or whether the developments
were independent but parallel. Clearly they must have been
parallel as the time from August 1953 to March 1954 was
much too short for America to develop the new method from
the start. In any case, there seems nothing in the above
account of the functioning or the bombs which does not seem
reasonably plausible to a physicist like myself with no
specialist knowledge; and I am prepared provisionally to
accept the account as substantially true. Very likely, however, the story as told in these articles is incomplete, and it
may be that the lithium 6 deuteride bomb is more complicated than is here indicated.

There is, indeed, one report of another supposed Soviet
development which, if true, might make hydrogen bombs
still cheaper. The source is an article in *The New York
Times* of 31 March by Harry Schwartz. The article quotes a

[5] *Time*, 12 Apr. 1954.

" source " as indicating that the 1953 Soviet bomb may have been triggered by a chemical explosion rather than by an A-bomb. In some other papers the use of a " hollow charge " explosion is mentioned. Schwartz writes: " The Soviet explosion last August is therefore believed to have consisted of three stages, with the initial chemical triggering technique setting off tritium and deuterium, whose explosion in turn sets off the light metal component." However, as I think most physicists would not expect the method to work, I will assume the story incorrect unless further confirmed by other evidence. A common American comment on the position as revealed by this story is that, while the U.S.S.R. may have overtaken the U.S. qualitatively, the U.S. has a bigger manufacturing capacity for H-bombs and at present a better power of delivery.

It is not of great importance whether the technical details of the new types of H-bomb, as given in the various articles quoted, are entirely accurate. Probably they are not. But there seems little doubt of the main fact: with the discovery of the lithium 6 deuteride process, H-bombs have become relatively cheap and easily available to any nation able to make plutonium or uranium 235. As to the explosion power, we may assume a thousand times that of the 1945 atomic bomb—though bigger bombs could no doubt be built. Such a bomb would lead to complete destruction up to a radius of some ten miles, and so an area of some 300 square miles. This is about the area of Greater London.

III

When I first planned the last of these three articles, I intended to pursue further the argument outlined in the first that the discovery of how to make cheap hydrogen bombs has made it necessary to revise radically our present defence strategy as outlined in the recent White Paper. Now the Prime Minister has stated the case for such a revision in impressive words. " But I had not held my mind closed to the tremendous changes that have taken place in the whole strategic position in the world which make the thoughts, which were well founded and well knit together a year ago, utterly obsolete and which have changed the opinion of every competent soldier that I have been able to meet . . ." " . . . how utterly out of proportion to the Suez Canal and the position which we held in Egypt are the appalling spectacle which imagination raises before us. Merely to imagine in outline the first few weeks of a war under conditions about which we did not know when the session commenced and about which we had not been told . . ."[6]

I have no means of knowing, of course, what precise facts the Prime Minister had in mind when he spoke these ominous words, but I will only assume that they were substantially those which I have outlined in my two earlier articles: the most important of these assumed facts are that the U.S.S.R. has probably now attained equality in H-bomb development, though probably not in number of ordinary A-bombs, and that it would be wise for defence planning purposes to assume also approximate equality in the power of delivering them.

Clearly it will be a long and difficult task to work out a new defence policy appropriate to the new situation. Very many complex facts and possibilities will have to be the subject of intricate thought, and it would be clearly presumptuous for me or any single individual to propose any simple or ready-made solution. Moreover, there are a number of broad political and strategic consequences likely to result from the assumption of H-bomb equality which will take time both to mature and to be fully appreciated. I intend, therefore, to confine myself to some of these general probable consequences rather than to suggest changes in our defence policy.

The first and most important of these conclusions is that there is now no possibility of success for any tough diplomatic policy aiming at rolling back without war the Soviet power to the Russian ethnic frontiers and so liberating the satellite States. Still more is a preventive war off the map, in spite of the efforts of some vociferous advocates.

[6] Speech by Churchill, Aug. 1954.

4

Roll-back or liberation policies were much canvassed in America during the 1952 presidential election, and even earlier were often advocated in many British and American papers as the main objective of the rearmament campaign. Once the West had sufficient strength on the ground to enable it to use safely the threat of atomic war, the U.S.S.R. was to be told to retire to her own frontier and accept Second Power status—or be destroyed. "The year of decision," when the West would be ready for a show-down, was often held to be 1953 or 1954.

Clearly the Soviet progress in atomic bombs has made this policy impracticable. Many important consequences follow —perhaps the most important may be in connection with the situation in Western Germany.

To see what this effect might be, it is only necessary to remember the essential incompatibility between the present Western German policy of close military alliance with the NATO Powers and that of attaining unity with East Germany by peaceful means. A few years ago, while the A-bomb superiority of the West was a fact, there were three possible ways by which Western Germany could seek unity with the Eastern Provinces: by a NATO victory in a third world war; by the success of a roll-back policy achieved through the threat of preventive war; and by a bargain with the U.S.S.R. Now, with H-bomb equality a fact, there is only the last way.

It seems almost certain that this issue of how to attain unity will dominate the political scene in West Germany in the next few years. So it seems inevitable that West Germany will start exploring all possible avenues to a bargain with the U.S.S.R. and in so doing will become an unreliable ally to the NATO Powers. I cannot see clearly how any change in NATO defence or foreign policy can prevent this situation coming about.[7]

In the Far Eastern part of the Cold War the chief effect of the development of hydrogen bombs has, I think, been to

---

[7] Where I went wrong in this prediction was greatly to underestimate the tenacity with which the West would cling to the doctrine that German reunification could be achieved within the Western defence system without a major war or major concession elsewhere to the U.S.S.R. Only recently, that is some seven years later, has this doctrine been effectively abandoned.

make it still more dangerous for the West to use or threaten to use even ordinary atomic bombs tactically. Undoubtedly plans were far advanced to drop atomic bombs from U.S. aircraft carriers on the Viet Minh armies round Dien Bien Phu. It is not difficult to guess what the British Government said to this proposal of Admiral Radford. Where would it stop? Would Canton and Peking be the next targets—and then might there not be a Soviet counter-attack on the quite defenceless port of Singapore? If so, then perhaps Moscow would be the next target for American bombs, and in reply perhaps London and Paris for Soviet ones.

Similar considerations apply to Europe though perhaps less immediately. For it is certainly a fact that both A- and H-bombs and atomic shells fired from cannon could be in some circumstances a valuable tactical weapon in a land battle in Europe. They would be of some use in offence but be much more useful in a defensive action.[8] Since NATO planning for land war must certainly be mainly concerned with a defensive campaign, and since, moreover, America probably has now many more ordinary atomic bombs than the U.S.S.R., in the case of war the West might gain considerably by using atomic bombs tactically. However, the NATO planners must be greatly inhibited in planning for the tactical use of atomic weapons because of the uncertainty as to whether wider strategic considerations would actually allow their use. If the tactical use of atomic shells by the West in a land battle was likely to lead to the strategic use of A- and H-bombs against cities, the tactical gain by using atomic shells would have to be compelling.

Another most important consequence of the development of H-bombs by both East and West is to reduce drastically the military value of many exposed overseas air bases. For if the bases in Britain are doubtfully defensible, how much less defensible would be bases in Iceland, Turkey, Cyprus, the Middle East, the Phillipines, Formosa or Japan. The defence of even a single air base against atomic attack involves an extensive radar installation as well as many fighters and guided missiles. The cost of the equipment and the number

[8] I later decided I was wrong on this point: see Chapter 5.

of highly trained personnel required are too high to make feasible the effective defence of a large number of advanced bases. Even if such a base itself were adequately defended, this is hardly likely to be so for the cities of the country in which the bases are situated. So the U.S.S.R. could use the policy of the Great Deterrent in reverse: it could threaten atomic attacks on neighbouring cities if and only if the local government had allowed American or British atomic bombers to use the bases for atomic attack on a Soviet country. There is no doubt that the neutralisation of many advanced bases could, in certain circumstances, be achieved in this way. Thus the NATO Powers may be forced to rely increasingly on relatively safe bases in America itself or advanced bases in relatively uninhabited lands, where there is no civil population to be considered.

The virtual writing off of the Suez military base, with its huge investment of military capital, is likely to be paralleled elsewhere.

Before it is possible to start thinking about possible changes in our defence policy it is necessary to analyse in some detail what is the real strength and weakness of the policy of the Great Deterrent as applied to British policy and what are its likely consequences. Now the primary aim of all the armed forces of any nation which considers itself peacefully inclined is, of course, to deter an enemy from attacking: it is only when the deterrent fails to operate that the armed forces have actually to fight. If, in recent years, the Soviets had envisaged the invasion of Western Europe with land forces they would undoubtedly have been deterred from so doing by the existence of the American atomic stockpile. Likewise, if the Western allies had envisaged the invasion of the U.S.S.R. they would have been deterred from so doing by the strength of the Soviet army. Thus these two factors, the American atomic bombs and the Soviet army, have certainly acted as effective deterrents to a third world war breaking out in the past few years.

The H-bomb now available to both sides will undoubtedly constitute a powerful deterrent to the outbreak of a major war in the future. Yet, on the other hand, it has little relevance to the possible outbreak, or conduct of, any minor wars. The weakness of the Great Deterrent as the main basis of NATO defence planning is that by concentrating so much material effort on the deterrence, by threat of atomic bombardment, of the U.S.S.R., from a full-scale attack on Europe, it weakens our ability to play an effective role in many parts of the world where minor wars may and do continually occur. So, by reducing relatively the land forces, tactical and transport aircraft, etc., required to fight minor wars, we may find it difficult to prevent such minor wars spreading into bigger wars. In this way, the policy of the Great Deterrent may make a major war more rather than less likely. Serious military and moral problems have already arisen, in Indo-China, due to the fact that the only force available to intervene in a crisis were atomic bombs.

In more broad terms, by expanding strategic atomic air power at the expense of ground troops and air defence, our present defence policy seems a sure recipe for losing most small wars for lack of troops and for finding ourselves unable to fight a bigger war for lack of defence of our cities.

Before the advent of the H-bomb, it was often argued that the lack of defence of our cities was not important and did not inhibit our use of atomic attack on the Soviet Union, because our initial atomic attack would be so devastating as to prevent the enemy replying in kind against our cities. This I always thought dangerous nonsense. For airfields and bases can be far too dispersed and numerous to make possible the interdiction of them all in a short time. Now with H-bombs available to the U.S.S.R., so that far fewer aircraft are needed to destroy our cities, there is no hope at all of preventing atomic counter-attack by attacking enemy bases in the first few hours or days of an all-out war.

Suppose, for instance, that the armed forces of Russia, or another Communist country, invade in force with ground troops some country in the Western orbit. Then the essence of the New Look policy would be for the West to use atomic bombs on targets in the U.S.S.R. Sir John Slessor makes perfectly clear that the readiness to be the first to use atomic bombs strategically is an essential element in this policy. The

U.S.S.R. would be likely to reply in kind, and the cities of Western Europe would be easy targets. Thus if the New Look policy goes according to plan, any armed aggression by Soviet Communist land forces anywhere, even in relatively small force, would lead, in all probability, to the destruction of London, Paris, and other big European cities. European governments would, of course, be bound to try to stop any atomic attack on the U.S.S.R. in order to save their cities from destruction, and so would try to prevent the New Look policy from being put into operation. One concludes from this that, in any circumstances other than a full-scale Soviet attack on the West, the New Look policy will be found at the critical moment to be a bluff.

It is in the light of such sombre conclusions as these that a new military defence policy for Britain must be worked out, and with it a new orientation of our foreign policy. Both sets of changes will take time to work out and may prove highly uncongenial to many cherished dogmas. For the last nine years military and political thinking in Britain has assumed the decisive superiority of America over the U.S.S.R. in atomic weapons. Now, with H-bomb equality an assumed fact for planning purposes, a drastic and perhaps painful rethinking of this problem is necessary.

Four

Scientific Method and the Study of War[1]
1955

At the present time the study of war seems to me to have become both more important and more difficult than at any period in our history. I want to make it clear that I am now taking a utilitarian view of the value of the historical analysis of war. Certainly such a study can also be of the highest intellectual interest: here I am concerned with it as a guide to future action.

For it is clear that the only way to attempt to estimate the future is to understand the past. Since all practical executive action—for instance, deciding the make-up of our armed forces—involves estimates of the likely course of future wars, the study of past wars becomes the essential basis of practical statesmanship.

The study of war has become more important than in the past not only because of the terrific destruction involved in modern war, but also because the preparation for future wars now affects the whole social life of a nation, even in peace time. The length of the call-up; the fraction of our national income to be devoted to armaments; the measure of the disturbance of our social life demanded by a civil defence programme; the part of our inventive resources to be devoted to weapons and other military devices—all these questions are the subjects today of acute technical and political controversy.

The study of war has clearly become more difficult because of the rapid change in the technique of war and so of the increased difficulty of predicting the future from the past. Some would say that it has become impossibly difficult. This

[1] B.B.C. Third Programme. *The Listener,* 10 Nov. 1955.

47

is a counsel of despair. Without prediction, practical action
becomes a matter of pure guesswork: one might as well toss
a coin to decide, for instance, how to apportion our air effort
between the offensive and defensive roles. The fact that
rational prediction of the military future has become more
difficult owing to the advent of revolutionary weapons means
not that we must abandon it but that we must put more
effort into it.

Let us turn from these generalities to the outstanding
problem of present-day military planning. The major fact
which has emerged during the last two years is that atomic
and thermo-nuclear weapons are available to both Western
and Eastern power groups. Moreover, their numbers are
probably sufficient, in relation to the powers of defence, to
produce, in the event of all-out war, extreme devastation to
the countries and populations of the opposing groups. In
contemporary political jargon, some kind of balance of
atomic destructive power has come about. This has led to a
marked change in the international atmosphere.

The post-Geneva atmosphere has recently been described
in the words: " with each side accepting that the other has
(at least for the time being) renounced the arbitrament of
nuclear war without abandoning its main objects of policy."
If this is a correct interpretation, what military policy follows
from it? I do not think it possible to attempt to answer this
question in detail at the present time. The situation is too
new and unfamiliar, and I think we must live with it for a
time before we can expect to develop a rational defence
policy which really fits the new situation. Any defence policy
must, of course, depend on the outcome of the current
negotiations for the limitation and control of armaments in
general and nuclear weapons in particular. However, the
proposals for such control put forward by each of the great
powers are necessarily based on their own estimate of the
role of atomic weapons: and these estimates will rest on their
own reading of history.

So we come back to the importance of the historical study
of war as a basis for urgent political decisions. In discussing
the study of the history of war as a basis for contemporary

action, there are two major aspects which require careful analysis. First, there is the study of the political, economic, and personal causes of the recent major wars of history, and of the political, economic, and personal consequences of these wars. War is and has been for centuries an integral part of the national life of organised nations. Wars are fought for certain social objectives and achieve certain often very different goals. The relation of means to ends is here of extreme importance, particularly now that nuclear weapons have made the destruction of national life a technical possibility.

The second aspect of the study of war, which is the one I wish to discuss here, is the broad statistical and numerical analysis of what actually happens in wars. It is easy sometimes to think that because war is a complex phenomenon, involving very many individual actions, including the military genius of some people and the military mistakes of others, therefore little useful quantitative knowledge can be acquired. History refutes this. For the very magnitude of the scale of modern war brings about an averaging process, which makes the broad course of a war more understandable and more predictable than sometimes is thought. So it comes about that simple arithmetical methods of analysis are often extremely useful tools to apply even to some of the more complicated aspects of modern war. This was proved up to the hilt by the success of many operational research groups attached to the armed forces during the Second World War. Moreover, I find that a grasp of some of the simple numerical facts of modern war and of atomic bombs does materially help to understand many things that have been rather unclear in the international history of the post-war period.

Ever since the first use of atomic bombs in 1945, by far the greatest uncertainty underlying all military planning has been that of the military potentialities of atomic weapons. For what military tasks are they suitable and for what unsuitable? How many bombs are required to achieve some specified military result? Many of these questions are hard to answer today because of the very limited use up to now of atomic weapons in actual war. In fact, the only two so far

used, at Hiroshima and Nagasaki, were employed in such
special circumstances as to provide, by themselves, a not very
reliable guide to future action.

However, valuable lessons can be learned from the detailed
study of the strategic bombing offensive with chemical bombs
against Germany and Japan during the last war. The history
of these campaigns provides the only information available
to us of the behaviour of a civilian population under a heavy
and prolonged aerial attack designed explicitly to break its
morale and to bring industry to a stop. Just because these
campaigns were directed against the social life of the enemy
rather than against the traditional target of armed action—
the enemy armed forces—they became the subject of acute
controversy in military circles. A consequence was that the
bombing offensive became perhaps the most numerically
analysed aspect of the whole Second World War.

The United States Government sent into Germany immediately after the war strong teams of observers and
analysts to find out the effects of the bombing. Many of the
results have been published. Of particular interest is the
Over-all Report of the United States Strategic Bombing
Survey, which gives in great statistical detail the effects of
the Allied bombing offensive on all the major parts of the
German economy. Unfortunately, these important publications are hard to obtain, and so are little known.

One learns, for instance, from these analyses of the Allied
bombing offensive the weight of ordinary bombs which was
successfully withstood by a disciplined and determined
population provided with effective shelters. I know of no
other reliable method of estimating this essential figure
except by such numerical analysis of past events. The
million and a half tons of chemical bombs which were dropped
on Germany undoubtedly greatly helped the attainment of
military victory in the land war, but did not by itself prove
decisive. Since other special investigation has shown that
some 2,000 tons of ordinary bombs are required to produce
the same area of material destruction as one 1945 atomic
bomb, the equivalent number of these bombs which would

have produced about the same area of material destruction in Germany was about 700.

To achieve decisive results by atomic bombing alone against a continental power such as the U.S.A. or the U.S.S.R., assuming them to be well prepared and with high morale, would certainly run into a few thousands of the 1945-type atomic bombs. For both countries are much bigger than Germany in both area and population. Though by about 1947 the American stockpile was probably large enough to act as a massive deterrent against aggression, it was certainly not until 1952 or 1953 that it was large enough to be decisive in an inter-continental war. Thus, during the whole early period of the negotiations for the control of nuclear weapons, the aggregate power of the existing American bombs was not adequate to admit of their use to enforce a policy which was described at the time as including the possibility of " condign, immediate and effective penalties against violation of the future international scheme of control." So the Soviet Union was in a position to reject the Atomic Energy Commission's proposals for control, which she probably felt would have kept her in a position of atomic inferiority, and get on with her own atomic programme. This we now see involved the attempt to catch up with the West in atomic matters as soon as she could.

It is necessary to comment on the rather special problem of the defence of the United Kingdom against atomic weapons. By her small size (one-thirtieth of the area of the United States, with one-quarter of the population) and her geographical position she is especially vulnerable to this form of attack. Less than, say, a hundred old-type atomic bombs might inflict a decisive injury on Britain, even if well prepared and disciplined.

By about 1953 the United States must have accumulated a stockpile of atomic bombs (many of a greatly improved type) running into many thousands, and so, according to our arithmetic calculations, of potentially decisive importance in an inter-continental war. On the other hand, the U.S.S.R. must by then have built up a stockpile of smaller but still substantial size. For the first Soviet experimental bomb was exploded in 1949.

The facts of geography, taking into account the present performance of aircraft, make all the cities of western Europe relatively easy targets for atomic bombs. So a balance of a kind was attained between the smaller Soviet stockpile and the greater American one. We see, then, that even without hydrogen bombs, some kind of precarious balance of atomic destructive power between East and West would have already emerged. With hydrogen bombs now available to both sides, the balance became still further stabilised by a greatly increased destructive power of each bomb. The greater destructive power of a single H-bomb means that far fewer bombing aircraft have to reach their target to produce a given amount of damage. The task of providing an effective interception and defence system is thus made correspondingly difficult.

Published estimates rate a typical hydrogen bomb as having an explosive power of rather less than a thousand times that of a 1945 atomic bomb, and consequently an area of destruction about fifty times greater. Thus one hydrogen bomb will destroy the same area as fifty old-type atomic bombs. Roughly speaking, a 1945 atomic bomb destroys about six square miles and a hydrogen bomb about 300 square miles. The number of hydrogen bombs required to inflict lethal damage on a continental power is not, however, reduced quite in proportion to the increased area of destruction, since the number of vital targets enters into the calculation. Estimates have been made in America that some twenty to forty hydrogen bombs delivered to their target would inflict decisive injury to a continental power such as the U.S.A.: some five to ten would be likely to be adequate against this country, say, one for each of the main cities. So the hydrogen bomb has not so much created a new strategic situation as confirmed one already coming into existence owing to the growing size of the stockpiles, both in the West and in the East, of ordinary atomic bombs. The marked improvement in the past year in the relations between East and West is without doubt largely due to the general recognition of the implications of this, however precarious, balance of power.

In a real sense, however, this new and hopeful improvement makes the task of evolving a sensible policy for the armed forces of this country even more difficult than it was before. For what now is a rational military objective? If offensive destructive power has widely outdistanced defensive possibilities, what proportion of national effort should be devoted to improvement in offensive power and what to defence against air attack? Will, perhaps, the requirement of old-fashioned wars, as exemplified by Korea, Indo-China, and now North Africa, begin to loom larger for planning purposes than in the recent past? It is, however, pertinent to remark that in so far as a tendency develops to place on high priority the requirements of old-fashioned colonial-type wars, and other wars of limited objective, then the study of past wars becomes again of unquestionable importance. Moreover, such lessons are relatively easy to apply to the future. Can one, however, imagine more wars of these types breaking out and not developing into an all-out war of world destruction? The Korea and Indo-China wars did occur without becoming general and without atomic weapons being used either strategically or tactically.

A very interesting question is what would have happened if atomic bombs had been used tactically, say at Dien Bien Phu. Would this local war have then developed into a third world war? This question is typical of many which the military historian and planning staffs must study if a national defence policy is to be worked out.

Five

Nuclear Weapons and Defence:
Comments on Kissinger, Kennan, and King-Hall[1]
1958

In view of the millions of words which have already been written on all aspects of nuclear weapons, some justification is required for adding some more. Almost every aspect has been ably argued and equally ably refuted, and it is not unusual to find oneself convinced one week by an advocate of some specific policy, only to remember later that the week before one had been equally convinced by some advocate of its exact opposite. So when I hear the words "the Great Deterrent," "Massive Retaliation," "Graduated Deterrence," "Limited Nuclear War," etc., I sometimes share the feelings of Eliza Doolittle: "Never let me hear another word again! There isn't one that I haven't heard: say one more word and I'll scream." So if any of you feel like screaming I shall sympathise. May I remind you, however, that sometimes, as another great lady, the White Queen, knew so well, it is better to scream before one is hurt than after: with atomic warfare one is unlikely to scream afterwards.

The three authors enumerated in the sub-title of this address have been chosen as having written books[2] which seem to me to be the most suitable now available to stimulate a critical diagnosis of our present defence position. If the authors of these three books were here today, I would tender

---

[1] Address at the Royal Institute of International Affairs, 28 Apr. 1958. First published in *International Affairs*, XXXIV, No. 4 (Oct. 1958). A shorter version was published in *The New Statesman and Nation*, 17 May 1958.

[2] Henry A. Kissinger, *Nuclear Weapons and Foreign Policy*, New York and London 1957; George F. Kennan, *Russia, the Atom, and the West* (The B.B.C. Reith Lectures, 1957), London and New York 1958; Sir Stephen King-Hall, *Defence in the Nuclear Age*, London 1958.

my apologies for any unintentional imputation that they thought alike. They do not, on many vital issues: that is why I have chosen these books for detailed comment. In a real sense, however, they are complementary to each other.

Dr Henry A. Kissinger's book *Nuclear Weapons and Foreign Policy* merits attention because of its great length, wide erudition, and keen analytic power. It arose out of the serious deliberations over many months of a study group sponsored by the American Council on Foreign Relations. In this group were many of the most distinguished American military and political writers, and its chairman was Gordon Dean, former Chairman of the American Atomic Energy Commission. Thus the arguments in the book must be taken as commanding a substantial amount of influential support in the United States. Indeed Mr Foster Dulles's article in *Foreign Affairs* (October 1957) seems likely to have been influenced by the book.

The main conclusion of Kissinger's argument is that America's defence policy has reached a desperate impasse resulting from over-reliance on total war, with the consequential almost complete divorce of power from policy. He thinks that this impasse can only be broken by reliance on tactical nuclear weapons in limited war. This remedy is emphatically rejected by Mr George F. Kennan in his little book *Russia, the Atom, and the West,* based on his remarkable Reith Lectures, and by Sir Stephen King-Hall in his recent book *Defence in the Nuclear Age.*

Kennan does not elaborate in great detail his ideas as to what medicine to prescribe for our nuclear ills, in view of his belief that Kissinger's prescription would prove fatal, but he said enough to raise a storm of criticism, the legitimacy of which it will be necessary for us to examine. His past experience as Russian scholar, one-time American Ambassador in Moscow, and State Department expert on Soviet affairs, together with the unexampled impact made by his lectures, are sufficient to make us study very closely what he said.

King-Hall has had a very different experience from the other two authors, having been a professional sailor, an M.P., and a well-known publicist. His uneven book contains much which I think is important and courageous, though I also think it includes much that is untenable.

The problems which I intend primarily to discuss, in as professional a way as an amateur like myself can hope to do, are just the problems of military planning which I presume our professional military planners are in fact studying. The factual background assumed will be the real world of today, with vast strategic nuclear destructive power in the hands of the United States and the Soviet Union and with quite a lot in the hands of Britain. Moreover, I will restrict my discussion to the situation in Europe alone and I will assume that both the NATO and the Soviet land forces are already armed with tactical atomic weapons or soon will be. I will not mainly discuss what weapons we ought to have or ought not to have, but I will discuss the limited but highly important problem of how we should use, or not use, those we have got.

Kissinger's first thesis amounts to a total dethronement of the concept of the threat of total war as an effective instrument of policy, in any but the most unlikely of all circumstances. Of great interest is the emphasis he puts on the lengths to which the doctrine of all-out war, divorced from political considerations, was carried by the American armed forces, particularly by the Air Force:

> Alone among the services its Strategic Air Command has been able to maintain the " pure " doctrine, the secret dream of American military thought: that there exists a final answer to our military problem, that it is possible to defeat the enemy utterly, and that war has its own rationale independent of policy. . . The notion that a new war would inevitably start with a surprise attack on the United States has been basic to postwar United States strategic thought.[3]

This must be met by building up the maximum possible strategic nuclear power to be able to strike at Soviet vitals and so to deter such an attack. Kissinger accepts the necessity of having such capability of all-out war, but emphasises over and over again the extreme limitations of this doctrine,

[3] Kissinger, *Nuclear Weapons and Foreign Policy*, pp. 25, 30.

except in the most unlikely event of a " pure " case of all-out aggression.

Since the doctrine of total war includes little or no provision for any threats less than the almost wished-for case of " pure " aggression, it left the United States practically powerless to use its great military power in any less vital circumstances. Of the period of atomic monopoly, when Kissinger implicitly assumes that the United States could have destroyed the U.S.S.R. easily and cheaply, he writes: " We never succeeded in translating our military superiority into a political advantage." This passage shows a *naïveté* of thought unexpected in so sophisticated a thinker. It is indicative of the almost mystical American belief in what technology can achieve: its implication is that it was reasonable to expect that the United States should have been able to use its monopoly of the bomb to gain permanent political advantage, without having to wage war or even threaten it. In particular, Kissinger points out that the American monopoly did not prevent the U.S.S.R. from producing its own atomic bombs in 1949 and so profoundly altering the balance of power, to America's detriment. " No conceivable acquisition of territory—not even the occupation of Western Europe —could have affected the strategic balance as profoundly as did the Soviet success in ending our atomic monopoly."[4]

The divorce between planning and policy became still more flagrant with the outbreak of the Korean War. America was forced to fight a war limited in terrain, limited in weapons, and limited in aims, and to accept an armistice far short of even local victory without using her nuclear power. Never was the contrast greater between the humdrum exigencies of the real world and the dream world of American military thought. Kissinger emphasises the vital necessity to develop strategic methods and weapons systems which do not paralyse the will by the horror of putting them into effect. He is at his most passionate and most convincing when castigating the pure doctrine of total war and the associated policy of massive retaliation, and is most eloquent when he pleads with his countrymen to find some workable way of

[4] *Op. cit.*, p. 9.

exerting power, between all-out destruction on the one hand and appeasement on the other.

His second main thesis is that a way out of the impasse can only be found by the West relying on tactical nuclear weapons to eke out its deficiencies of mobilised manpower. He elaborates possible "rules" for the waging of limited nuclear war with tactical nuclear weapons, to which he believes the West can make the U.S.S.R. conform by the threat of all-out nuclear war. Very similar conclusions are reached by R. E. Osgood in a very able book, *Limited War*.[5] He stresses the view that the idea of limited war is profoundly antithetical, both morally and emotionally, to the American way of thinking, but asserts his own opinion that "the deliberate, scrupulous limitation of warfare [is] an indispensable condition of American security." Gordon Dean, in the preface to Kissinger's book, expresses the same view.

Thus there appears to be almost unanimous agreement among serious writers on the subject that total war as an instrument of policy paralyses the will on any occasion but the least likely one (that of total aggression), encourages nibbling and indirect attack, deters local defence and resistance, and plays into the hands of an enemy commanding more flexible military power. The importance of achieving an understandable doctrine of limited war is rammed home repeatedly by Kissinger, who considers that the survival of NATO as an effective military organisation depends on doing so. He emphasises the well-known contradiction that Western policy at present attempts to convince the U.S.S.R. that any attack on Western Europe would bring on an all-out war, and at the same time tries to persuade the Continental Powers that it won't—that is, that a Soviet attack can be contained on the ground.

When the tactical use of nuclear weapons in land warfare was first seriously canvassed in the United States about 1950, I believe it represented a militarily feasible policy and in a certain sense an advance on the previous doctrine. It was

[5] Robert E. Osgood, *Limited War: the Challenge to American Strategy*, Chicago and Cambridge 1957.

then a feasible policy for the West because the U.S.S.R. had very few atomic bombs to use in reply, and it could be held to be sensible because it was at least a step away from the rigidity of planning only for all-out war. Discounting its political disadvantages, it remained perhaps a possible military policy for a few years more—while, in fact, the West had a big numerical preponderance of nuclear weapons. For then it could be argued that the threat of massive retaliation by the United States Strategic Air Force was adequate to make the U.S.S.R. conform to the West's own set of rules for waging limited atomic war. But, even during this period of numerical superiority, detailed studies—for instance, that of Sir Anthony Buzzard and the Chatham House study group *On Limiting Atomic War*,[6] by Richard Goold-Adams, and my nearly contemporary book *Atomic Weapons and East-West Relations*[7]—revealed the complex and arbitrary nature of the rules required. As one of the participants in the Chatham House discussion group I came more and more to the conclusion that the power of the American Strategic Air Force to force Soviet compliance with the West's own set of rules for limited war was probably then a thing of the past and would certainly soon be so. Now, with effective parity, for planning purposes, of mutual destructive power, I think it has vanished. Further, I believe that the Soviets' superiority in land forces combined with atomic parity may put them in a position to try to force the West to comply with their own set of rules for limited war, which in some circumstances might well exclude the use of tactical nuclear weapons.

In the United States the doctrine of limited nuclear war clearly commands wide support. One reason is that it seems to provide a course of action which might restore to the United States the possibility of exercising its military power, while avoiding the twin horrors of America being atom-bombed or of the necessity of raising bigger armies.

Europeans cannot but look on the matter rather differently. The doctrine of limited nuclear war, as opposed to

[6] Royal Institute of International Affairs, London 1956.
[7] Cambridge 1956.

the older doctrine of massive retaliation, might deflect the bombs from both America and the U.S.S.R., but it would certainly bring them down on the densely populated and highly vulnerable countries of Western Europe. Nevertheless, tactical nuclear weapons have become accepted in NATO forces, even though no rational theory of their use exists.

For limited war in Europe with tactical atomic weapons to be a policy which the West should initiate, clearly the following conditions would have to be fulfilled. First and most obviously, the West must be convinced that the war could be kept limited and that the chance of it spreading to all-out war and so to the destruction of European cities must be negligibly small. Secondly, the initiation of the use of such tactical nuclear weapons must be reasonably likely to give some military advantage to the West.

It is one of Kissinger's main theses that the West should use tactical nuclear weapons in limited war *even if the enemy does not.* The issue is so important that I will quote his actual words:

We should leave no doubt that any aggression by the Communist bloc may be resisted with nuclear weapons, but we should make every effort to limit their effect and to spare the civilian population as much as possible. . . . We could announce . . . that we would not use more than 500 kilotons explosive power [25 times that at Hiroshima] unless the enemy used them first; that we would not attack the enemy retaliatory force or enemy cities located more than a certain distance behind the battle zone . . . (say, five hundred miles); that within this zone we would not use nuclear weapons against cities declared open and so verified by inspection, the inspectors to remain in the battle zone even during the course of military operations.[8]

It will be noticed that on Kissinger's proposed rules for limited atomic war in Europe, American and Soviet cities would be excluded as targets but nearly all European cities would be legitimate targets—unless declared open and verified by inspection. Kissinger believes that the West has a reasonable chance of inducing the enemy to conform to such a set of rules, because the West holds the ultimate sanction of threatening all-out nuclear war if it does not. As already

8 Kissinger, *Nuclear Weapons and Foreign Policy*, pp. 231-2.

mentioned, I believe this to be incorrect today even if perhaps it was once true in the past. I will return to this point later.

Kennan too concedes that the attempt to find a more discriminating alternative to the H-bomb as a basis for national defence may have been at least a step in the right direction, in the sense that it recognised the bankruptcy of a policy relying only on H-bombs and long-range missiles. However, he vigorously attacks the advocates of limited atomic war in the following sentences:

It appears to be their hope that by cultivation of the tactical weapon we can place ourselves in a position to defend the NATO countries successfully without resorting to the long-range strategic one; that our adversaries can also be brought to refrain from employing the hydrogen bomb; that warfare can be thus restricted to whatever the tactical weapon implies; and that in this way the more apocalyptic effects of nuclear warfare may be avoided.

It is this thesis which I cannot accept. That it would prove possible, in the event of an atomic war, to arrive at some tacit and workable understanding with the adversary as to the degree of destructiveness of the weapons that would be used and the sort of target to which they could be directed, seems to me a very slender and wishful hope indeed.[9]

Let us consider now what might happen if tactical atomic weapons were used in Europe by both sides. It is customary to assume that their use would favour the side which is strategically on the defensive—that is, according to the common assumption, the West. This argument has always[10] seemed to me rather weak, particularly where, as in Europe, or for that matter in Korea, the Western military effort must be supplied through a few ports. For these would, on almost any set of rules for limited war, be allowed as targets for tactical nuclear weapons. The use in Korea of tactical nuclear weapons by both sides would probably have been fatal to the West, because of the vulnerability of the ports on which its military effort depended.

On the battlefield itself, atomic weapons may perhaps sometimes favour the side which is tactically on the defensive,

[9] Kennan, *Russia, the Atom, and the West,* p. 59.
[10] My recollection was here at fault: see Chapter 3, § III.

since they would make too dangerous the massing of large numbers of troops for a conventional type of attack. It is not at all clear, however, that tactical atomic weapons could not be integrated very effectively into a tactical offensive: according to reports from neutral observers, this is being done in the Soviet Army, and no doubt also in the NATO forces.

As a matter of fact Kissinger, in his advocacy of limited atomic war, does not rely on the argument that their use would favour the defence. He is logical in doing so, for he envisages limited nuclear war as a fast-moving fluid affair of small independent units acting largely on their own initiative. In such a war, of course, the units on the side with an overall defensive strategy will, as often as not, take the tactical offensive.

He is led therefore to look for some other factor which will make the use of tactical atomic weapons of more value to the West than to the East. He finds this in the belief that Western soldiers will be much better at tactical nuclear warfare than Soviet soldiers. He contrasts the flexibility and self-reliance of the American officer corps, " drawn from a society in which individual initiative has traditionally been encouraged," with the rigidity of Soviet military organisation. " The Soviets may be able to train units for limited war, but the pattern of operation for such a conflict would not come ' naturally ' because the Soviet human material would possess no instinct for this kind of warfare."[11]

To be quite frank, I think this argument of Kissinger's is, from the planner's point of view, plain poppycock—and very dangerous. To one who remembers similar beliefs about British personal and technical superiority current before the first World War, and remembers the outcome, I can only comment: " This is where I came in." First we rely on our atomic monopoly to offset the greater number of Soviet soldiers; when the atomic monopoly is lost, we rely on having more bombs; when numbers become unimportant, we rely on better bombs; when this technical superiority is lost, we rely on the superiority and quality of the few individual soldiers

11 Kissinger, *Nuclear Weapons and Foreign Policy*, p. 400.

we do have. Superiority in character, like superiority in weapons, is something to be trained for and worked for. When achieved it should come as a welcome windfall profit, but it should not be counted upon in planning.

I conclude from this analysis that it is by no means certain that if tactical atomic weapons were used by both sides in Europe, they would favour the West. Personally I would go further and hold that the NATO forces even in their present state would probably put up a better defence if neither side used them than if both did. But this must remain a matter of conjecture.

We see, therefore, that neither of the two conditions which must be satisfied if the West is to gain by the initiation of limited nuclear war can be proved true: it cannot be shown that the war could be kept limited, and it cannot be shown that the use of tactical atomic weapons would favour the West. Thus the initiation by the West of tactical nuclear war might either hasten military defeat, or lead to the destruction of Europe by H-bombs—or both.

Something must be said of the probable destructive effects of using tactical nuclear weapons on the battlefield. Since they have never been used in real war, reliance must be placed on exercises, of which two have been reported in the press, both in 1955. In operation Sage Brush, in Louisiana, 275 tactical nuclear weapons of from 2 to 40 kilotons (one-tenth to twice that of the Hiroshima bomb) were exploded in a limited military operation. The assessors reported that the destruction was so great that no such thing as limited or purely tactical nuclear war was possible in such an area. In a similar exercise, Carte Blanche, in Western Europe, 335 bombs were used in 48 hours, and the estimated civilian and military casualties were 1·7 million Germans killed and 3·5 million wounded. One reported conclusion was that, given military equality in all fields between opponents in atomic war, an attacker could always defeat a defender.

We see, therefore, that even if, in spite of my arguments, limited nuclear war in Europe could be kept limited, and even if it did militarily favour the West, the reluctance of Continental peoples, especially West Germans, who live in the area where the battle would be fought, to entrust their safety to such a destructive means is easily understandable.

King-Hall argues the case against initiating nuclear war in a realistic manner as it could appear to military planners.

If a conflict started between the Soviet Union and the West, the Soviet Union might say: " We do not intend to use nuclear weapons of any kind unless they are used on us." It would be to their advantage to say this because they would have a superiority in non-nuclear force, and the NATO powers would be in an awkward position. Are we to suppose that they would reply: " We intend to use nuclear tactical weapons in order to counter-balance your superiority in non-nuclear forces "? This would mean that the West was deliberately making the war a nuclear event and this would have serious disadvantages from the western point of view. First, it would put the West in the wrong with uncommitted world opinion; secondly, it would lead to a split of opinions in western countries; thirdly, it would open the United Kingdom to nuclear attack and this is a form of attack against which we are defenceless. My surmise is that if the Soviet Union were clever enough to make a statement about not using nuclear weapons and live up to it we should have to follow suit, even though today we claim that *we must and will use* tactical nuclear weapons in a NATO war."[12]

It is clear that there are a number of perfectly possible and even likely disturbances, for instance in Eastern Europe, which might be the starting point of a limited war in which the land forces of NATO would engage probably superior Soviet forces. Current Western doctrine suggests that SHAPE would at once use tactical nuclear weapons. If there were any serious intention of keeping the war limited, it would certainly be necessary to make some announcement to the enemy of just what the West intended to do. Since no one has agreed what ought to be announced on such occasions, there would be endless wrangling and confusion. By the time agreement had been reached, the enemy might well have achieved his limited objectives.

For such reasons as these I am convinced that it is on the whole unlikely that Britain or America would, in fact, initiate the use of tactical nuclear weapons if a limited war broke out in Europe. I think that at the last minute they

[12] King-Hall, *Defence in the Nuclear Age*, p. 140. Author's italics.

would have to leave the land forces to fight without nuclear weapons. I believe this in spite of the official statements to the contrary, in spite of the conventional status which tactical nuclear weapons have achieved in SHAPE, and in spite of the fact that the training of the troops is being largely based on their use. I do not think they would be used for much the same set of reasons which led to their not being used in Korea, Indo-China, and Suez. In these three campaigns, stalemate, partial defeat, and complete withdrawal respectively were accepted by nuclear Powers without nuclear weapons being used.

If through some circumstances some NATO forces did use a few tactical atomic weapons in Europe, I believe the British Government would immediately announce to the world that it was taking active steps to try to stop any more being used, and that no strategic nuclear weapons would be launched from British bases against the Soviet Union in any circumstances other than that several British cities had already been destroyed by Soviet bombs. There would seem to me to be no alternative course of action in view of the lack of any effective civil defence. It seems to me impossible to imagine a limited nuclear war in progress in Europe without the overwhelming British concern being not what happened in the battle, but to prevent Britain being destroyed. In such a tactical nuclear war there would be many Western aircraft with nuclear bombs in the air and in the sole control of individual men who might mistake their targets, misread their orders, or deliberately ignore them. If one such man attacked a major Soviet city, it would appear to the U.S.S.R. as deliberate aggression and a violation of the assumed rules of limited nuclear war. Could the British Government leave London at the mercy of one such man? It seems clear enough that the American Government is extremely unlikely, in fact, to use the threat of all-out war by the Strategic Air Command in order to assist NATO to keep a limited war in Europe limited. This is because of the risk of Soviet nuclear attack on the U.S.A. It has been estimated by an American writer that in the first two days of an all-out war between America and Russia about 100 million Russians might be killed—but also about 20 million Americans! Another recent estimate is that 250 Soviet H-bombs reasonably placed on their targets would kill 70 million Americans. The figures may well be quite wrong, but the effect of their publication without effective refutation can only be to prevent the threat of total war being used effectively by America to keep a limited nuclear war limited. In such calculations it is becoming customary for convenience in the United States to make use of a new unit of numbers of killed—this is the Mega-death.

It is useful, if obvious, to note that a decision to initiate the use of tactical nuclear weapons in Europe would not be taken by an anonymous "they" but by individuals—perhaps someone here today. May I talk for a moment to such an imaginary person. Under precisely what circumstances would you initiate the use of nuclear weapons in a limited war in Europe? If you did, what would you say to the country? I hope you will excuse a certain flippancy in what follows. After all, atomic weapons are far too horrific to be treated entirely solemnly. Would you say: "There is no danger at all of the war spreading: carry on your work and living as usual"? If not, perhaps this: "I fear there is an imminent risk of the war spreading to British cities. Unfortunately, we have not found it politically possible to make any serious preparations for atomic attack on Britain, so you will have to fend for yourselves. I am glad to announce that the Government is issuing free to every householder an excellent pamphlet on Civil Defence, from which you will be able to discover the best statistics available as to how many of you will be killed and how. I may add that the Government has set up an expert committee to consider whether cyanide pills are to be issued free through the Health Service for use by those who survive immediate incineration."

Leaving flippancy aside, such arguments amount to asserting that the inhibition which Britain must have against authorising the use of tactical atomic weapons in Europe seems to me to be nearly, if not quite, as strong as are her inhibitions about launching a strategic attack on the Soviet Union. It can never be quite certain that a tactical nuclear war would, in fact, turn into a strategic one; but the likelihood is sufficiently high to make it absolutely necessary to plan for the probability that it would. Failure to do so would seem to me extremely dangerous.

So far, I have discussed the situation as it is today, with the main NATO forces beginning to be trained in the use of tactical atomic weapons, but with the nuclear warheads remaining under American and British control. The policy recommended by Kissinger and, as far as one can learn, likely to be carried out if the present policy is maintained, is to train the land forces of all the fourteen nations of NATO in the use of tactical nuclear weapons. This implies that the warheads will have eventually to be put under the control of the local national commanders. As soon as this has happened then all the already strong inhibitions against SHAPE authorising their use will be greatly magnified. For now the possibility of any set of rules for limited nuclear war being maintained will be much reduced, due to the increased likelihood of the major cities of contestants being attacked, either by mistake or deliberately. Britain, for instance, might find her national survival hazarded by any one of many fanatical fingers of many nationalities on hundreds of nuclear triggers.

As the tactical nuclear armament of NATO forces progresses, I am convinced that the increasing concern of each member State at a time of international tension will become less and less with the military intention of the Soviet bloc and more and more with the dangerous consequences of possible individual action by other NATO countries. When this happens NATO ceases to exist as a unified military force and becomes an uneasy agglomeration of nuclearly armed States relapsing into frightened isolationism.

Moreover, if and when tactical nuclear weapons become conventional among the fourteen NATO Powers, it is hard to imagine that they will not be found to have spread to non-NATO Powers, for instance all over the Middle East. When this happens, it is easy to predict that both the Western and Eastern blocs will become less worried about each other's intentions and more and more worried about the possible activities of other nations. They may well find themselves forced together into *joint* attempts to keep general order in the world. In one of his most moving passages Kennan implores the West to realise the extreme danger of its present policy of spreading tactical nuclear weapons around the world.

The logic of this argument is that on strictly military grounds Western countries have to face the fact that tactical nuclear weapons provide little hope, at any rate in Europe, of compensating for the West's disinclination to mobilise its superior manpower to produce adequate land forces. It follows that in certain circumstances Western countries may have to accept military defeat and thereafter possible occupation.

Both Kennan and King-Hall have made courageous contributions to the problems that then arise. In studying what they say, it is well to remember that they are not speaking only of Britain, but implicitly also of the other European NATO countries. Some Britishers may well prefer to contemplate now the thought of British national suicide rather than that Britain should be occupied. Far fewer will be found to prefer British national suicide rather than, shall we say, that Turkey should be occupied. The Turks might well reciprocate these feelings.

Kennan states clearly that circumstances could arise in which European countries would have to accept defeat and occupation. This follows from his view that the West is unwilling to provide enough soldiers, and will be found to be unable to remedy this deficiency by the use of tactical nuclear weapons.

> . . . the problem of defence for the continental nations would be primarily one of the internal health and discipline of the respective national societies, and of the manner in which they were organised to prevent the conquest and subjugation of their national life by unscrupulous and foreign-inspired minorities in their midst. What they need is a strategic doctrine addressed to this reality.[13]

Then come the much-criticised remarks about the possi-

[13] Kennan, *Russia, the Atom, and the West*, pp. 64-5.

bility of relying more on territorial militia type of forces, on the Swiss model, as contrasted with the regular military units of the last war. I agree to some extent with many of the critics of Kennan that he tends to place too much emphasis on para-military forces rather than on strengthening conventional forces.

King-Hall discusses shrewdly the relation between nuclear war and possible occupation.

It is an open question whether Britain could rely on the Americans to make the war nuclear to save us from an occupation and whether it would be in our best interests to ask them to do so, and I am more sure that the British Government would think twice before taking such a step. My vote would be against it because I am convinced that as between Britain occupied by the Russian army and a Britain a smoking radioactive charnel-house the former is the lesser of the two great evils. . . . The people of the U.K. must recognize that they are liable to invasion to a greater extent than ever before in their history. This is a strange idea to most Englishmen but the notion that one's country is liable to be invaded is familiar to Continental Europeans, Middle Easterners, Africans and Asians. We are unique amongst nations, not in the Western hemisphere, in not reckoning invasion of our homeland as one of the normal hazards of international life. We are no longer amongst the privileged class in this respect and should face this fact and take it into account in our defence plans.[14]

He proceeds to elaborate possible methods of carrying on the struggle after military defeat and occupation, using in a most interesting and critical manner the experience of successful and unsuccessful resistance movements of recent history. His conclusions are, briefly, that active resistance is unlikely to pay, and resort must be had to some form of passive resistance which may have to last for years or decades. Finally, he advocates the study of, and the training in peace-time for the carrying out of, passive resistance.

There is one general criticism of King-Hall's book with which I am entirely in agreement. He places much too much hope on the efficacy of propaganda and political warfare, except in rather special circumstances. He also underrates the value and possibility of stronger conventional forces.

[14] King-Hall, *Defence in the Nuclear Age*, p. 141.

The main attack on both King-Hall and Kennan is that the peoples of Western Europe are not heroic enough or impervious enough to Communist pressure to sustain a long passive resistance. This view may perhaps prove true, if ever put to the test. However, it seems to me clear that they are even less likely to be heroic enough to will their own certain destruction to avoid the possibility of occupation. One remembers the well-known democratic principle of " No annihilation without representation." When it comes to the critical moment, the admittedly heroic tasks of passive resistance may seem less formidable and farther distant than that of embarking on all-out war. The policy of those critics who decry beforehand the possibilities of continued resistance and refuse to think about its problems seems well designed to make quislings of most Europeans.

Some may feel that the discussion of such grim situations and the pin-pointing of such appalling national and personal dilemmas is not in the national interest: that it is better to leave things vague and undefined: that any attempt to analyse in detail the sort of situation with which one may be faced will only raise doubts as to the national will to survive. I respect this view, but cannot share it. To me it has too big an ingredient of bluff and of the attitude " It will be all right on the night " to form the basis of a rational military policy. Perhaps, too, I am influenced, as no doubt Sir Stephen King-Hall is, by a professional training and service as a sailor. Pre-eminently a sailor's training is to anticipate in detail the emergencies which may occur, and to have a drill ready and trained-for to meet each one of them. In my view, one of the greatest contributions Britain can make to her own great future and that of the world as a whole is to chart realistically the dangers ahead of us, and so to provide the basis for working out a realistic defence policy which does not put the ship of State unnecessarily in hazard of extinction.

My three selected authors, Kissinger, Kennan, and King-Hall, have all, in their very different and often contradictory ways, exposed some of the foundations on which such a policy could be based. But there is much further study and hard work to be done. I am convinced that unless we face realistically the possible situations which we may encounter, Britain may find herself led by events beyond her control into political and military fiascos compared with which Munich will appear to future historians as a monument of courage and Suez as a triumph of military planning.

Kissinger's greatest achievement lies just in his greatest failure. If such ability, such knowledge, and such dedication can only make so fragile a case for limited nuclear war as a policy for the West in Europe, then we can safely reject it: and, incidentally, forgo the tedium of reading other writers on the subject. Kennan and King-Hall have had the courage to face up to the implications of the end of the great illusion that a now non-existent technological superiority is a match for trained soldiers.

Let me leave this grim prospect and end on a less serious note. When grappling with these important but intricate arguments as to the role of nuclear weapons in Western defence policy, it is useful to keep in mind a few numerical facts and certain deductions from them. One remembers that the main argument for spreading tactical nuclear weapons among the nations of NATO is that they would enable the West to use its superior technology to defeat the hordes of Soviet soldiers. On the other hand, Osgood quotes the actual population of the NATO countries as 430 million, which is over 50 per cent. higher than the 280 million in the U.S.S.R. and her European satellites. Thus the role of the assumed superior technology, which certainly existed ten years ago, was to compensate not for a deficiency of manpower but for the disinclination of Western peoples to serve as soldiers. Today no important degree of military technological superiority can safely be planned for, and military planners must revert to traditional practice of assuming technological parity.

Unless present tendencies are changed, technological superiority may well pass to the U.S.S.R., since they are training more engineers and applied scientists than the Western world, and have shown a marked aptitude for concentrating their efforts on to a limited number of important technological targets, such as nuclear weapons, aircraft, and the sputniks. So future military planners (taking an optimistic view, which I share, that the world is rather unlikely to blow itself up) may find themselves faced with the task of how the West can mobilise its superior manpower to offset the achievements of the hordes of Soviet technologists.

Six

Atomic Heretic[1]
1958

During nearly twenty years of my lifetime of sixty years, I have been either training for war, fighting wars, or studying and thinking about them. In between, I became an experimental atomic physicist. Because of the dominating significance and danger of atomic weapons today and of the intricate military problems to which they give rise, I intend to talk here mainly about my military career rather than my scientific career.

In 1910, at the age of thirteen, I became a naval cadet. For the next four years I received, at Government expense, an excellent modern and scientific education, with a background of naval history, and the confident expectation that the naval arms race with Germany then in full swing would inevitably lead to war. When, in August 1914, it came, I found myself sailing for the South Atlantic, where my ship took part in the Battle of the Falkland Islands, three weeks after my seventeenth birthday.

Then, in June 1916, I watched the opening phases of the Battle of Jutland, the greatest sea fight of history, from the *Barham*, flagship of the Fifth Battle Squadron. I saw the oily patch where the battle-cruiser *Queen Mary* had blown up a few minutes before. The shock to the widespread complacency about British naval technological superiority due to their heavy tactical defeat was profound. In the first three-quarters of an hour of the engagement between six British battle-cruisers and five similar German ships, two of ours blew up, while little damage was inflicted on the enemy. The new German navy, without tradition or experience, had proved itself superior in gunnery and in ship construction.

---

[1] B.B.C. *The Listener*, 11 Sep. 1958.

It was only the marked superiority in numbers of British ships that sent the German High Sea Fleet scuttling back to harbour, and so brought strategic victory.

Early in 1919, after eight years in naval uniform, I found myself an undergraduate at Cambridge studying physics under one of the greatest experimental physicists of all time, Ernest Rutherford. I was indeed lucky to take part in the wonderful developments of nuclear physics in the Cavendish Laboratory between the wars, which laid so much of the scientific foundations on which many years later were built both atomic bombs and atomic power stations. For seventeen years I forgot war and hugely enjoyed myself as experimental physicist and teacher. Then in 1936 the growing threat of Hitler's Germany, and the ever-growing dangers of air warfare, brought me back into military affairs as a member of Sir Henry Tizard's famous Air Defence Committee, which, amongst other things, fathered the development of radar and vigorously encouraged the application of scientific method to the study of war.

I spent the five years of the Second World War mainly applying scientific methods to the study of the tactics and strategy of air and anti-submarine warfare. I worked in turn for the Army, the Air Force, and the Navy. Under the name "operational research," scientists were put into a position to study and analyse the planning and operational activities of the military staffs, thus encouraging numerical thinking and helping to avoid running the war on gusts of emotion. Towards the end of the war many of the operations of war, especially those concerned with aircraft, were kept under close scientific scrutiny and control. This was the era of the so-called slide-rule strategy.

With the end of the war in 1945, I went back to my laboratory, but not to forget about war. For the atomic bombs on Hiroshima and Nagasaki in August brought a new dimension of destructiveness and horror to warfare and set the world problems which it has so far signally failed to solve. Speeches, editorials, articles, and headlines were full of such ideas as "The absolute weapon," "Armies and all other weapons are obsolete," "Russia has been reduced to second-class status overnight," "World government imposed by atomic bombs is the only solution."

When, soon after Hiroshima, the basic facts about the damage produced by an atomic bomb were published, it became possible to think quantitatively about the probable effects of atomic bombs in future wars. I felt impelled to try myself to make such an analysis: for, as far as I knew, I was the only atomic scientist brought up as a professional fighting man and I had specialised, during the war, in just this type of analysis. Since the U.S.S.R. had now replaced Germany as the potential enemy for military planning purposes, the military problem was how to estimate the role of nuclear weapons in a possible future war between the U.S.S.R. and the West.

During the first two years after the war I gave much thought to this problem, and gradually came to certain conclusions that were in marked conflict with official British and American opinion. Very much simplified, my main points of disagreement were as follows. I held that official opinion over-estimated the decisiveness of atomic bombs of the Hiroshima type in a major war against Russia, unless used in very large numbers—that is, many thousands, which were not available. I also thought that the importance of strong land forces was being greatly underestimated, and in particular that the effective military use of even a large number of atomic weapons would be very difficult without strong land forces to follow them up. I guessed that the Soviet High Command would have reached similar conclusions and that therefore the Soviet Government would certainly stall on the West's proposals for international control of atomic weapons until they had built up their own stockpile. This is what they did, and I am convinced that Britain and America, if in the same situation, would have done exactly the same.

In more general terms I feared then, and still do today, the consequences of staking the survival of the Western way of life on the maintenance of technological superiority in atomic weapons and in the aircraft and rockets to carry them: I remember Jutland only too well. Though warned often by their statesmen that the atomic monopoly could not last, the West behaved as if it would. I concluded that at that time there were three main courses of possible action open to the West: to attempt to negotiate a horse-deal with the U.S.S.R.—I mean by this an agreement embodying a real bargain of mutually acceptable concessions; to attempt to use the temporary atomic bomb monopoly to force a show-down with the U.S.S.R. by the implied threat of waging preventive war; or, finally, to wait until the U.S.S.R. had herself become a strong atomic power and then have to negotiate from a very much weaker position.

When I published these views in a book in 1948 I was not altogether surprised to be violently attacked from many quarters. For it was perfectly true that my conclusions did conflict directly with important aspects of Western policy. This policy appeared to be based on the assumption that a major war against the U.S.S.R. could be won quickly and cheaply by relatively few atomic bombs, and that strong land forces were not needed. As a result of these military views the Western Allies in effect tried to force or bluff the U.S.S.R. into accepting a state of permanent atomic inferiority, which would incidentally also have deprived her of the possibility of building up her own atomic power industry. This Western policy, which amounted to attempting to snatch permanent political advantage by exploiting a temporary atomic superiority, seemed to me bound to fail, as it indeed did.

Although in my book I inevitably made many errors of detail and emphasis, on re-reading the criticisms I find that my critics made more errors and more serious ones. During the ten years since my book was published more and more of my military views seem to have become generally accepted. This, of course, made my crime in 1948 still more grievous, since what can be more tactless than to be right at the wrong time? I had committed the unforgivable sin of being a premature military realist. I like to claim, like J. M. Keynes, that " orthodoxy keeps catching me up." What better evidence of my present—relative—orthodoxy could there be than that I am talking to you now!

Where all the prophets went wrong, including myself, was in expecting the U.S.S.R. to take longer than she did to produce a nuclear bomb. She did this in 1949, four years after the first American bomb and three years before the first British one. The other unexpected fact was the technological break-through which allowed both the United States and the U.S.S.R. to produce H-bombs within a year of each other in 1953-4. H-bombs are a thousand times as powerful as the first atomic bombs, and a single bomb could destroy Greater London and kill perhaps a few million Londoners. A third unexpected factor was the technological success of Russia in the field of aeronautics and of rocketry, as exemplified by the sputnik last autumn. These add up to the fact that the West can now assume no technological superiority over the East in military matters, and may find itself inferior in some respects. I think I am quite orthodox in holding that H-bombs are so powerful that they could not be used against another H-bomb Power by any nation that wanted to survive.

Thus land forces again become of dominating importance. Where I am still in disagreement with official policy is in disbelieving that the West can solve its military problems by reliance on tactical atomic weapons to offset the lack of soldiers. For instance, I believe that the initiation by the West of the use of small tactical bombs on a battlefield in Europe would prove disastrous to NATO forces and would lead either to quicker defeat in the field or to Britain being destroyed by H-bombs, or both. So I seem once more to be an atomic heretic. However, I confidently expect orthodoxy to catch me up again, sooner or later.

Seven

Thoughts on British Defence Policy
1959

*Depend upon it, Sir, when a man knows he is to
be hanged in a fortnight, it concentrates his mind
wonderfully.*—Samuel Johnson.

The recent improvement in the international atmosphere
may lead some to think that there is now less need for a
coherent and intelligible defence policy for the West
as a whole and for Britain in particular. This is not so, if
only because it is essential to make use of the improved
relations between the Eastern and Western blocs to make
concrete progress in disarmament, and this is much more
likely to be achieved if the nations concerned have realistic
views about the relative military importance to them of the
various weapons of war. It is thus essential to have a coherent
and intelligible defence policy. In my opinion neither the
western alliance as a whole, nor Britain in particular, has
one.

Inevitably the main features of the controversy in Britain
about what our policy should be have run parallel to that in
progress in the United States. However, there are some
important differences of emphasis, which directly derive
from the very different economic and geographical situations
of Britain compared with the United States. Perhaps the
single most important reason why British defence policy is
of great international significance today lies in her key situation in relation to the spread of nuclear weapons to other
nations. As the third nuclear power, and the first of the
medium-rank nations, as measured by population and wealth,

---

[1] *The New Statesman,* 5 Dec. 1959.

to produce bombs, Britain can have a decisive influence, for good or ill, on the vital task of attempting to check their spread.

In one respect Britain can draw on experience possessed by no other country: she was not only the first medium-rank nation to have her own atomic stockpile, but she was the first atomic power to find herself indefensible against a potentially hostile and much larger atomic power. So, by accident of geography and history, Britain has been forced to think clearly on the possibilities and limitations of the wielding of atomic power by a country which could be completely destroyed in the event of their being used against her.

When Britain started her own atomic weapon programme in 1946, it was no doubt expected both that the Western monopoly would last many years and that Britain would in due course become atomic power Number Two. Neither of these expectations was fulfilled, since the first Soviet bomb was tested in 1949 and the first British one not till 1952. So it came about that by the time Britain had acquired a sizeable stockpile, she had become so vulnerable to Soviet bombs as to make any possibility of their independent use against the U.S.S.R. equivalent to national suicide. Since about 1957 Britain has been within the range of Soviet medium-range missiles with nuclear warheads, against which no defence exists and none is in sight.

Now that both the United States and the U.S.S.R. possess the atomic capability to devastate each other, an uneasy strategic stalemate, or balance of terror, prevails.

A few figures will give an indication of the technical possibilities which lie behind this balance of terror. One American analyst estimated that in the first two days of an all-out war between Russia and America, about 100 million Russians might be killed—but also 20 million Americans. This was two years ago and now the score in mega-deaths might be even larger and nearer. The Federal Civil Defence Administration has computed that an attack on the industrial complex and air bases of the United States with 250 H-bombs each of 10-megaton power would be likely to kill some 40 million people immediately, that is by blast, thermal and direct radiation effects, and another 30 million in the next two months by the delayed effects of radiation and by the radiation from fall-out. Comparable numbers of Russian dead would result from a similar attack on the Soviet industrial complex and air and missile bases.

Reactions in Britain to this situation and to the role of British atomic weapons are many and various. Some hail the hydrogen bomb as a heaven-sent device to free mankind from the age-old curse of war. Such optimists are apt to be somewhat evasive as to what practical steps should be taken in relation to British defence policy on the one hand and to Britain's disarmament policy on the other. Others see the present strategic stalemate as intrinsically unstable and liable to collapse at any moment into all-out atomic war. Amongst this group are some who seek salvation in an intensified arms race on the lines recommended by the advisory council of the Democratic National Committee in their recent pamphlet *The Military Forces We Need and How to Get Them*. This programme has the stated objectives of attempting to catch up with the present Soviet lead both in long-range missiles and conventional weapons. Some hold that it would be dangerous to attempt to negotiate a general settlement of East-West differences till these missile and conventional war gaps are closed, which cannot be until about 1964.

A small but active minority in Great Britain consider that Britain should opt out completely from both the atomic arms race and effectively also out of NATO.

Probably the largest group in Britain take a middle line: neither seeing H-bombs as the salvation of mankind; nor holding that the strategic balance will be drastically changed by each technical advance in rocket motors or electronic guiding systems; nor believing that a massive rearmament programme is either militarily necessary or politically possible. This group is worried about the following three main points: the dangers arising from the West's weakness in conventional armaments; the danger that the use of tactical atomic weapons in a limited war may lead unintentionally to all-out war; finally, the dangers arising from the spread of atomic weapons to many more than the present three atomic powers. It is with the fears and the hopes of this group that the main arguments of this article will be chiefly concerned. The first problem to be discussed will be that of the role of tactical atomic weapons in land war.

The relevant steps by which the present dilemma arose are worth recalling. About 1954, when it was assumed that the West had still a marked quantitative superiority in both strategic and tactical atomic weapons, the military doctrine seems to have been as follows: any major aggression by the conventional forces of the U.S.S.R. would be met by the use of tactical atomic weapons on or near the battlefield to strengthen the Western land forces; the danger that the U.S.S.R. might reply by atomic attack on Western cities would be met by the threat of much greater devastation of the Soviet homeland by the Strategic Air Command. This doctrine amounts in effect to the use of the still assumed superior strategic atomic power to attack the enemy homeland to make it safe for the West to use its assumed superior tactical atomic power on the battlefield. This was perhaps militarily tenable till about 1956: it then became less plausible since it was no longer possible to make the essential assumptions of atomic superiority at both the strategic and tactical level. So a new doctrine had to be sought. None has found general acceptance, though many have been suggested.

One school of military theorists, conceding that the West could no longer impose on the enemy its own chosen limitations on the use of tactical atomic weapons, holds that some kind of tacit agreement could be arrived at with the U.S.S.R. on rules for their use. However, so far no agreement has been reached even by the theorists in the West as to what type of rules to suggest, and most professional military men seem determinedly sceptical of the validity of any such approach. The official publicised Soviet view is that limited nuclear war is not possible—their actual military doctrine for planning and training purposes may perhaps be essentially different. Thus, it would not be far wrong to state that there is no clear doctrine in the West at present as to whether the initiation of tactical atomic war by the West would or would not lead to atomic attack on western cities.

Many writers have assumed that, in some way or other, limited atomic war can be kept limited, and have discussed the conditions under which it would pay the West to initiate it. It is clear that the immediate problem for the West is not whether to have tactical atomic weapons—they already exist on both sides—but whether, when, and how to use them. It is believed that the Soviet armies are supplied with tactical atomic weapons and are fully trained to fight either offensively or defensively and either with or without them. In the event of armed conflict the Soviet command is likely to attempt to exploit its superiority in conventional land forces, so possibly leaving the West with the desperate choice of having to accept military defeat in the field or initiating tactical nuclear war. If the U.S.S.R. initiated their use, clearly the West would follow suit. The immediate key problem is what the West should do if the U.S.S.R. does not use them.

Many attempts have been made to demonstrate that the mutual use of tactical atomic weapons would favour the side with the fewer troops. However, strong criticisms of this view are now being made and many Western experts now seem to agree that the use of tactical atomic weapons would require not less but more troops. This has long been the published Soviet view and may well be one of the reasons why the U.S.S.R. kept its army strength to a high level during the period of United States atomic superiority. One of the main reasons for greater numbers of troops required is that larger reserves are needed to replace the very heavy casualties expected in tactical nuclear war.

Others argue that the initiation of the use of tactical atomic weapons by the West would be advantageous because their use would favour the side which is on the strategic defensive—by definition the West. This argument stresses that the existence of tactical atomic weapons would prevent the great concentration of troops required for the successful offensives of the last war, and so on balance would favour the defence. This view has also come in for sharp criticism. It is pointed out that such large concentrations might not be needed for a successful offensive because of the increased fire power produced by atomic weapons. Moreover, the defending side would also have to keep widely dispersed, thus facilitating tactics of manoeuvre and encirclement. It is also emphasised that tactical atomic weapons can undoubtedly be used very effectively in an offensive operation—Soviet military writers also stress this.

The American report already referred to discusses carefully the role of tactical atomic weapons and arrives at the conclusion ". . . that NATO cannot overcome its relative weakness, *vis-à-vis* the forces of the other side, by the simple expedient of committing itself to the use of nuclear weapons. On the contrary, the commitment to nuclear weapons inevitably increases the relative advantages of the other side—provided Russian forces are equipped with nuclear weapons, as we know they are. . . ."

It seems possible that, if a limited conventional war was turned into a tactical atomic war, the logistic supply of the armies in the field would become impossible, thus bringing operations to a halt and so favouring the side on the defensive. However, it has been pointed out that in many possible cases the Western communications would be much more vulnerable than those of the Soviet armies, because of the greater role of sea-borne supplies through ports. It is generally agreed that, if in Korea both sides had used tactical atomic weapons, the ports on which the Allied effort depended would have been unusable and the Allies would have had to accept defeat.

Even if the initiation by NATO, say in an initially conventional war in Germany, did bring operations to a halt, the cost would have to be taken into account—this might amount to several million German civilian dead, as is shown by the exercise Carte Blanche. Germany has survived total defeat in two major wars. Would she survive a tactical atomic victory?

Even if it could be demonstrated that the initiation of the use of tactical atomic weapons would favour the side on the strategic defensive, there are possible situations when the West would wish to engage, albeit locally, on large-scale offensive land operations. Suppose a political rising occurred in East Germany and Soviet land forces proceeded to suppress it. Then West German forces might intervene and would bring strong pressure on NATO to support them. Then suppose that the Western forces which were attempting to reach the centres of the East German uprising found themselves blocked by Soviet armies: the decision would then have to be made as to whether to initiate the use of tactical atomic weapons to attempt to compensate for the West's inferiority in ground forces.

I think it most probable that the decision would be against doing so and that the West would accept limited defeat rather than take the three risks inherent in initiating tactical nuclear war: the risk of accelerating defeat in the field: the risk of obliterating the people whom one is attempting to defend or to protect; and the risk of starting the process of escalation towards total war.

Returning to the general problem of possible advantages and disadvantages to the West resulting from the initiation of tactical nuclear war, I am convinced that the most important certainty is that there would be uncertainty; and that this uncertainty would prevail and lead to inaction, whatever the consequences.

Military caution would suggest that the attempt to distinguish operationally between tactical and strategic atomic weapons should be abandoned and that tactical atomic weapons should therefore be kept under the same rigid control as strategic weapons; or in the language of deterrence, the little deterrent must be considered in practice as part of the great deterrent.

I think, moreover, that NATO would be well advised to announce that in no circumsatnces would it initiate the use of tactical nuclear weapons, though it would use them if the Soviet forces did.

Clearly, the only sensible military policy for the West would be to attempt as soon as possible to match more nearly the strength of the Soviet land forces in Europe and to provide the equipment and training for land war both with and without tactical atomic weapons.

To end this survey of the West's attempt to gain military advantage by exploiting a now non-existent technological superiority, it may be worth while to draw attention to some purely military merits of conventional land war as practised during World War II. For there is a wealth of experience to prove the great advantage of defence over the offence: it was quite usual for a position to be successfully defended against an attacking force outnumbering the defender by three or even five to one. Perhaps conventional war is after all the best military way for the West to solve its self-set problem of how to be safe without becoming soldiers.

Without a shadow of doubt the West, since the war, has committed a vast military blunder in neglecting adequate preparation for land warfare in the mistaken view that atomic weapons would do instead. Moreover, there is no quick way to close this conventional-war gap which has been allowed to come into being, in spite of a considerable Western superiority in manpower and in spite of a large industrial superiority. Not only has the West fewer divisions but many of those it has are markedly less well equipped than those of the U.S.S.R.

The raising of more NATO divisions, the re-equipment with modern weapons of existing forces, the qualitative improvement of conventional weapons by a crash-programme of research and development; all these would take at least a few years to implement. In the meantime the West has to live with effective atomic parity and with conventional war inferiority. No one can restore to us the years that the locust hath eaten.

We have now to look at recent British defence policy in the light of some of these considerations. For our purposes it will be sufficient to go back only as far as the Defence White Paper of April 1957, entitled *Outline of Future Policy*. As is well known, the most important provisions were the plans for the ending of the call-up for National Service in 1960, the reduction of the British contribution to the ground forces of NATO in Europe, the emphasis given to the fact that it was not possible to defend the British population against nuclear attack, and the reliance to an even greater extent than formerly on the deterrent power of nuclear weapons to prevent major aggression.

The main criticisms of this policy were threefold: it went far to disrupt NATO planning for adequate land strength in Europe; consequently, it forced NATO to rely increasingly on tactical nuclear weapons, just at the time when their possible advantage to NATO was becomingly increasingly problematic; and finally, to prevent major aggression, it re-emphasised reliance on nuclear retaliation against the sources of power in the U.S.S.R. at a time when putting it into effect would mean the destruction of Great Britain. It was claimed that these changes enabled the 1957 defence budget to be kept below £1500 million, instead of the £1700 million which it would have had without these changes, thus saving £200 million a year.

The policy of the White Paper was in fact neither new nor confined to Britain, but constituted an important step in a process of gradual increasing reliance on atomic weapons, which was also markedly evident in the United States at the same period. It is clear, in retrospect, that such a forthright formulation just at that time of this policy was based less on defence than on political considerations. For Great Britain was still in a state of humiliation and financial crisis, as a result of the Suez campaign of the previous autumn, and the Government's popularity had reached its lowest ebb. Thus for both internal and external political reasons it was essential that the Government should not increase the defence budget, and should, at the same time, appear to be strengthening the military power of Britain. The solution was to reduce British real military strength, particularly in ground forces in Europe, and to attempt to make the reduction palatable by announcing increased reliance on nuclear weapons.

Another strand of thought may possibly have also been of importance in leading to the 1957 policy. The British Government may well have held that a Soviet attack in Europe was highly unlikely, so that there was very little chance of the military deficiencies of their policy ever being found out. However, they may have been inhibited from saying so publicly for fear of offending those elements in

America who base their plans on the assumption that the U.S.S.R. was awaiting the first favourable moment to launch a full-scale attack.

On the whole the political objectives of the new policy were achieved. The arms budget was not increased, the storm of home and foreign military and political criticisms was left to spend its force, and the electoral prospects of the Government party increased notably.

Britain was left without an operational defence policy—I use these words to denote a body of military doctrine on which realistic military planning and training could be based. There is no doubt that this deficiency is fully realised in some Government circles and that important changes in policy may be under consideration. So far there has been no hint as to what these changes may be.

It is clear that the British nuclear stockpile cannot in fact deter any other country from a hostile act unless there is some chance, even if only a very small one, that, in given circumstances, the bombs would be used. Much discussion, much of it very evasive, has taken place on the question as to what such circumstances might be: a common conclusion is that a major Soviet attack even with conventional forces would unleash a British atomic attack on Soviet cities. Leaving out the difficulty of deciding just what constitutes a major attack, it seems very hard to think out realistically the circumstances in which the British Government would in fact dispatch nuclear weapons from British soil against the U.S.S.R., knowing that within a few hours London and other major cities could be destroyed. Until clarity is achieved on this point, Britain cannot be said to have an intelligible defence policy. It may be that there is a clear and confidential doctrine in the Defence Ministry, but this seems unlikely, because, long before any preparatory action to use atomic weapons was taken, the British public would have to be told something of what was in store for them. Not to give them a clear warning would be irresponsible in the highest degree.

Any possible doubt about what the official British defence policy amounts to was removed by the statement in the 1958

White Paper that "A full scale Soviet attack could not be repelled without resort to a massive nuclear bombardment of the sources of power in Russia." There is no room for doubt that in practice, if not in intention, the phrase "sources of power in Russia" was a euphemism for Russian cities. No doubt other targets such as airfields, missile bases and other military establishments would also be attacked, but it is undeniable that the main sources of power in the U.S.S.R., as in other industrial countries, lie in her cities. Thus the putting into effect of the official British defence policy would be likely to lead, in the event of a major Soviet aggression on land, to the obliteration of Britain. In fact, it is clear that this aspect of British defence policy is not an action policy to be put into effect under certain circumstances but a declaratory policy to deter a major attack. In my view there is much less danger of a mutual holocaust than of a Western military and political débâcle arising from the failure to work out a viable military policy to deal with foreseeable types of events. When official policy is to do impossible things, then, if put to the test, nothing is done.

Though, of course, all the views that I have expressed are still highly controversial, I do consider it fair to hold that the criticism of the 1957 and 1958 White Papers is overwhelming. In my view the card house of our defence policy erected on a base of bluff and politics has collapsed and will never be resurrected in its old form. I will proceed, therefore, on the basis that there is at present in Britain no consistent and intelligible operational defence policy. Nor is there, in fact, in the United States, and for precisely analogous reasons. Now that it is believed that Soviet long-range ballistic missiles with atomic warheads, against which no defence is possible, can reach American cities, in addition to the possibility of attack by manned bombers, against which there may be a rather good but not 100 per cent. defence, America is now essentially in the situation in which Britain found herself in 1956 or even earlier.

Before discussing in detail possible modifications of Western defence policy it may be useful to say something more of the historic steps by which the West has reached its present awkward military situation.

Since the end of the Second World War there have been three occasions on which, following the Western military doctrine of the time, the use of atomic weapons to redress the balance in a limited struggle was seriously contemplated. The Western world owes much to the restraint of President Truman that atomic bombs were not used in Korea, and to President Eisenhower that they were not used in Indo-China or during the Quemoy struggle. It appears that in Indo-China, America came very close to using tactical atomic weapons against the North Indo-Chinese forces besieging Dien Bien Phu. The use for the second time of atomic weapons by white people against coloured would have been a major moral and political disaster for the West, and quite likely would not have saved the French base.

The rise in the West of the doctrine of winning wars quickly and cheaply by air attack on the enemy's war-making capacity rather than against his armed forces arose out of the long struggle of the early military airmen to break through the military conservatism of the soldiers and sailors. This struggle convinced them, probably at this time rightly, that the air arm would remain backward technically if left under the control of the army and navy. Air attack on the enemy's war-making capacity rather than his armed forces provided a military role for air power which could be exercised independently of the two older services. Tactical support of land forces was excluded as a major role of British and American air power (but not of German or Russian) as it would have made the air force strategically subordinate to the army.

In my view, no real military theory of the " exercise of true air power," as it later come to be called by some British writers, was ever achieved: in effect, what passed for one was a theory of the exercise of air superiority, that is, how best to destroy the enemy's war-making capacity when the enemy could not destroy yours. No complete theory of such an independent strategy was ever formulated because it could not be kept within the air force's own province: for it would

7

have been necessary to include in it the passive defence of one's own civilian population. This is so because it soon became clear that air attack on the enemy's war-making capacity generally led to attack on cities and so on the civilian population. If the usual military principle had been adopted, that of preparing to be attacked with the same weapons with which one is preparing to attack an enemy, then the huge cost of an adequate civil defence system would have had to be incurred.

This doctrine of the independent use of air power against the war-making capacity of the enemy long pre-dated atom bombs and was, of course, the foundation of the area bombing offensives of the last war; it reached its peaks of esteem after 1942 in the Second World War, when Germany could not afford a serious counter-attack due to her heavy involvement in a vast land war in Russia, and during the period of atomic monopoly and marked quantitative superiority (1945-53) when no serious atomic counter-attack was possible.

It was towards the end of this period that the doctrine of massive retaliation at the times and places of our own choosing was formulated—it is said, by British strategists. This policy was generally understood to mean the use of atomic air attack on the enemy's war-making capacity rather than on his armed forces to make him abandon some military action which the West could not defeat by conventional means. Actually this policy had been effectively accepted all through the period of atomic monopoly, when in fact it was a militarily feasible policy. But its formulation in about 1954 in these memorable but disastrous words came just when it became militarily absurd due to the growth of the Soviet atomic stockpile. And today, with effective parity in atomic destructive power between East and West, the exercise of air power has become inextricably entangled with the preservation of the civil life of the country. Since most Western countries have made no attempt to provide any significant civil defence—even a moderately effective one would be enormously expensive and take many years to produce—they are not in a position to withstand the type of attack which they have planned to be able to inflict on the enemy. The exercise of true air power no longer appears so easy or cheap a road to victory.

It is important to discuss the possibility of distinguishing between atomic attack on the enemy's war-making capacity and deliberate attack on cities and the civilian population. Much stress has been placed by military analysts on this distinction between these two policies, that is, between a counter-force and a counter-city strategy. First, we note that the scale of a nuclear attack on the enemy's air and missile bases, to destroy his power of nuclear counter-attack, would have to be of such a scale as to lead to many tens of millions of enemy civilians killed, and would not differ in this respect greatly from a direct attack on his cities. Moreover, the likelihood of such an attack succeeding is very small, and so to launch one would be immensely risky.

Another logical distinction of current importance demands some mention: this is the distinction between preventive war and a pre-emptive first strike. Preventive war can be defined as an aggressive war undertaken by a power which considers itself temporarily superior to a hostile power, but knows that this superiority will not last. On the other hand, a pre-emptive first strike is an attack on the enemy made to forestall the attack which you know he is going to make on you. Since the Western world has often stated that it will never wage aggressive war, a preventive war is ruled out; on the other hand, clearly there can be fewer moral scruples against being the first to strike when, if you don't, you will certainly be destroyed. From the logical and moral standpoints the distinction is clear: in the actual world of real life and death the distinction can easily dissolve into nothingness in the inevitable fog of political crisis and war preparations. Consider such a time of crisis, with news of political uprisings, of troop movements reported by neutrals of dubious reliability, of radio interception, of disputed radar echoes, of widely diverging intelligence appreciation: if one considers such a situation, one will realise that it is unlkely that one will be certain enough of the enemy's intention to make it possible to base action policy on a distinction between preventive war and pre-emptive first strike. It may be that some future historian, if any survive the holocaust, may conceivably dig out of the ashes records by which he will be able to sift the conflicting evidence for or against the view that nation A immorally waged preventive war against nation B or morally made a pre-emptive first strike.

From such dilemmas as these comes the theory of deterrence; that is, that the role of atomic air power is no longer to win wars but to make them impossible. Thus came into existence an excessively complicated set of theoretical and numerical arguments essentially dealing with such problems as the extent to which a military threat which one dares not implement can deter an enemy from an action which you do not want him to take, or force him to do something which you want him to do. The ramifications of such theories and calculations have reached scholastic subtlety and are expressed in a formidable jargon: such as the numerical balancing of the enemy's pre-emptive first strike counter-force atomic capability against one's own second strike counter-city atomic capability, or vice versa; theorising which, however necessary it is, in my view is hardly likely to provide the military and civil heads of governments with the basis of practical decisions in a crisis—where the penalty for a miscalculation is annihilation.

If there are in any country, whether Soviet or Western, military strategists or operational analysts who favour a first strike counter-force attack, I think they would be guilty of staking the fate of civilisation on a game of atomic roulette played on electronic computers.

What is curious in this story is that the professional soldiers as a whole (with a few notable exceptions) put up such ineffective opposition to the official adoption of a doctrine with which most must have been in violent disagreement. Perhaps their predecessors' opposition to the legitimate demands of the rising air forces to a place in the military sun checked them from effective opposition to the later wild extravagances of air power theory.

If a scientist may be forgiven for mixing his classical metaphors, one might think of the earth-bound soldiers as becoming beguiled by the sirens' song of their airmen colleagues, who, spiritually intoxicated by flight at 50,000 feet in a jet bomber with an H-bomb in the bomb bay, sang of the ease with which they could keep erring mankind in order by threatening them (as if they were Jove himself) with atomic thunderbolts. This Jupiter complex of the airmen came to dominate disastrously the military thinking of much of the Western world and was an important factor in bringing about the present Western inferiority in conventional weapons. A comparison between national pride and service pride may not be inapt. Nationalism has been and still is one of the creative forces of history; but also, in extreme form, the seeds of its greatest disasters. So also pride in the role and tradition of a fighting service is the mainstay of its efficiency and morale: yet one must recognise that recent forms of extreme inter-service rivalry have had a disastrous effect on the whole structure of Western defence policy.

In fact the soldiers, even the greatest and most hard-headed, did get out of their depth when faced with the problems of air and land war in an age of atomic weapons. Without caricature one can construct out of military doctrine a few years ago the following propositions: If the enemy attacks with conventional forces, we will reply with atomic bombs on his cities. If his cities are attacked, the enemy will attack ours. If a country has no effective civil defence against atomic bombs and its cities are attacked, it will be defeated. None of our cities has any civil defence. The military doctrine might well be called ensuring defeat by syllogism.

Just what is the present policy of NATO with regard to the use of tactical nuclear weapons is not easy to discern. In some unofficial formulations one finds the assertion of the intention of the West to initiate the use of tactical nuclear weapons in certain circumstances, combined with the belief that limited nuclear war in Europe is not possible. This seems to come perilously close to another version of ensuring defeat by syllogism. Admittedly the NATO planners are faced with an intolerable problem through the refusal of their member states to provide adequate ground forces. But this fact does not make their apparent present policy sensible.

Parallel with the acceptance of a policy which amounted to attack on enemy civilian populations, as a reply to a hostile military attack, even made only with conventional forces, went inevitably a transformation of ethical standards. Within a few decades, most official, military, religious and moral leaders of the West came to accept as justifiable a military doctrine which previously they would have denounced as wicked, nauseatingly immoral and inconceivable as a policy for the West. If, in response to a Soviet aggression with conventional forces, the American and British atomic bombers had been set in motion to carry out the plans for which they are trained, then the six million victims of Hitler's gas chambers would be hardly remembered: the humane and civilised West would have sunk below the level of Genghis Khan.

To justify to the tender consciences of Western peoples the deliberate plan, in certain military circumstances, to annihilate tens of millions of Russian men, women and children, it was necessary to believe the U.S.S.R. to be innately aggressive and wicked. Once a nation pledges its safety to an absolute weapon, it becomes emotionally essential to believe in an absolute enemy.

At the intellectual level, it came to be believed that the U.S.S.R. might attack the West as soon as she estimated that she had a marginal superiority in military power; this is sometimes expressed in the current jargon by alleging that her intentions would become equal to her capability. On this view, the slightest falling behind of the West in military power would precipitate a holocaust. It was this set of beliefs which in 1957 led to the violent reaction to Sputnik I and which leads today to what I feel strongly is an excessive concern with the precise relative strength of the American and Soviet atomic striking power.

The era of the most fervent belief in the aggressiveness of the U.S.S.R. did, in fact, last from about 1948, when America had acquired a sizeable stockpile of atomic bombs, to about 1956, when the Soviet stockpile also became quite large. Now with the acceptance of effective atomic parity and the continued failure of the West to match the U.S.S.R. in land forces, a change in attitude towards the U.S.S.R. is politically necessary. For sound practical reasons the West is finding it necessary to abandon the moral consolation of having an absolute enemy. For there are clear political disadvantages in estimating the U.S.S.R. as both innately aggressive and possibly militarily stronger. Corresponding changes in the U.S.S.R. are clearly in progress and, under the influence of the immense destructiveness of American H-bombs, the Communist concept of Western capitalism as being inevitably aggressive is also under modification.

Till recently and with a few notable exceptions, there has been a surprising lack of protest from the moral leaders of the Western countries, whether in or out of the churches, against the gradual growth of policy of atomic attack on enemy civilian population; or of emphasis on the moral abyss into which the Western powers would have fallen if ever it had been put into operation.

Not infrequently the thesis has been upheld that national suicide was preferable to defeat. It is essential to understand that, while individuals can commit suicide, nations cannot: what is meant by this phrase, if anything at all, is that rather than accept defeat, the few individuals composing a government of a country would be justified in acting in such a way as to kill everybody. In fact, much of such talk was only moral boasting. It is interesting to speculate how many of the individuals who mouth these brave words would, in fact, individually commit suicide in the event of defeat—history suggests only a very few.

More than once I have heard my airmen friends pursue the logic of their thought to the point where they almost seemed to hold it the duty of their nation to accept destruction in order to validate the theory of true air power.

The policy of massive retaliation at the times and places of our own choosing, which in practice would in many circumstances have meant atomic attack on civilians, however much this fact had been clothed euphemistically as attacks on the enemy's war-making capacity, contradicted every moral and international obligation. It is ironical that this doctrine was the chosen slogan of Mr Foster Dulles, the most passionate political moralist of our times. There is a deeper irony in the fact that it was not the first use of the atomic bomb in 1945, but the loss of its monopoly by the West, which sent the moralists back to their morals and the theologians back to Grotius's formulation three hundred years ago of the *Principles of the Just War* in not so very different circumstances from today.

Quite recently a more forceful expression of the ethical view has been given by Lt.-General Sir John Cowley in a lecture to the Royal United Service Institution:

Before finishing this lecture I must say a word about the ethical problems which are raised by weapons of mass destruction, as I believe these to be extremely important and relevant to the whole business of future warfare. . . . The choice of death or dishonour is one which has always faced the professional fighting man and there must be no doubt in his mind what his answer must be. He chooses death for himself so that his country may survive, or on a grander scale so that the principles for which he is fighting may survive. Now we are facing a somewhat different situation, when the reply is not to be given by individuals but by countries as a whole. Is it right for the government of a country to choose complete destruction of the population rather than some other alternative, however unpleasant that other alternative may be? Should we in any circumstances be morally right to choose not only the termination of our own existence as a nation, but also the existence of future generations of our own countrymen and even of the whole civilised world? To take an example from history, it might well have been that the inhabitants of the Roman Empire, threatened with inevitable conquest by the barbarian hordes, might have considered that the total destruction of humanity would be preferable than the immediate prospects that faced them. How wrong they would have been. The human race can in time recover from almost anything, but it cannot recover from universal death.

As a result of these events, the utmost confusion reigns in the West about the basis of military planning, with a corresponding confusion in the political field—this has been designated by an American wit as a " state of agonised paralysis at the times and places of our own choosing."

As a result of growing awareness of the dangers inherent in the Western defence policy, the Labour Party in 1959 proposed a plan for a non-nuclear club, which may be aptly called a plan for maintaining a Great Power Safety Catch. This proposal has often been dismissed as insincere on the ground that the party leaders well knew that countries like France and Sweden might not agree to give up their prospects of nuclear weapons. I agree that, if the idea were abandoned merely because one or more countries declined to participate, the allegation of insincerity would have some foundation. But it seems clear that even a few members of the club would be better than none. It is entirely irrelevant at the moment whether the great majority of the weaker or smaller nations of the world are members or not, provided both great powers agree not to give any of them atomic weapons for their own independent use. The more important countries are those which could make their own within a few years, and every effort would have to be made to recruit as many of these as possible as members. But if a few are recalcitrant, harm, but not fatal harm, will be done. For even a club of limited membership means that the number of independent national fingers on nuclear triggers will be reduced, and so the overall risk will be less than if the spread of privately owned bombs is unchecked. Moreover, if the two great powers use their influence wisely they can certainly do much to make non-membership of the club less attractive. Some risk is inevitable in an age of atomic weapons—the risk that Britain might be atom bombed by France or Sweden is one which we may not be able to do anything about—but it won't disturb my sleep.

Since, then, the already existing nuclear stockpiles of the great powers must be counted in tens of thousands, a fraction, say ten per cent., would mean many thousands, and if these were given away to the complete control of smaller powers they would far outnumber those which are likely to be manufactured by any of the smaller powers for many years. So the immediate step in the problem of checking the spread of bombs in the West is not so much the checking of independent manufacture but of maintaining vigorously the present American ownership of all its nuclear weapons.

I conclude from these considerations that Britain should content herself with (a) inducing as many as possible medium and low rank nations to join the Great Power Safety Catch

Club; (b) obtaining a reasonable promise from both great powers that no atomic weapons will be given to any other powers, free of their own safety catch: this assured, Britain should follow the Labour Party proposals to cease production of her own A- and H-bombs, dismantle her stocks and submit her atomic installations to international inspection, as would all other members of the club. No alteration in Britain's relation to United States atomic bases or to NATO is implied by these first steps.

As has already been explained, there is no military method of closing rapidly the conventional weapon gap, and for the time being the West must learn to live with it. Moreover, one must not underestimate the political, financial and diplomatic difficulties of even starting the process of closing the gap. For this would involve an increased arms programme which would be hard to make acceptable just at a time when there is a real improvement in East-West relations and a real possibility of at least limited disarmament. In the case of Britain, some of the increased cost of strengthened land forces could perhaps be partly offset by reduction or elimination of her atomic weapon programme.

However, I do not believe that a marked increase of British land forces is a possibility, either for internal or for external political reasons, unless combined with a definite and drastic reduction of the West's dependence on atomic weapons. As already mentioned, I think that the minimum condition would be the public decision that the West would not be the first to use atomic weapons of any kind. In the disarmament discussions now in progress, the renunciation by the West of the first use of atomic weapons would be a powerful argument to negotiate a reduction of Soviet land forces in the European sector: for the Soviet military hold that conventional land warfare requires fewer troops than tactical atomic warfare.

In the past, one of the main arguments for an independent atomic capability for Britain has been that it could be used to force the United States to use her strategic atomic power on our behalf. In the dream world of some present-day military theorists the argument goes somewhat as follows. The value to

Britain of an independent atomic capability is that it could be used to trigger off the American Strategic Air Command if a crisis arose in which the President would not order it into action unless his hand was forced. For instance, if Soviet radar picked up a missile travelling from Britain, the U.S.S.R. would assume that a general attack had begun and retaliate against the whole Western system—or America would assume that they might assume this and immediately join in. So the British H-bomb was held to have a catalytic function in the sense that it gives Britain a share in the physical control of the Strategic Air Command far more convincing than any formal agreement with the United States.

Even in the era of atomic monopoly this argument seemed more than doubtful: in an era of atomic parity it is not only nonsense but the direct opposite of sense. For there cannot be the slightest doubt that if any medium-rank power initiated atomic warfare with the intention of involving a great power, the inevitable reaction of the latter would be to disclaim immediately all responsibility and to state emphatically by all available means that it was taking no part. The same course would be true if France tried to involve Britain in the same way or vice versa. No country will allow itself to be led by other countries to destruction without making every possible attempt to take evasive action. Just as atomic bombers have a technical fail-safe device which recalls them from a mission if anything goes wrong, so it is inevitable that every country will have to devise its own political fail-safe policy, designed to insulate itself from the dangers due to other countries' actions. This is the reason why the giant powers are bound to be the best disposed to non-nuclear allies. However much one may hope that the rigid national divisions of the world today may be softened, one inalienable right of the sovereign state is likely to remain for long: that is the right of a government to obliterate its citizens only at the times and places of its own choosing.

There can be little doubt that if nuclear weapons do come into the sole possession of many NATO powers, either by independent manufacture or by gifts from the giant powers, then a common defence policy for Western Europe will become very difficult and NATO may tend to break up into a number of nuclearly armed and mutually suspicious states: in fact, possibly more suspicious of each other than of the U.S.S.R.

In my view this situation cannot be altered by the building up of the much-discussed European as opposed to NATO deterrent—meaning by this a strategic and tactical nuclear capability under exclusive European control. I have failed to envisage any possible way in which a dozen independent nations could make arrangements for the joint control of such nuclear forces, which avoided on the one hand the danger of such divided and ponderous control as to remove its military value, and on the other, the much greater danger of careless or irresponsible action by one nation involving the others.

In fact, I can see no plausible way in which the European defence community can survive either with its own jointly owned nuclear forces or with individual national nuclear forces. I feel that the present situation, with an American safety catch on all its own nuclear weapons, wherever situated, is much more stable than either of the above alternatives. However, to keep it stable, it is essential for Britain to renounce her own nuclear forces, otherwise their spread to other countries will never be checked.

Eight

Tizard and the Science of War[1]
1960

It is sad indeed that the newly founded institute for the study of war (the Institute for Strategic Studies) should so soon have to mourn the loss of one of its most distinguished members. I wish to attempt to assess the nature of Tizard's direct personal contribution to the Allied victory in the Second World War and to trace the great influence he exerted on the general study of war, which is, of course, the explicit object of the Institute for Strategic Studies. All men's careers have much that is accidental in them, and no doubt there was an element of chance in the selection in 1934 by the Air Ministry of Sir Henry Tizard, then Rector of the Imperial College of Science and Technology, as chairman of the Committee for the Scientific Survey of Air Defence. But there was none in the brilliant and decisive manner in which Tizard exploited the opportunities thus given him, at a decisive moment of world history.

The military and political outlook of the middle 1930's was indeed ominous. The world economy was just beginning to stagger uncertainly out of one of the most disastrous slumps of history: Hitler had come to power in Germany and was openly preparing for war; the advance of aeronautical science and engineering had at last gone far enough to make it possible that air power might be a vital factor in a major war—if this were so, then the extreme vulnerability of Great Britain with her high population density and her close proximity to the mainland of Europe, which only too easily might fall into enemy hands, became of major

[1] Tizard Memorial Lecture delivered before the Institute for Strategic Studies on 11 Feb. 1960. Published in *Nature*, Vol. 185, No. 4714, 5 Mar. 1960, pp. 647-53.

military importance. As far as there was a military doctrine of the day, it seems to have been expressed in Baldwin's famous phrase in 1933 that "the bomber will always get through."

This, then, was the background to the first meeting in January 1935 of what became universally known as the " Tizard Committee "; its official terms of reference were: " To consider how far recent advances in scientific and technical knowledge can be used to strengthen the present methods of defence against hostile aircraft." In addition to the chairman there were originally only three members: H. E. Wimperis (then director of research at the Air Ministry), A. V. Hill (physiologist at University College, London) and myself, with A. P. Rowe (later to become the director of the famous Telecommunications Research Establishment) as secretary.

During its five years of existence—the Committee was dissolved during the first years of the war—four things of major importance were achieved, mainly through Tizard's vigorous and persuasive personality. Radar, which in Great Britain originated with Robert Watson Watt at the Radio Research Laboratory of the National Physical Laboratory, was energetically supported and, with the enthusiastic support of senior airmen, introduced secretly into the Air Force. When war came in 1939 the whole east and south-east coasts of England had their radar chains operational, and this was a decisive factor in the winning of the Battle of Britain in 1940.

The second indirect but very real achievement was to bring the senior officers of the Armed Services into much closer intimacy with the research and development scientists in the Government establishments. Tizard's gifts, which will be referred to again, of inspiring confidence in young and old, in those in authority and in those at the bench or on the gunsites: his passion for getting things done and his flair for interpreting the military requirements to the bench worker, and the technical possibilities to the Service chiefs: all these greatly enlivened and made more productive the scientific and technical side of the Air Force in the first instance, and then by example the other two Services.

The third achievement was the creation of mutual confidence and understanding between serving officers and university scientists; so that, when need arose, and it did arise very soon, many of the best academic research workers flocked out of the universities into radar stations, and later into service experimental establishments, where they became a vital part of the brilliantly creative, and sometimes obstreperous, teams, whose work had so profound an effect on the waging of the war.

The fourth achievement was the recognition that scientifically trained research workers had a vital part to play, not only (as of course was traditional) in the development of the weapons and gadgets of war but also in the actual study of operations. It was due to Tizard's personal initiative as early as 1936, before, in fact, radar data on approaching aircraft were available, that civilian scientists were attached to the fighter station at Biggin Hill to study the art of controlled interception, as it would have to be done, when a year or two later the radar chain would become operational. This experiment seems to have been the first official recognition that the actual operations of modern war are so complicated and change so fast that the traditional training of the serving officers and personnel is inadequate. In fact, many of the operational problems which arise when new equipment comes into service require for their solution the aptitudes of the scientific research worker: for he is trained to apply scientific methods to elucidate hitherto unknown and complex phenomena.

The Biggin Hill experiment was the first step towards the fully fledged Operational Research Sections attached eventually to all the major commands of all three services. A further important step was taken when, at the outbreak of the War, A. P. Rowe, then in charge of radar research at Bawdsey, sent a small group of scientists to Headquarters Fighter Command to study the actual use of the radar data so as to keep the radar scientists in the establishments briefed both on the actual performance of the sets in operations and on the real operational needs of Fighter Command. Out of this group grew the Fighter Command Operational Research Section as an integral part of the Command organisation. Analogous developments took place at Anti-Aircraft, Coastal and Bomber Commands, and also at the Admiralty and the War Office. These developments implied a great measure of mutual trust and understanding between the senior service officers and the often brash and initially very ignorant scientists—ignorant, that is, of most things that went on outside a university research department. This intimate relationship between professional fighting men in charge of operations and research scientists proved highly profitable, and some of the later operations of the war were carried out under a close scientific and statistical scrutiny. The pattern of organisation and method worked out in Britain during the first years of the war stimulated similar developments in the United States. Hitler's Third Reich saw no such collaboration. No doubt the almost unbroken German military successes of the first war years confirmed the highly competent military staffs in the view that they had no need to seek help from outside scientists, however brilliant. When the tide of war swept against Germany it was too late. Luckily for the Allies, Germany never produced its Tizard.

The importance of bringing scientists into close touch with operations had been clearly foreseen during the early days of the Tizard Committee. It was well expressed by the Secretary of State for Air, Lord Swinton, then Sir Philip Cunliffe Lister. In his book *I Remember* he wrote: "There was nothing new in the use of men of science as advisers to Service Departments and to the Committee of Imperial Defence. . . . There was nothing new, therefore, in calling in science to help; but from the moment I went to the Air Ministry, I felt that in the air, with all its unknown possibilities, we wanted a much closer and more intimate relationship. The scientists who were to work with us must be from the start an integral part of the Air Staff." Of the Tizard Committee he wrote: " . . . they were at the heart of operational planning. That relationship was, and I believe always will be, the key to success in scientific co-operation."

Prominent among the senior Air Force officers who welcomed and co-operated closely with the Tizard Committee were Air Marshal Sir Cyril Newall, chief of the Air Staff 1937-40; Air Marshal Sir Hugh Dowding, Air Member for Research and Development 1930-36 and then Commander-in-Chief Fighter Command, and so the first operational user of radar; Air Marshal Sir Wilfred Freeman, who succeeded Dowding in 1936 as member for Research and Development; Air Marshal Tedder (now Lord Tedder), who was Director-General for Research and Development during 1938-40; and Air Marshal Sir Philip Joubert, then Air Officer Commanding Fighting Area and later Commander-in-Chief Coastal Command.

Unfortunately, Tizard published little about his own contribution to these developments, though no doubt much of great interest will be found in Whitehall files, when these become available to historians. So far as I know, his lecture to the Royal United Service Institution in 1946, entitled "Science and the Services," and his Haldane Memorial Lecture at Birkbeck College in 1955, entitled "A Scientist In and Out of the Civil Service," are almost all that are available: and in these, with characteristic modesty, there is little about his own achievements. So the history of these vital years has to be pieced together from personal memories.

Although the Air Defence Committee started up in January 1935 with only Tizard, Hill, Wimperis and myself as members, in July of the same year the Secretary of State for Air, under pressure from Mr Winston Churchill, enlarged it by the addition of Professor F. A. Lindemann (afterwards Lord Cherwell). It was not long before the meetings became long and controversial: the main points of dispute concerned the priorities for research and development which should be assigned to the various projects which were being fathered by the Committee. For example, Lindemann wanted higher priority for the detection of aircraft by infra-red radiation and for the dropping of parachute-carrying bombs in front of enemy night bombers, and lower priority for radar, than the other members thought proper. On one occasion Lindemann became so fierce with Tizard that the secretaries had to be sent out of the committee room so as to keep the squabble as private as possible. In August 1936, soon after this meeting, A. V. Hill and I decided that the Committee could not function satisfactorily under such conditions; so we resigned. A few weeks later Lord Swinton re-appointed the original Committee without Lindemann, but with Professor E. V. Appleton, and a few months later with Professor T. R. Merton, as additional members.

During the years 1935-39 the Committee investigated and assessed a large number of projects, good and bad; we visited many establishments and discussed all aspects of air defence problems with air marshals, with pilot officers and with scientists in their laboratories. Pre-eminent, of course, was radar, both ground and air-borne. The story of radar has often been told, and all I wish to emphasise is the vital part played by the confidence which Tizard did so much to build up between the senior airmen, the research workers and the responsible Cabinet ministers. The full backing of the Committee became an effective way of getting high priority given to a project. Without such mutual trust the scientific development of radar could not have forged ahead at such speed, nor would the tens of millions of pounds have been provided so rapidly and secretly by the Treasury to build the radar chain.

In 1937 Tizard was made chairman of another Committee, this time for the Scientific Survey of Air Offence, modelled on the lines of the Air Defence Committee. However, it failed to come to grips with the problems of the use of bombers and made no decisive impact. Possibly Tizard himself was too heavily involved in air defence problems easily to switch his interest: possibly the failure was partly due to the not very sympathetic response by those in the Air Force then concerned with bombing policy. Whatever the cause, I think it would be fair to hold that until the war was well advanced, Bomber Command was less scientifically minded than either Fighter, Coastal or Anti-Aircraft Command. Moreover, it was just this failure to think and analyse scientifically which delayed for too long the recognition of the extreme ineffectiveness of our early bombing offensive.

Sir Winston Churchill tells how Professor Lindemann in 1941 informed him that, of the bomber crews who thought they had found their target, it had been shown by analysing flash photographs that two-thirds were not within five miles of it. Once these facts were fully recognised, high priority was put on navigational aids of various kinds, and matters greatly improved.

In November 1939 Tizard, then scientific adviser to the Air Ministry, suggested that A. V. Hill should go to Washington to act as scientific adviser to work with the Air Attaché, so as to get scientific help on defence problems from the United States. Since scientific developments were likely to play a major part in determining the issue of the war, the importance of attempting to get official approval for Britain to tap the vast scientific resources of the United States was very great. In a typically apt phrase Tizard described his policy as that of " bringing American scientists into the war before their Government." In this he succeeded in a startlingly successful manner. When A. V. Hill reached Washington, he realised that this objective could only be attained if a complete interchange of scientific secrets between the two countries could be arranged. With the help of the British Ambassador, Lord Lothian, President Roosevelt became convinced of the importance of such interchange, as were also the American Service chiefs. On the other hand, the task of convincing the British Government that it was useful and safe to entrust our most closely guarded secrets to the scientists and Armed Services of a then neutral country, with not a few anti-British elements in it, was not easy. But at last Tizard succeeded; and in September 1940, as the " Blitz " on London started, the Tizard Mission, with Cockcroft as second in command, set out for the United States with the famous black box containing samples, blueprints and reports on nearly all important new British war devices. These included radar, fire control, under-water detection, aircraft turrets, Whittle's jet engine and, above all, a sample 9·1 cm. resonant cavity magnetron.

Within a few days American scientists had the magnetron working, to find it gave a thousand times the power formerly available. This remarkable invention, due to Randall and Boot working in Oliphant's laboratory at the University of Birmingham, was called by Watson Watt " a radically new and immensely powerful device which remains the heart of every modern radar equipment." An assessment of the importance of this interchange of secret military information is given in James Phinney Baxter's book *Scientists Against Time*, published in 1946 with a foreword by Vannevar Bush. The writer comments on the contents of the black box as " the most valuable cargo ever brought to our shores " and " the single most important element in reverse lease lend." He goes on: " In the early days of scientific interchange, the British gave more than they received." Later the debt was repaid many-fold; in particular, for example, by the superb centimetric anti-aircraft radar set SCR-584 and the proximity fuse which together led to such brilliant successes by Anti-Aircraft Command during the V1 attack on England in 1944. The former set was a product of the famous Radiation Laboratory at the Massachusetts Institute of Technology, which was, in fact, founded as a result of a meeting of the Tizard Mission with American scientists in September 1940.

This imaginative act of trust, which Tizard and A. V. Hill first envisaged and finally forced through Whitehall, had immensely beneficial effects on the scientific aspects of the Allied war effort. Cockcroft reminds us that the mission was magnificently organised by Tizard and that he had the inspiration to bring a mixed team of serving officers and scientists. For the first time our American friends heard civilian scientists discussing authoritatively the instruments of war and then heard the Service people following on with practical experience.

When Tizard returned to England in September 1940 on the completion of his American mission, he worked full time at the Ministry of Aircraft Production and later became a member of the Air Council. The Air Defence Committee itself died a natural death, since an advisory committee of part-time members was not useful under fully mobilised war conditions.

There is little doubt that Tizard found less than satisfaction in what he could achieve during the years 1941 and 1942. In spite of his wide knowledge of the Government machine, he seems to have been genuinely disappointed to find that the Air Council rarely discussed strategy or tactics, but often minor administrative matters: he related that at one meeting of the Air Council the main business was the inspection of an exhibition of different designs of W.A.A.F. underwear! A deeper difficulty underlay the frustrations of this period. For it was not at all easy for a Service Ministry to incorporate a man as senior as Tizard in its taut, executive, war-time machine. On one hand he was too senior to do his own devilling among the files at the lower levels of the machine, where much of the real work of a department is done—to be sure, he was too impatient to have been very good at this—and on the other hand, he had too much self-respect to acquire influence by becoming a courtier. Tizard evidently felt that he was not wanted in Whitehall and so he accepted the presidency of Magdalen College, Oxford, where he remained, apart from some Government advisory work and several important visits abroad, until after the end of the war.

Shortly before he went to Oxford, Tizard became involved in a controversy about bombing policy which had far-reaching consequences. The interest of this story is not only its importance at the time, but also that it concerned problems of the theory and practice of bombing which, now with the advent of nuclear weapons, is giving rise to so much deep thought, subtle analysis and high controversy, carried on not least by members of the Institute for Strategic Studies.

As I remember it, what happened was this. In the early spring of 1942 the Prime Minister was extremely anxious that everything possible should be done by Bomber Command to help the hard-pressed Soviet armies at Stalingrad. About April a Cabinet paper (which was known to have been written in Lord Cherwell's office, Cherwell then being Paymaster-General and the Prime Minister's scientific adviser) was issued on the probable effect on Germany of the British bombing offensive over the next eighteen months, that is, until the early autumn of 1943. The paper laid down the policy of directing the bombing offensive primarily against the German working-class housing—middle-class housing was too spread out to be a good target and factories or military installations were too difficult to find and hit. So far as my memory goes, the paper claimed that it should be possible within the stated period to destroy 50 per cent. of all houses in all towns of more than 50,000 population in Germany, if Britain concentrated all her efforts on the production of bombers and used them for this purpose. Tizard studied this paper in detail and concluded that the estimate of the number of houses likely to be destroyed in the next eighteen months was five times too high. At that time I was director of Operational Research at the Admiralty, and I was also asked to comment on the Cabinet paper. I came independently essentially to the same conclusion as Tizard—I think I estimated the error as sixfold. The main mistake made in the Cabinet paper was to assume that all bombers which would be delivered from the factories in the next eighteen months would in the same period have dropped all their bombs on Germany. The year or more from the completion of a bomber to the completion of its average operational life of twenty sorties had not been fully allowed for. The bombing survey after the war showed that the number of houses actually destroyed in the assigned period was only one-tenth of the estimate in the Cabinet paper: this agreed rather closely with Tizard's and my estimates, allowing for reduced numbers of bombers actually supplied to Bomber Command.

By this time a certain allergy to arithmetic was spreading in Whitehall, and our numerical forebodings went unheeded: the Air Ministry agreed with the Cabinet Office paper, and the policy of dehousing the German working-class population, with the object of lowering its morale and will to fight, became a major part of the British war effort.

The story goes that at that time in the Air Ministry it was said of anyone who added two and two together to make four, " He is not to be trusted; he has been talking to Tizard and Blackett." Less agreeable stories circulated: that anyone who made such calculations must be a defeatist.

So far as I know, Tizard never wrote anything of this period and spoke but sparingly; but he did comment after the war in his Royal United Service Institution lecture on the theory and practice of aerial bombing. " Experience has shown that a nation, with toughness, stamina and a will to live and work, can stand far more punishment in the form of bombardment of cities and homes than most people thought possible before the trial. No one thinks now that it would have been possible to defeat Germany by bombing alone. The actual effort in man-power and resources that was expended in bombing Germany was greater than the value in man-power of the damage caused. . . ."

If only Tizard's Offence Committee had succeeded as well as his Defence Committee, and if as a result a strong and trusted operational research section had been earlier established at Bomber Command, I think it likely that the numerical error on which the area bombing campaign was initiated would not have been made and that great advantage to the war effort would have resulted.

Whether or no this bombing controversy in 1942 was the decisive factor, there is little doubt that at that time there was not room enough at the top in Whitehall for both Tizard and Cherwell. The incompatibility of these two brilliant men, and one-time intimate friends, proved a calamity to the nation.

Too much, however, must not be made of personal factors, strong as these no doubt were. For the entry of academic scientists into fields of military strategy and tactics brings to them responsibilities for advising on courses of action on which the survival of one's country—or, today, in an age of nuclear weapons, the survival of civilisation—may depend. So real differences of technical judgment become allied to differences of temperament and lead to lasting and often bitter struggles. The war-time controversy on bombing policy with conventional explosives and the strains that it engendered in Whitehall were but a minor foretaste of the still more bitter controversy, particularly in the United States, engendered by atomic weapons, which has left such a trail of personal antagonisms behind it.

The result of the 1945 General Election, with the consequent return of Cherwell to Oxford, opened the way for Tizard to return to Whitehall. The opportunity soon presented itself, for in 1946 the new Government, headed by our President, Lord Attlee, invited him to become chairman of two new high-level advisory bodies, the Defence Research Policy Committee and the Advisory Council on Scientific Policy. Widespread acclaim from both scientists and military greeted the formation of these bodies and the choice of Tizard to head them. Thus Tizard, for the third and last time, became a full-time civil servant. What he achieved in the six years to his retirement in 1952 was by no means the least of his service to the nation, for there is no doubt that a great part of the credit for the growth to maturity of these two committees must go to him.

These last six years of his active life were in a real sense the fulfilment of his quarter-of-a-century-old belief in the importance to the life and prosperity of Great Britain of a close relationship between the administrative and scientific worlds, a belief which was one of the factors which led him in 1920 to forsake an academic for a Civil Service career.

It would probably be generally agreed that the Defence Research Policy Committee has proved a more effective instrument than the Advisory Council on Scientific Policy. This is certainly mainly due to the much narrower and administratively well-defined field of its activity. The executive authority residing in the Defence Ministry and the Chiefs of Staff, together with the related financial power of the Supply Ministries, gives them almost complete control of all defence matters, whether in the Government or in industry. So any advice from the Defence Research Policy Committee, on which these Government bodies are represented, is likely to be relevant and acted upon. Some of those who were intimately concerned with the working of the Committee hold that Tizard moulded it into the finest organisation for co-ordinating the scientific and technical aspects of war policy which has ever existed in the Western world. During his time as chairman, from 1946 until 1952, Tizard's influence was exercised over a wide range of important and complex problems, including those arising from atomic weapons, super-sonic fighters, V-bombers and guided missiles. He shared much of the responsibility for developing the rocket range at Woomera, and when some Australians were worried that it would cost them a lot of money and perhaps no one would use it, he told them not to worry as it would attract work and men as a magnet atracts iron filings. A good example of his flair for the important practical action arose out of a discussion concerning the rocket and guided missile programme. After years of intricate debate on what the research and development programme should be, when a practical plan was eventually hammered out, Tizard ruled that the implementation of the programme should be carefully watched but that there should be no alteration or even discussion of the basic programme for two years. This ruling is reminiscent of his advice to fishermen: " Don't waste time changing flies and always know what the fishes are doing."

In his Haldane Memorial Lecture at Birkbeck College in 1955, Tizard referred to the creation of the Defence Policy Research Committee thus: " It was a revolution in organisation. It was not until a short time before the Second World War started that scientists began to exercise an influence on the tactical use of weapons and later on strategy. I believe I can truthfully say that the very idea that they should interfere in such matters was repugnant to senior officers twenty years ago. It was the experience of war that caused the revolution and the appointment of the new Committee, far from being resisted by the Chiefs of Staff, was, in fact, initiated by them." " The Chairman . . . has full access to all relevant information, and attends the meetings of the Chief of Staff Committees not only when he is specially asked to do so, but whenever he judges that his presence will be useful. No major recommendation on Defence Policy is made by the Chiefs of Staff without his knowledge and assistance."

The role of the Advisory Council on Scientific Policy, on the other hand, was much more difficult to define. Its advisory activities ranged over a wide field, including scientific and technological education and manpower, the organisation of Government science and indirectly the efficiency of research and development in private industry. Taking into account the rigid autonomy of Government Departments and the privacy of private enterprise, the Advisory Council, with neither money nor executive authority, had from the beginning and still has, a difficult task. Perhaps its main success has been in the field of scientific and technical manpower. Its relative lack of impact on the national life is not to be attributed to lack of ability or Tizard, but to the essential difficulty of injecting a small degree of direction into a social system where, outside a few fields such as education and defence, the word planning is not seldom used as a term of ridicule. These difficulties are currently receiving much public attention, stimulated by the vast scientific and technological power of the United States, by the much faster industrial growth of some of our European competitors and by the massive technological and economic advance of the highly directed economy of the Soviet countries. Here are problems galore for Tizard's successors on the Advisory Council on Scientific Policy to solve.

The changes that have taken place in the world of military science in the past twenty-five years, that is, since Tizard's Air Defence Committee was formed, have indeed been immense. The revolution in weapons is, of course, the most obvious, and the ultimate origin of the other organisational and psychological changes. In the 1930's it was certainly important in Great Britain to bring into the defence field from academic life as many highly trained and critical minds as possible; now in 1960 the outburst of analytical thinking and writing on military subjects by scientists, lawyers, historians, psychologists and philosophers, and, of course, by retired generals, is becoming almost overwhelming and is one of the fundamental causes of the foundation of the Institute for Strategic Studies. No serving officer could possibly find the time to read all the current literature; those amateurs like myself who write on these matters have no time to read all that the other amateurs write. The flood is greatest in the United States, where many universities have their military or foreign policy research groups or institutes, where brilliant academic minds analyse and dissect our present Western military discontents and are by no means shy of ingenious solutions. Traditionally, Britain has been averse to thinking about war in between fighting wars; once they are over we tend to forget them until the next time. Even today there are only two academic posts in our universities concerned with military studies. The Institute for Strategic Studies is attempting, and I think successfully, partially to fill this gap.

This huge expansion of thinking about military subjects is, of course, largely due to nuclear weapons, and is to be welcomed as a sensible response to a highly complex and dangerous situation. On the other hand, I cannot convince myself that the practical content of the response has every-where proved adequate to the challenge. The intellectual level of much of this discussion is of the highest, so high that I find much of it very hard to understand, and I wonder sometimes whether it is all rooted in military and political reality. The policies recommended by many of these studies seem not always to have been felt through to actual potential action. I think the essential prerequisite of sound military advice is that the giver must convince himself that if he were responsible for action, he would himself act so. During the war, when the Operational Research Group at the Admiralty had proved intellectually to themselves that big convoys were safer than small ones, before we advised the Navy to make this major change, we had to decide whether we really believed in our own analysis. I personally convinced myself that I did, by the conviction that if I were to send my children across the Atlantic during the height of the U-boat attacks I would have sent them by a big rather than by a small convoy. I think that occasionally analogous personal tests of belief in one's own recipes may be useful in the study of nuclear war. Perhaps part of the fault has been the relative silence of some professional fighting men, often may be for good Service reasons.

What I feel is needed now is more effective analytic activity within the Armed Services by those senior officers who would have, in the event of war, the actual responsibility of waging it—and conceivably of pressing nuclear triggers. All generals will agree that atomic war is much too serious a matter to be left to professors.

History has shown that Wimperis's choice in 1934 of Tizard as chairman of the famous Air Defence Committee was a very wise one: he had just the right mixture of academic and military background to enable him to build a bridge between these two very distinct worlds. Son of a captain in the Navy, who had been navigator to the *Challenger* Expedition and later Assistant Hydrographer, and who was also a Fellow of the Royal Society, the young Tizard had also been destined for the Navy but had been rejected because of eyesight. This, however, did not prevent him from becoming a pilot in the Royal Flying Corps during the First World War, where he rose to the rank of lieutenant-colonel and was awarded the Air Force Cross. Previously to this he had taken both mathematics and chemistry at Oxford, had spent a year in Berlin with Nernst, and had made researches in both physical chemistry and physics. Early in 1917 he was put in charge of all experimental flying at Martlesham Heath and later in the year went to headquarters of the Ministry of Munitions. In his lecture to the Royal United Service Institution in 1946, Tizard, commenting on his experiences at Upavon as a young Royal Flying Corps pilot, wrote of the " absence of any sign of interest on the part of the War Office . . . in the scientific development of the new fighting arm . . . as for air fighting, the enemy called the tune and we danced to it." Thus his early experiences in the Royal Flying Corps must have fixed as firmly in his mind the danger to the nation of technological inferiority in war as my experience in the Navy did in mine.

There is a well-known story of his Martlesham time. Just as he was about to take off to test a new Sopwith Camel fighter, a formation of Gotha bombers approached London. Tizard had the untested guns loaded and intercepted the bombers on their return, only to find that his guns jammed immediately. So he joined the formation and made notes about the speed and performance of the Gothas, which information was badly needed. He then waved good-bye. His most important contribution during the First World

War was the development of a hitherto non-existent system of performance testing, so that afterwards no new design went into production without proper testing.

After the war he returned to Oxford and to physical chemistry, but only for a short time, as in 1920 he became assistant secretary of the Department of Scientific and Industrial Research, and secretary in 1926. Then in 1929 he became Rector of the Imperial College of Science and Technology, where he remained until 1942. In 1933 he was appointed chairman of the Aeronautical Research Committee and held the post for ten years. He was thus very knowledgeable about all aeronautical matters.

With such experience and such interests it is not surprising that Tizard exploited so brilliantly the opportunity which Wimperis afforded him by making him chairman of that " grand body," as Rowe once called it. Tizard knew the Government machine well enough to realise that all committees could not achieve such great things, and in his Haldane Lecture one finds a good example of that dry wit which all his friends remember as one of his most endearing characteristics and which we all mourn to have lost. In writing of the early thirties and of the gradual growth of a machinery for scientific advice to the Government, Tizard refers to one committee in the following words: " The Committee on tsetse fly control was still sitting in 1938 without any noticeable effect on the expectation of life of these pests."

Tizard's outstanding achievement in bringing civilian scientists and serving officers into such fruitful contact was based on personal qualities of a high order. Though fundamentally of a conservative temperament and a great admirer of the virtues of tradition in national life, he was a radical in technological matters, and approached new problems and possibilities with courage, enthusiasm and originality. It is true that he often followed up too many ideas at the same time and sometimes bewildered his colleagues by alteration of course induced by the almost gad-fly quickness of mind. One reason for this was his instant readiness to look at anyone's bright ideas and to see whether they could be made to work. It is these qualities which perhaps led to him being considered a poor administrator by some people—it is true that he would sometimes chase some hare for a few weeks and then switch his interest suddenly to some more profitable quarry. However, these intellectual escapades were seldom fruitless and were an essential part of his method of spotlighting the really important problems. When he himself had sifted the ideas thrown up by his own exuberant technical and administrative imagination he was exceedingly practical.

Throughout our long friendship, which began in 1934 when I became a member of the Aeronautical Research Committee of which he was then chairman—and what an admirable chairman he was—I have never failed to find stimulus, entertainment and enlightenment from his company. Though sometimes a little irritable, he was essentially warm-hearted and very wise. Of the individuals who have influenced me by their personality, I think Tizard comes next to Rutherford. As has already been emphasised, he had a most unusual ability to establish immediate and mutually stimulating contact with anyone doing a job; he seemed as genuinely interested in talking to a college porter, an aircraftman or a young scientist as to a crack pilot, a professor or an air marshal. A visit with Tizard to an experimental establishment was an exhilarating experience; he left behind him a newer awareness of the tasks and a new keenness to get results.

Along with the great encouragement he so often gave to the younger men in the Services and in academic life, and his gift for inspiring them with his own enthusiasm for getting things done, his flair for setting the cat among the official pigeons, and for ignoring the normal channels, made him not always popular with the upper hierarchy. His sharp incisive wit was often exercised at the expense of the complacent, the pompous and the incompetent—among these he undoubtedly made enemies—but I have never heard of it being used at the expense of the young, the vigorous or the keen. There is a story which shows his ready wit, dating from the meeting of the British Association in Canada before the war. Tizard and a colleague inadvertently crossed over into the

United States near Niagara. When challenged by a police-
man, and not having their passports with them, they produced
their British Association membership cards. When the police-
man told them that " The American Government doesn't
recognise British Science," the lightning reply came from
Tizard, " Oh, that's all right, neither does the British Government." As Linstead, the Rector of Imperial College, recently
wrote, Tizard himself played a major part in making the
crack less applicable today.

In his Haldane Lecture, Tizard pays the highest tribute to
Lord Haldane for his achievements over four decades ago, in
making official circles in Britain first conscious of the national
implications of the scientific-technological revolution. In a
sense Haldane was the first British Minister for Science:
Tizard was his disciple and we today are his. I will conclude
by quoting to you, as expressing most aptly what many of
his intimate colleagues feel about Tizard, what he felt about
Bertram Hopkinson, Professor of Engineering at Cambridge,
and one of the outstanding pioneers in Great Britain of the
application of science to war, and whose death in an aeroplane accident in 1918 was a real calamity. Tizard wrote:
" He had not only the position, but the qualities, to command respect from soldiers and scientists alike: and those
who served under him, and who have been able to do anything for the Services in later years, have owed our own
capacity largely to his leadership and inspiration."

Nine

Science and Government[1]
1961

To the people making it, history is a long series of decisions: whether to do this or to do that; whether to take one road or another; whether to be bold or whether to be cautious; whether to make war or to make peace; or, in this nuclear age, whether to live or to die. H-bombs have made us all decision-conscious. All decisions must start with an analysis of the past, for without understanding the past it is not possible to predict the future, and without some prediction of the future no rational decisions can be made. The decision to take one course of action rather than another implies the prediction that the one chosen will produce more favourable results than the one rejected. Unless one can make some such prediction, one has to rely on a guess; when this is successful, history calls it inspired.

How have the important decisions of the tumultuous past three decades actually been made? What sort of people made them? How much part did calm and detached thought play, and how much instinctive feelings or plain emotion? To what extent did personal loyalties and personal hates dictate the pattern of world events? To what extent did the decision makers think out the complex consequences of their actions and plan accordingly? Or did they stake their country's— or indeed mankind's—future on a gamble? Or were the decision makers perhaps more like players of chess than of poker?

All these questions came into my mind as I read C. P. Snow's *Science and Government*,[2] originally presented at Harvard University as the Godkin Lectures. Snow is prim-

[1] *Scientific American*, Apr. 1961.
[2] Cambridge, Mass. and London 1961.

arily concerned with understanding how some of the important decisions of our time were in fact made. His training
as an experimental scientist, his years as a Civil Servant in
close touch with the British scientific effort during the war
and after, his experience as a director of a major engineering
firm and finally his authorship of many successful novels—
have given him a background that no contemporary, either
in Britain or the U.S., has had. Moreover, his main interests
as a novelist have been concerned less with the relationship
between men and women than with the relationship between
men and men, as they live their professional lives in government departments, in scientific laboratories, in the board
rooms of industry or the common rooms of universities. The
interplay of personalities and policies, of abilities and ambi-
tions, the actual functioning of that remarkable abstraction,
the so-called British Establishment, were among the interests
that have made Snow the novelist of committees and court
politics in this scientific age.

Snow analyses in detail two major decisions of British war
policy: the decision made between 1935 and 1937 to give
the development of radar the highest possible priority, and
the decision in 1942 to make the bombing of German cities a
major part of the British war effort. In the conflicts that
preceded these two fateful decisions, two outstanding and
very different scientists, Henry Tizard and Frederick Lindemann, played a major role. Much of Snow's book is concerned
with the clash between these two strong personalities. By
various accidents I was personally involved in both conflicts,
and I can vouch for the fundamental truth of Snow's account
of what went on. Moreover, I think that his description of
the conflicts and his penetrating insight into the characters
of the two men is brilliantly carried out: this is a first-rate
piece of writing. One quotation must suffice here:

" Judged by the simple criterion of getting what he
wanted, Lindemann was the most successful court politician
of the age. One has to go back a long way, at least as far
as Père Joseph, to find a gray eminence half as effective.
Incidentally, there exists a romantic stereotype of the courtier
—as someone supple, devoid of principle, thinking of nothing

9

except keeping his place at court. Now Lindemann was, in functional terms, a supreme courtier; and yet no one could be more unlike that stereotype. Life is not as simple as that, nor as corrupt in quite that way. Throughout his partnership with Churchill, Lindemann remained his own man. A remarkable number of the ideas came from him. It was a two-sided friendship. There was admiration on Lindemann's side, of course, but so there was on Churchill's. It was a friendship of singular quality—certainly the most selfless and admirable thing in Lindemann's life, and in Churchill's, much richer in personal relations, it nevertheless ranked high. It is ironical that such a friendship, which had much nobility and in private showed both men at their human best, should in public have led them into bad judgments."

There is no doubt that Tizard must be given a major part of the credit, and Lindemann none, for the radar chain. When war came, Britain had an operational early-warning radar system all around its east and south coasts; moreover, it had fighter squadrons trained to intercept the German bombers by using radar plots. Our edge over the enemy was more in massive deployment and operational training than in the basic knowledge of electronics. Tizard, above all others, was responsible for the high priority that led to the rapid development and installation of the radar system. Without it the Battle of Britain in 1940—a near thing at best—might have been lost, with incalculable historic consequences. As Snow points out, this particular decision was not technically a difficult one, being in effect a choice of doing something that might work as against doing nothing. The conflict over the decision, which was very real and in slightly different circumstances might have gone the wrong way, appears in retrospect to have been at the bottom purely personal. At that time Lindemann opposed anything suggested by his former friend Tizard.

Tizard's second vital contribution related directly to the United States. In the summer of 1940, soon after the fall of Paris, he persuaded a reluctant British Government to send to the United States a mission headed by himself with the famous black box containing samples, blueprints and reports on nearly all important new British war devices, including the magnetron.

By 1941 Tizard was widely recognised as the ablest British scientist to apply himself to the problems of war. He was popular both with scientists and with the armed services; he had two major achievements to his credit—the radar chain and the American mission—and in addition he had done much to make the services scientifically minded. Two years later he was effectively out of the war effort. How this came about is a major theme of Snow's book. The cause of this disastrous turn of fortune—in my view disastrous for the whole British war effort—was another conflict of judgment on priorities, this time about the bombing offensive. As I was deeply involved in this, I can add something to Snow's vivid account. I will also say something of the historic background and of the aftermath of the decision to concentrate a major part of the British war effort on the destruction of German housing. So far as I know, it was the first time that a modern nation had deliberately planned a major military campaign against the enemy's civilian population rather than against his armed forces. During my youth in the Navy in World War I such an operation would have been inconceivable. Incidentally, the German air attacks on London from September 1940 to May 1941 were undertaken with little serious planning, and they were called off when the Germans attacked the U.S.S.R.

I remember fire-watching on the roof of a block of flats in Westminster in September 1940, on the evening of the day the " blitz " began. We were watching the glow from the burning East London docks, and bombs were falling on central London. A young bomber pilot by me said: " I can hardly bear to wait till we can do it back to them." Such understandable sentiments do not necessarily make good strategy, nor does the commonly used argument: What else could we have done?

The origin of the Allied bombing offensive goes much further back. It was a product of the rise of the air forces of the world and of their determination to evolve a strategic role for air power that would made them independent of the

two older services, the army and the navy. Since this requirement excluded co-operation with either of these two services
as its major role, the air force sought the strategic role of
attacking the sources of economic and military power in the
enemy country. When this policy was first put into effect
in the early summer of 1940, it was gradually realised that
the accuracy of navigation was far too poor to allow our night
bombers to hit anything smaller than a fair-sized town—and
generally not even that. So the attempt to hit military
installations, factories and transport centres was abandoned
for a general attack on the centres of civilian population.
Until 1943 the effort was on such a small scale and was so
ineffective as to have negligible military effect. The decision
to make the dehousing of the German working-class population, with the object of lowering its morale and will to fight,
a major part of the British war effort was made in the spring
of 1942, as Snow relates.

From my talks with Lindemann at this time I became
aware of that trait of character which Snow so well emphasises: this was his almost fanatical belief in some particular
operation or gadget to the almost total exclusion of wider
considerations. Bombing to him then seemed the one and
only useful operation of the war. He said to me (unfortunately I have no record of this conversation, but he probably
said the same to others) that he considered any diversion of
aircraft production and supply to the anti-submarine campaign, to army co-operation or even to fighter defence—in
fact, to anything but bombing—as being a disastrous mistake.
Lindemann even suggested that the building up of strong
land forces for the projected invasion of France was wrong.
Never have I encountered such fanatical belief in the efficacy
of bombing.

The high priority given thereafter to everything pertain-
ing to the bombing offensive made it very difficult to get
adequate air support for the vital Battle of the Atlantic.
If this had got worse there would have been no more bombing
offensive for lack of fuel and bombs, and no invasion of
France in 1944. I remember that during the winter of 1942
and 1943 the Admiralty had to enlist President Roosevelt's

personal influence to ensure that a squadron of that admirable anti-submarine aircraft, the B24, was allocated to Coastal Command (where they were brilliantly successful) and not, as the Air Staff wanted, sent to bomb Berlin, for which they were not very suitable. However, at the Casablanca Conference in January 1943, a combined American and British bombing offensive was formally adopted as a major part of the British war strategy.

No part of the war effort has been so well documented as this campaign, which had as its official objective " the destruction and dislocation of the German military, industrial and economic system and the undermining of the morale of the German people to the point where their capacity for armed resistance is fatally weakened." Immediately after the war the U.S. Strategic Bombing Survey was sent to Germany to find out what had been achieved. A very strong team (which included two men who are now advisers to President Kennedy, J. K. Galbraith and Paul Nitze) produced a brilliant report, which was published in September 1945. Without any doubt the area-bombing offensive was an expensive failure. About 500,000 German men, women and children were killed, but in the whole bombing offensive 160,000 U.S. and British airmen, the best young men of both countries, were lost. German war production went on rising steadily until it reached its peak in August 1944. At this time the Allies were already in Paris and the Russian armies were well into Poland. German civilian morale did not crack.

Perhaps it is not surprising that the report of the Strategic Bombing Survey seems to have had a rather small circulation; it is to be found in few libraries and does not appear to have been directly available, even to some historians of the war.

If the Allied air effort had been used more intelligently, if more aircraft had been supplied for the Battle of the Atlantic and to support the land fighting in Africa and later in France, if the bombing of Germany had been carried out with the attrition of the enemy defences in mind rather than the razing of cities to the ground, I believe the war could have been won half a year or even a year earlier. The only major campaign in modern history in which the traditional military doctrine of waging war against the enemy's armed forces was abandoned for a planned attack on its civilian life was a disastrous flop. I confess to a haunting sense of personal failure, and I am sure that Tizard felt the same way. If we had only been more persuasive and had forced people to believe our simple arithmetic, if we had fought officialdom more cleverly and lobbied ministers more vigorously, might we not have changed this decision?

Snow devotes the last part of his book to extracting from these two cautionary tales, as he calls his accounts of the radar and the bombing conflicts, some lessons for the future. He wisely warns us of the danger of what he calls the euphoria of gadgets, meaning by this the tendency on the part of some scientists—and not only scientists—to believe that a new device, or a new tactic, is a solution of all our defence problems. This was fundamentally the error behind the over-concentration during the war on the area bombing of enemy cities. It is worth remembering that Germany never did this. Her remarkable military successes of the first years of the war were achieved by brilliant co-ordination of armour, artillery, infantry and close air support. The same was true of Russia. When she finally drove the German armies back from Stalingrad into Germany, this was achieved by the co-ordinated use of land and air power. In fact, Germany was eventually defeated primarily by the methods that had brought her such startling successes earlier. Of the three million German war dead and missing up to November 1944, 75 per cent. were on the Russian front. This is an indication of the extent to which World War II was primarily a land war. The air operations of the bombing offensive carried on independently of military operations did begin to have an important effect during the summer of 1944. However, by this time the German armies had been decisively defeated both in the East and in the West.

This is not the place to attempt to apply in detail some of these lessons to post-war defence problems. There is, however, one comment that must be made. Never have Snow's twin warnings, of the danger of thinking that one weapon will solve our problems, and of the illusion that one can rely on maintaining technical superiority, been more vividly illustrated by the early years of nuclear weapons. Here the euphoria both of gadgets and of secrecy reached their highest and most disastrous intensity. Through a blind obeisance to a single weapon the West let down the strength of its conventional forces and failed even to develop prototypes of modern weapons for land warfare. In spite of the vast technological strength of the Western world, its ground armies in Europe are not only much smaller but also much inferior in equipment to those of the Soviet army. This has led the West to a reliance on nuclear weapons that is certainly dangerous and could be suicidal. A calm contemplation of the last fifteen years makes one remember the cynical comment that the only lesson ever learned from history is that no one ever learns from history. But unless we do, there will be no more history. Snow's little book, with its wisdom and penetration, should do much to stimulate serious thought on these vital problems of decision making.

Ten

Critique of Some Contemporary Defence Thinking[1]
1961

The impact on Western opinion of the Soviet A-bomb in 1949, the H-bombs in 1953-54, and the Sputnik in 1957 acted as a powerful stimulus to new thought on the fundamental bases of Western foreign and military policy. After a gradual start, the output of articles and books rose rapidly to a veritable flood. The main authors are either academic civilians writing in their spare time, or civilians working full-time in special institutes, often attached to universities.

The writings of these civilian military analysts contain many wise and highly relevant studies of the problems raised by nuclear weapons: however, some of them contain some conclusions which seem to me wrong and dangerous. I propose to examine some of these conclusions in detail. Before doing so, however, I will make a few remarks on the analytic methods by which these complex problems of nuclear war can be approached. As no large-scale nuclear war has ever occurred, there is no body of operational data on real events on which to base a common-sense analysis, such as was available to the Operational Research Groups attached to the Services during the long-drawn-out operations of the last war. It is difficult, therefore, to avoid using some type of theoretical approach, in which the vast complexities of the real world are at first set aside and an attempt is made to construct a simplified model which will represent the real

---

[1] *Encounter,* Apr. 1961. Another version of this article was delivered as a lecture to the Royal United Service Institution on 22 Mar. 1961, with the title " Operational Research and Nuclear Weapons," and printed in *Journal of the Royal United Service Institution,* Aug. 1961.
One footnote from this version is incorporated here (note on p. 137).

problem in as many essentials as possible. When such a model has been set up, either verbal or mathematical arguments are used to deduce conclusions on points of practical importance.

The essential difficulty of this method is to know whether the model which has been constructed is sufficiently like the real events which it purports to represent to allow conclusions which have much relevance to executive action. When a highly simplified model has to be used, any prediction made by its use is likely to be so uncertain that it is essential to check it against the conclusions reached in a more intuitive manner by attempting to envisage the situation as a whole.

One of the most important lessons, which the war-time operational research groups had to learn, was that there were only a few problems, perhaps only one-tenth, where they could add something useful to the decisions arrived at by the trained Services staffs through the exercise of their traditional military judgment and wisdom. This small fraction arose because in most operations the staff themselves got the right answers, or because there was not enough factual data of past operations to extrapolate from, or because the operations proposed by the staffs were too novel to allow realistic predictions of the likely results. It is thus clear that the work of the operational research groups was an addition to, and not a substitute for, the exercise by the trained staffs of their conventional military wisdom.

In the present world of nuclear plenty, when both Western and Soviet blocs have the power to destroy each other many times over, it is clear that, to a degree never before equalled in history, there can be no military policy independent of both home and foreign policy. Thus any purely military analysis will almost certainly leave out of account some vital factors and so can lead to fallacious results. Again, just because the life of a nation is involved, any military analysis which leads to definite recommendations for decisions must be readily intelligible to the political and military leaders who have the responsibility for executive action. It would be almost true to say that in the field of major strategy, as opposed to weapons design and tactics, the only good arguments are simple arguments. If they are not simple, they will not be generally understood and so no action should be taken on them.

Because of the essential complexity of real events, many of the most important decisions of war have necessarily to rest on rough calculation. It is certainly a duty of an operational research group to help the staffs to improve on these, but when they cannot, they should keep silent: never should they fall into the trap of decking out what is essentially only a hunch with a pseudo-scientific backing.

When I come to study in detail some of the arguments of these new military writers about nuclear war, I will necessarily have to adopt many aspects of their own methods and terminology, that is, I will have to meet them on the methodological ground of their own choosing. I want therefore to apologise in advance for the nauseating inhumanity of much of what I will have to say.

I will start by dicussing some aspects of the influential article "The Delicate Balance of Terror" by Albert Wohlstetter of the Rand Corporation, published in *Foreign Affairs* in January 1959. This contains many cogent arguments and analyses, but it also contains at least one important conclusion which I believe to be fallacious. A key part of the arguments rests on the enormous advantage which it is alleged the possession of thermo-nuclear weapons gives to an aggressor. Other writers who take a similar view are Klaus Knorr and Oscar Morgenstern of Princeton University, Herman Kahn and Bernard Brodie of the Rand.

Mr Wohlstetter starts by listing a large number of people who in one way or another have stated the view that the present nuclear balance is relatively stable against rational acts by America or Russia. He then sets out to refute this view and to substitute for it the thesis that the stability was then in 1959 very precarious, in fact more so than previously, and that, unless very drastic steps are taken, will be still more precarious in a few years' time.

Though there are many acute statements and much quoting of the details of numbers of weapons and their performance, etc., there is little attempt to envisage realistically the whole situation which would arise in the event of the present balance being really unstable. Instead one finds a number of verbal statements, some of which I will analyse in detail, and which are explicitly directed towards reversing the commonly held view, which, in his own words, "would make aggression irrational or even insane." As we will see, Wohlstetter puts much emphasis on the circumstances in which nuclear aggression would be, in his view, both rational and sane.

Let us look at the verbal statement of the alleged enormous advantage to the aggressor in the light of some numerical figures, which may be plausibly assumed to have some relation to the reality of the present strategic nuclear balance between the Western and Soviet blocs. I will start with a highly simplified abstract model and then bring in step by step some additional features.

Suppose firstly that two major and similar hypothetical countries can inflict 100 million deaths on each other by an all-out attack on the other's population, and secondly, that if either launches a surprise attack on the enemy's retaliatory force, it can destroy the high fraction of 90 per cent. of it. Then the victim's counterblow against the aggressor's cities will amount to 10 per cent. of what it otherwise would be, so that the retaliation will only inflict 10 million deaths on the aggressor.

If, however, anything goes wrong with the preparations for this surprise attack, so that the intention to strike becomes known to the intended victim, the latter will be likely to make a forestalling blow with everything it has, directed against both cities and retaliatory forces; this would, in our model, produce 100 million killed. If, on the other hand, the hypothetical aggressor does not strike at all, there will be no reason to suppose that the hypothetical victim will be attacked—at any rate, not then.

So, at any rate, in the short run, the political leaders of the potential aggressor have to make the choice between not attacking, and so having no killed, and of attacking successfully, and so having 10 million killed, and attacking unsuccessfully, that is, losing surprise, and so having 100 million killed. In this simple numerical model, the aggressor could hardly be considered sane if it made such an aggression. If now one works through this model with a variety of different numerical assumptions, the enormous advantage the aggressor would gain by making a nuclear attack still seems a bit elusive.

For instance, suppose, to take an extreme case, that the aggressor could hope to destroy 99 per cent. of the enemy's retaliatory forces, then the result of the three possible eventualities mentioned above could be 0, 1 and 100 mega-deaths respectively. However, no military planners would ever expect to pull off such a fantastically successful first strike.

Alternatively, let us go back to our 90 per cent. assumption but suppose that the aggressor's nuclear strength was five times that of his victim so as to allow him to inflict 100 mega-deaths, but that as his enemy is only one-fifth as strong, his full retaliatory capacity would kill only 20 million. Then in this eventuality, no attack, successful attack and unsuccessful attack, would lead to 0, 2 and 20 mega-deaths respectively.

The above calculations underestimate the destruction suffered by the aggressor in the case of a successful first strike, because the victim country is likely to concentrate its remaining retaliatory force against the most worthwhile target, for instance, the big cities. Because of this, the casualties suffered by the aggressor might be as much as twice as high as indicated above.

Actually I have made my first model look much too favourable to the aggressor. For I have spoken as if its High Command could be *certain* to reduce the enemy's retaliatory power to 10 per cent. of its initial capacity, so as to be able to inflict only 10 million deaths on the aggressor. However, they could not be certain of this. All that the aggressor's operational analysts could justifiably conclude would be that 10 million would be the probable number, but that the essential uncertainties of such an operation and of the calculations would not exclude the possibility that it might reach, say, 30 million or more.

Even this is too favourable to the aggressor. For, consider the nature of the intelligence about the enemy's retaliatory force which its High Command would have to rely on to make the calculation which I have assumed leads to 10 million as the most probable number. How could their Intelligence Service obtain sufficiently reliable and up-to-date information of all the multitude of facts necessary for a successful first strike? The whereabouts of every long-range bomber, the location of every missile site, the deployment of all medium-range fighter bombers with nuclear warheads —all would be needed, accurate up to the last hour. Aircraft aloft would clearly be immune to attack. It must not be forgotten that 100 fighter bombers, perhaps flying low, armed with normal A-bombs, could, if they reached their city targets, kill 5 to 10 million people.

Wohlstetter expresses a qualitative truism when he writes: "A totalitarian country can preserve secrecy about the capabilities and dispositions of his forces very much better than a Western democracy." Can it, however, do this well enough? Is there no chance of there being a few dissident individuals, amongst tens of millions of people, who would notice the not inconsiderable preparations for such a massive operation as a first strike? Would any country seriously contemplate initiating a first strike, which would bring an expected 10 mega-deaths from the counter blow, without the slightest preparation or warning to its civil defence authorities? Consider the half-million tourists from the various Soviet countries, and the many thousands from the West, who visit the U.S.S.R. every year. Could the Soviet authorities be sure that there were no foreign agents among these? How could they exclude the possibility of a Western agent penetrating their high councils as successfully as their agent, Richard Sorge, did those of Japan for so many years?

The aggressor's enemy might be an "open" country, but this does not mean that the aggressor's agents would be left free to radio back every hour all the latest military movements. Intelligence from orbiting satellites or high-flying aircraft could be neither reliable enough nor comprehensive enough to be adequate. If a country spent a small fraction of what is now devoted to missile research to systematic camouflage and decoy schemes, it could do much to nullify confidence in satellite or aircraft intelligence. Thus any planned attack on the enemy's retaliatory forces would have to be preceded by a great increase of illicit radio signals from the aggressor's agents. This would certainly alert the enemy and thus surprise would be lost.

Another point related to this is the time factor in launching a surprise attack against enemy nuclear strength. Manned bombers could not be used, because radar warning would allow the victim country to get its nuclear bombers airborne, so that they would be able to retaliate. So a surprise attack would have to be done with missiles. Now the technical problem of launching a few hundred I.C.B.Ms. within a few minutes is severe. To spread the firings over half an hour or so is to lose surprise and so increase the retaliatory blow.

Let us now turn to another of Wohlstetter's statements. ". . . it takes great ingenuity at any given level of nuclear technology to devise a stable equilibrium." We have seen that when some plausible numerical figures are introduced into the balance of terror, it is clear that no country could make use of even a very substantial degree of nuclear superiority by staging a first strike without incurring a high probability of very heavy destruction. Moreover, this conclusion remains valid for a very wide range of numerical assumptions about the relative size of the nuclear strength of the two contestants. If then the present nuclear balance is rather stable, it follows that only some very big technological change could upset it. What sort of change? I think one can rule out the operational possibility of a near 100 per cent. anti-missile and anti-aircraft defence, which would allow the country which had it to attack with impunity another which had not. Improved accuracy of missiles or bigger explosive power at the same weight would make fewer missiles necessary to reduce the enemy's power of retaliatory to a given level, but would not alter fundamentally the numerical demonstration already given of the essential insanity of a first-strike policy.

I will now make some comments on Mr Wohlstetter's views about the effect of Russian history on Russian psychology. He says:

Russian casualties in World War II were more than 20 million. Yet Russia recovered extremely well from this catastrophe. There are several quite plausible circumstances in the future when the Russians might be quite confident of being able to limit damage to considerably less than this number—they make sensible choices and we do not. On the other hand, the risks of not striking might at some juncture appear very great to the Soviets, involving, for example, disastrous defeat in a peripheral war, loss of key satellites with danger of revolt spreading—possibly to Russia itself—or fear of attack by ourselves. Then, striking first, by surprise, would be a sensible choice for them, and from their point of view the smaller risk.

My first comment is that if the U.S.S.R. were involved in the disastrous situation depicted above, the Western world would be alerted and the utmost dispersal of nuclear carriers would be made, geographical security would be clamped down over large areas and all suspected Soviet agents would be rounded up. So the conditions for a successful surprise attack against Western nuclear forces would be absent. My second comment is that the suggestion that Russia, because she had suffered 20 million casualties in the last war, would willingly act so as to make probable a similar catastrophe seems to conflict with all common sense and all history. The history of Russia, both Tsarist and Soviet, tells of many invasions but few military aggressions. Military caution has been a marked characteristic, even to the point, as in 1941, of nearly fatal playing for time. As a suggested alternative to Wohlstetter's assessment of the influence of Russian history on Russian psychology, I put forward the following: "Any country which has experienced the horror of losing 20 million people in one war is very unlikely to take any avoidable risk of it happening again." I doubt the prediction value of any such verbal statements, but of the two I am sure that mine is nearer the truth. Wohlstetter's argument suggests to me that he has neither thought very deeply or imaginatively about the consequences of the nuclear war, nor has he ever imagined himself in the position of taking the action which he seems to think it sane for the Soviets to take.

In the list of imaginary circumstances which are depicted above as likely to provoke a Soviet strike, there is only one, in my opinion, which has any semblance of reality; this is the fear of an immediate attack by America. Clearly an urgent and major task of the Soviet and American Governments is to find ways of allaying each other's fears about such surprise attacks. In all negotiations towards this important objective, it is essential to start with a realistic view of the technical possibility of achieving a successful one. It is not likely to help the search for ways of reducing the chance of surprise attack to exaggerate greatly its military feasibility.

As regards the technical question of whether the U.S.S.R. has now, or is likely to have in the near future, a sufficient nuclear superiority to have any chance of making a successful first strike, the evidence is rather clear. For instance, Secretary of Defense Thomas S. Gates said to a House Sub-Committee on 13 January 1960: " It is the conclusion of those who have analysed the matter that even a surprise attack by all the missiles the Soviets could muster would not suffice to destroy enough of our retaliatory forces to enable him to make a rational decision to attack." The available evidence makes it certain that, in all-round nuclear strength, the U.S.A. is still markedly stronger than the U.S.S.R.

When Mr Wohlstetter wrote his articles over two years ago, in 1958, certainly the Soviet nuclear strength was weaker relative to America than it is today. Yet his articles gave the impression that he considered the balance of terror to be rather unstable. If he did think it then unstable, there seem only two alternatives: either he must have got wrong information about the relative American and Soviet nuclear strength, or he must have feared that America might under certain circumstances exploit her undoubted overall superiority to initiate nuclear war.

I want now to draw attention to a revealing sentence in the quotation given above about probable Soviet action. This reads: " . . . *they make sensible choices and we do not.*"[2]

Since the U.S.A. has certainly an overall nuclear superiority now, and had a still larger one a few years ago, then Wohlstetter's general argument suggests that it would have been a sane policy for the U.S.A. to have initiated a nuclear attack, but this was not made, presumably for moral reasons. In any negotiations with the U.S.S.R. about possible surprise attacks, the Western delegation would have to prove to the Russian that there is no possible chance that the moral inhibitions of America would ever weaken, so that it was perfectly safe for the U.S.S.R. to assume that the West would never take Wohlstetter's " sane " action.

This amounts in effect to asking the U.S.S.R. to base its military planning on the West's stated intentions. However, one of the doctrines of the academic theorists is that it is

---

[2] Mr T. C. Schelling, of Harvard, has pointed out that the passage from Wohlstetter which I quoted was taken from the version of his article as reprinted in *Survival* and that the word " if " in the original was left out. The original sentence in the article in *Foreign Affairs* reads: " There are several quite plausible circumstances in the future when the Russians might be quite confident of being able to limit damage to considerably less than this number [20 million casualties]—if they make sensible choices and we do not." Schelling states that in its correct form the sentence does not imply any moral asymmetry. I do not think this is correct for the following reasons. Without the word " if," the sentence stated that, in certain plausible circumstances, Russia *would* plan and wage aggressive nuclear war but that America *would not*. With the " if," it implies that Russia *would probably* do so, but that America *would probably* not. So the moral asymmetry remains, softened perhaps from a certainty to a probability. In fact the assumption of moral asymmetry is the key to Wohlstetter's whole argument. For if nuclear weapons gave as enormous an advantage to the aggressor as he holds, and in view of the undoubted overwhelming nuclear superiority of the U.S.A. in, say, about 1956, it can only have been moral restraint on the part of the U.S.A. which prevented them from being used. If the U.S.S.R. showed equal moral restraint, if and when she gets an overall nuclear superiority, then she would not attack. But Wohlstetter's whole theory is that he sees the main danger in that the U.S.S.R. would attack, even without overall nuclear superiority, relying on the alleged, but, in my view, fictitious overwhelming advantage to the aggressor. What greater mental and moral asymmetry is there than to contrast the fact that the U.S.A. did not attack some years ago when she had an overwhelming nuclear advantage with the expectation that the U.S.S.R. would do so in the future, even without such superiority?

necessary to plan on the basis of the enemy's capability, which one can know, and not on the basis of his intentions which one cannot. Wohlstetter's doctrine seems to be that the West must plan on the enemy's capability, but the U.S.S.R. should plan on the West's intentions. If the Western nations enter discussion on the surprise attack problem, the control of armaments, and disarmament, on the basis of this assumption of asymmetric morality, they are not likely to make much progress.

It is, of course, perfectly correct to bring into the analysis of the global situation the broader considerations of expediency, morality, and common sense. But these broader considerations must be brought in consistently and not arbitrarily just when it suits a particular argument. It is wholly correct that a nation should believe in, and pride itself on, the morality of its behaviour. It is an amiable and common conceit that one's own behaviour is better than that of one's opponent, and it may even be true upon occasion. What is absurd is that we should expect an enemy to base its military policy on our own estimate of our own moral character.

Let us now consider more fully the argument that the present nuclear balance is less stable against rational acts by the two giant powers than it was a few years ago, and that it is likely to get still more unstable in the next few years. During the earlier period, say 1954 to 1957, which has been often referred to as one of exceptional stability, the U.S.A. had a very large superiority of A-bombs, and of long-range aircraft deployed on dozens of bases around the perimeter of the Soviet Union. On the other hand, the U.S.S.R. could not then counter-attack seriously against America through lack of long-range aircraft. However, it was quite clear that this great relative nuclear superiority of America could not last long, and that therefore the diplomatic power and prestige resulting from it also could not last: so that, if no steps were taken by America, this power and prestige would be reduced. In military history, many wars have had such a preventive character. However, wider considerations, including no doubt moral ones, intervened, and preventive war was not waged. On the other hand, in 1954 A-bombs were very nearly dropped at Dien Bien Phu—it is said that the American National Security Council recommended this, but President Eisenhower rejected it. Thus close came a nuclear war—if only a small one—but with what vast possible consequences!

Again, the deep shock produced by the Sputnik in 1957 could have sparked off a drive in America to take the last possible chance of successful preventive war. This dangerous moment—dangerous, that is, from the viewpoint of all the tenets of the academic practitioners of theoretical warfare—passed. I consider that in both theory and fact the period 1954-57 was the most critical of post-war years. The crisis passed because American wisdom and good sense won the day and she did not behave like one of the amoral automata of the theorists.

I have no doubt that the balance of terror is now more stable *against sane actions of rational governments* than it was a few years ago, just because the two sides are nearer equal in nuclear strength. The increase in the number of Soviet missiles has markedly reduced the overall imbalance but certainly has not yet produced, nor is likely to produce in the near future, a marked imbalance the other way. Both common sense and the more detailed arguments of abstract military theory alike associate stability with near equality of defence capability. They therefore lead to the conclusion that the last few years have been a period of increasing stability against rational government actions. When Wohlstetter reaches the exact opposite conclusion, he does so by negating the conclusions of both common sense and of formal military theory by introducing a large and arbitrary degree of moral asymmetry between the two contestants. By this methodological device the period 1954 to 1957 is held to be a safe period because, though America had a large nuclear superiority, she was pacific, while the present time is dangerous because this superiority is less and the U.S.S.R. is aggressive.

The introduction of assumption of moral asymmetry into military arguments is full of pitfalls. Against the assumed moral superiority of the West, weight should be given to the very close integration of military and political policy in Soviet theory and practice. This implies that the probable consequences on the world situation of any proposed act will be carefully thought out.

If a man from Mars studied the history of the last few decades, what conclusion would he come to about the likelihood of East or West staking everything on a nuclear gamble? He might notice that poker is the national game of America, while chess is that of Russia, and that a country whose creed includes the inevitable triumph of its own social system is not likely to try to accelerate history by a nuclear gamble.

Klaus Knorr, in his book *NATO and American Security,* published in 1959, expresses views which are rather similar to those of Wohlstetter which I have criticised: Knorr considered that by the mid-1960's, the nuclear balance would be unbreakably stable due to improved missiles and greater dispersion and mobility. However, he held that the balance was then, in 1959, very unstable and would remain so until new technical developments came about. Thereafter the bases " would be protected against surprise attack and a counter-force strategy would no longer be attractive ": so in 1959 Knorr held surprise attack to be *attractive.* " However, known possibilities are such that the risk of Soviet surprise attack on the United States may well be substantial and, indeed, dangerously high." No convincing evidence is produced to suppose that it would be technically possible for Russia to achieve the near 100 per cent. effective first strike without which a surprise nuclear attack would neither be " sane " to use Mr Wohlstetter's word nor " attractive " to use that of Mr Knorr.

It may be objected that I am giving too much weight to the practical consequences of the wide dissemination of the military writings which I am criticising. Unfortunately, in my view, these writings have had a rather big influence. In *NATO in the 1960s* by Alastair Buchan,[3] we read: " It is this enormous advantage now accruing to the man who strikes first and the degree of surprise that the missile permits

[3] London and New York 1960.

that does more than anything else to create the instability of the strategic balance. . . ." The influence of the " delicacy of the balance of terror " thesis is found also in the study *Foreign and Military Policy for Peace and Security,* published in 1959 by the Advisory Council of the Democratic National Committee of the Democratic Party of America. This view that the next few years, that is, until improved Western weapons are available, are exceptionally dangerous, is stated clearly by Paul Nitze in a recent article in *Survival.* The same view is taken by John Strachey in a recent lecture at Chatham House, and is explicitly derived from Wohlstetter's and Morgenstern's books. All these documents are very serious works containing a great amount of cogent analysis. But they all, either implicitly or explicitly, support the thesis of the progressive worsening of the present situation unless there is a great increase of expenditure on research and development on long-range missiles, and a large increase in their invulnerability. I believe this thesis to be false, and that its promulgation by so many able people is likely to lead to wrong allocation of priorities as well as worsening of the international atmosphere.

One danger arising from the theory of " The Delicate Balance of Terror," assuming that it greatly exaggerates this delicacy, lies in the hope it gives that Russia and America might reasonably strive to acquire a first-strike capability. America had this in effect from 1954 to 1957, since Russia had no effective power of hitting America at all. If, however, as I believe, a successful first strike would now demand not only a very large margin but also a quite unattainable degree of Intelligence, then the attempt to achieve a first-strike capability would be fruitless.

Though the American Administration seems to have set itself firmly against attempts to regain a first counter-force capability by improved missiles and reconnaissance satellites, there seems to be a group which would like to try, and they must have been greatly heartened in their endeavour by the arguments that this can be done, given enough effort. This way leads to an endless and increasing arms race. Another group in America, who must welcome the " delicacy " school's conclusions, is the anti-test-ban lobby. The case for further tests—America is said to have made about 170 tests to the Soviets' 60, so presumably has better bombs—is that further improvements to existing nuclear weapons would be of decisive significance in relation to the present balance. Till recently this appears to have been the view of the Atomic Energy Commission. I do not believe this to be the case. Since the British Government has been all along one of the chief architects of the near-successful test-ban agreement, it has every reason to be wary of the conclusions of the academic military theorists, which have in fact often been used in favour of further testing.

If I personally believed that the present balance of nuclear terror was as unstable as these writers seem to think, I would in all seriousness conclude that the safest possibility for Great Britain, and ultimately for the world, would be for Britain to opt out completely from the nuclear arms race. Moreover, I myself would give up the arduous labour of studying the intricate arguments of these writers and devote myself to campaigning to achieve this.

By far the greatest danger of the " delicacy " thesis is its possible effect on negotiations for disarmament and arms control. It has, in fact, been widely used to suggest that serious negotiations with the U.S.S.R. should be postponed until the mid-1960's when the expected weapon developments will have occurred. For if the balance is really so delicate that it can be upset by some small increase in the numbers of deployed nuclear weapons on either side, or by some technical improvement in their performance, then it is clear that a degree of inspection and control would be required which might be unacceptable to both Soviet and Western blocs. Fortunately, I am sure that the present situation is rather stable, at least for the time being, and that the already grossly exaggerated feasibility of a successful surprise nuclear attack could be still further reduced by mutually acceptable control and inspection methods.

Belief in the thesis that the main danger to humanity at present is that Russia might find itself in a position to bring off a successful first strike and that it would be, in

Wohlstetter's words, a sane policy for her to do so, tends to divert attention from real and immediate dangers. I have not the slightest doubt that the main danger today is not from the rational act of responsible statesmen, but is due to essentially irrational acts of irresponsible, frightened, humiliated, revengeful or just mad people—or perhaps, more likely still, from the confused actions of well-meaning people overwhelmed by complex circumstances beyond their mental or moral ceiling. Clearly, the more nuclear weapons there are in the world, the more nations which possess them, the more will all defence systems become inextricably bound up with nuclear weapons, so that the number of fingers on nuclear triggers will grow and with it the danger of accidental or irresponsible nuclear war.

The present Western drive to make its nuclear bases more invulnerable is intended mainly to reduce the likelihood of a deliberate surprise counter-force attack by the U.S.S.R. If I am right in supposing that the arguments which suggested that this was the main danger are quite false, since the system as a whole is already invulnerable enough, then the urgency of further hardening becomes less. It should be noted that the invulnerability of bases is of no value against irresponsible or mad attack which could be made directly against cities.

The hardening of bases has also the role of reducing the necessity for quick decision as to whether and when to retaliate against a suspected " irresponsible " attack—I assume a " responsible " one is in the highest degree unlikely. So it is essential that the attempt to make the Western bases more invulnerable by hardening, dispersal and mobility must in no way increase the chances of accidental or irresponsible attack. This may be quite a difficult task.

Moreover, the danger of " accidental " war due to too quick reaction to false information, for instance spurious radar signals, is greatly increased by the belief that a surprise attack is likely to succeed. But if such an attack would lead to many mega-deaths to the attacker, then the advantage of reacting quickly is much less.

Looking broadly at the writings of this new school of academic military strategists it will be useful to try to detect how they have reached the false conclusions discussed above. I think the influence of the Theory of Games has been almost wholly detrimental. I can see little if anything in the methods outlined in such works as *Theory of Games and Economic Behavior* by J. von Neumann and Oscar Morgenstern,[4] or in *The Strategy of Conflict* by T. C. Schelling,[5] which are useful for making practical predictions. If they had, such methods would have become accepted by investors and card players. If such abstract theory cannot be applied in practice to such relatively simple activities, then it is clearly useless for the much more complicated problems of war. In fact the abstract theory of games is a branch of pure mathematics and almost wholly irrelevant to decision-making.

Then I think far too much is made of clear-cut logical distinctions in fields where a continuous gradation of facts and possibilities makes them inapplicable. It has been said that clear-cut definitions have little place at the beginnings of a scientific subject, and may be detrimental to progress. I believe this to be true of the present state of military analysis.

An example of this is the great stress laid on the distinction between vulnerable and invulnerable bases—a useful and common-sense distinction of venerable antiquity in military practice and theory. But when this distinction is carried too far in its application to practice, it can lead to absurdity. For instance, it is often concluded by these writers that the present Thor bases in Britain are now highly provocative because they are very vulnerable and so could only be used for a first strike. Thus—so the reasoning goes—their existence is a denial of the West's avowed intention not to make a first strike. In effect these writers are asking the U.S.S.R. to believe that the now alleged provocative nature of Western nuclear bases only began on the day when the Soviets acquired the power to destroy them. Would these writers have come to the same conclusion if the U.S.S.R. had produced nuclear weapons four years before the U.S.A.? Although

4 2nd edn., Princeton 1947.
5 Cambridge, Mass. 1960.

the more realistic of these writers do agree that the nuclear balance becomes more stable, the more invulnerable the bases of *both sides,* they do not always pay tribute to the Soviet insistence on keeping their bases relatively invulnerable by their system of geographical security: nor have I noticed any strong disapproval of those aspects of Western policies which attempt to destroy this invulnerability by ceaseless propaganda and by aircraft and satellite reconnaissance. If this objective were achieved, then the theorists must conclude that the balance would be upset. Then an American surprise attack on the U.S.S.R. would become, in Wohlstetter's phrase, a sane policy. Of course this conclusion is not made because at this point the assumption of moral asymmetry is quietly inserted into the amoral world of games theory. There are legitimate differences of opinion about the moral characteristics of different nations: however, where the verbal and scholastic bias of these writers has led them astray is in their failure to clothe the skeleton conflicts of the theory of games with the complex flesh and blood attributes of real nations; hence the bizarre nature of some of their practical conclusions.[6]

At the back of these mistaken practical judgments lies, firstly, the failure of these military analysts to imagine themselves in the position of having to take the executive action they recommend, and secondly, the failure to grasp the complexity of the problems with which they would then be faced.

Finally, I feel conscious of a strain of deep social pessimism combined sometimes strangely with an almost neurotic contemplation of destruction. Perhaps this is most marked in the remarkable last chapter of Morgenstern's book. Under the revealing chapter heading " The Fascination of War " are to be found some astonishing dogmatic statements, made usually without the semblance of proof.

The most interesting things in science at present are done only if they are related to war and war preparation. . . . Society does not accept the desire for knowledge unless it is in some way tied to war.

[6] See Chapter 7 for remarks on the danger of misusing the distinction between preventive war and a pre-emptive first strike.

These statements are just false in the West today. The exciting advances in high energy nuclear physics, in visual and radio astronomy, in organic and bio-chemistry, in molecular biology, in embryology and immunology and a dozen other fields are wholly independent of war preparations. In fact, the fields directly affected are rather few. Morgenstern continues: "War preparations are necessary in order to justify the deepest human desire for knowledge." Here Morgenstern gives a non-military justification for armaments and one, which if followed literally, would lead to an endless arms race unrelated to real military needs. It would follow that disarmament would be a scientific disaster. Would he have President Kennedy tell Mr Khrushchev that unfortunately America cannot reduce her armaments because this would mean falling behind in pure science? Some deep emotional factor must lie behind such absurdity.

If Morgenstern can make such gross mistakes about the rather simple facts of the effect of war preparations on modern pure scientific research, how can one trust his judgments on the far more complex and hypothetical problems of war? Temperamentally he seems to me to exhibit a deep social pessimism which contrasts flagrantly with the traditional extrovert optimism of America.

Some may think that the unexpectedly rapid deployment of Polaris-armed submarines has greatly improved the stability of the balance, so that it is only of historic interest as to whether the balance was stable or unstable a few years ago. I do not think this is correct. For one thing, the number of such nuclear missiles now deployed operationally is too small a fraction of the West's total nuclear strength to turn an unstable into a stable system. More important is the possibility that the arguments which have been, in my view, falsely used to prove the balance unstable in recent years may be used in the future to prove it again unstable, in spite of expected improvement of weapons. So the truth or falsehood of the delicacy thesis will remain for many years of vital importance.

Eleven

The Real Road to Disarmament[1]
1962

O wad some Pow'r the giftie gie us
To see oursels as others see us!
It wad frae mony a blunder free us
And foolish notion.
     —Robert Burns.

A military commander, in planning a campaign or a battle, attempts, as a matter of course, to envisage the situation as it must appear to his opponent. He has first to find out all he can about the material facts of his opponent's military deployment, and secondly he has to assess the probable intentions of his opponent for its use. This is the process which has been described as guessing what goes on the other side of the hill. A similar obligation rests on those who plan a disarmament negotiation. To succeed one must guess correctly what is going on the other side of the disarmament hill.

However, there are more serious obstacles to carrying out this mental process of " role reversal " in relation to the complex political and military aspects of disarmament than there are in relation to a purely military campaign. For a military planner can much more easily put himself mentally in the position of his military opponent than a statesman can think himself into the position of his opposite number; for a statesman must enter imaginatively into the political as well as the military thought processes of his opponent; this is a hard thing to do at a time of acute ideological struggle. However, it is essential that the military and

[1] *The New Statesman,* 2 Mar. 1962. A shortened version, entitled " Steps Towards Disarmament," appeared in *Scientific American,* April 1962.

political leaders of both sides do just this: in fact they should emulate the military objectivity which one might reasonably attribute to a military observer sent from Mars to report on the strange happenings on the earth.

In this article I shall be concerned mainly with the Western task of understanding the underlying facts about the Soviet military situation and their relation to the Soviet attitude to disarmament. It is useful to start by describing the most important elements in the military balance between the Soviet bloc and the Western alliance.

In recent months many important statements have been made about the nuclear weapons and their means of delivery, that is, missiles and aircraft, which are alleged to be possessed by both sides. On 12 November last year the American Secretary of Defence, Mr McNamara, said that the core of America's deterrent power, her nuclear strike force, consists of 1,700 intercontinental bombers including 630 B52s, 55 B58s and 1,000 B47s. In addition, he said there were several dozen operational intercontinental ballistic missiles (I.C.B.M.) in the United States, some 80 Polaris missiles in nuclear-powered submarines, about the same number of Thors and Jupiters, some 300 nuclear-armed carrier-borne aircraft with megaton warheads and, finally, nearly 1,000 supersonic land-based fighters with nuclear warheads. On 22 October the Deputy Secretary of Defence, Mr Gilpatric, said: " The total number of our nuclear delivery vehicles, tactical as well as strategic, is in the tens of thousands: and of course we have more than one warhead for each vehicle. . . . We have a second-strike capability which is at least as extensive as what the Soviets can deliver by striking first, therefore we can be confident that the Soviets will not provoke a major conflict."[2] The total American stockpile of nuclear weapons has been estimated as around 30,000 megatons, that is, enough for at least 30,000 one-megaton bombs. This amounts to 150 tons of T.N.T. equivalent for every man, woman or child in Russia.

Naturally no such precise figures of the Soviet strength are available, but estimates from Washington in the *New York*

[2] *The Times*, 23 Oct. 1961.

Times of 20 November and 6 January give some 50 I.C.B.Ms., some 150 intercontinental bombers and up to 400 medium-range missiles able to cover Europe, but not the United States. Intelligence estimates are reported to indicate that the United States may have a small lead over the Soviet Union in the number of intercontinental ballistic missiles. A few years ago the forecast was that the Soviet Union would have a four to one lead by 1962. A leading article in the same journal under the headline " Missile Gap in Reverse," asks why the Soviet Union has not built as many as it could have done and suggests that there may be an explanation which sheds important light on Soviet intentions. It is one of the purposes of this article to attempt to elucidate some of the Soviet motives. I have seen no reliable estimates of the Soviet nuclear stockpile, nor of her possible nuclear-armed submarine strength, nor of her nuclear fighter-bomber strength—these latter have too short a range to contribute to the Soviet strike power against America.

Even assuming that the Washington figures for the relative nuclear strength of the two sides are only approximately correct, the possibility of a rationally planned surprise nuclear attack by the Soviet Union on the nuclear delivery system of the West must be now, and always must have been, quite negligible.

There is, of course, the possibility that these new American estimates of the Soviet nuclear strength are too low. After all, firm information about Soviet military preparations is notoriously hard to come by. However, it seems certain that the United States Defense Department must believe the estimates to be roughly correct: for in the present political situation in the United States it would be politically disastrous for the administration to be found guilty of under-estimating Soviet nuclear strength.

At first sight there appears to be a contradiction between Washington's claim of a marked overall nuclear superiority and Soviet Defence Minister Malinovsky's recent statement that the U.S.S.R. has the power to destroy all the important industrial, administrative and political centres of the United States and whole countries which have provided their terri-

tories for the siting of American war bases. However, the
explanation may be as follows. To carry out the destruction
mentioned by Malinovsky would require not more than 1,000
megatons, say five megatons for each of 100 key targets in
America and another 500 megatons for western Europe and
America's overseas bases. At only 0·2 million dead per megaton, such an attack would kill 200 million people. But the
American stockpile is estimated as 30,000 megatons, that is,
30 times as great as Russia would need to carry out the
retaliatory blow described by Malinovsky. It will appear in
the course of the argument that the *New York Times*'s
question why the U.S.S.R. has built such a small nuclear
delivery system should perhaps be replaced by the question
why the United States has built such a big one.

Further light on the origin of the earlier high estimate of
the Soviet nuclear strength is given in a leading article in
the *New York Times* of 27 November:

The " missile gap " like the " bomber gap " before it, is now
being consigned to the limbo of synthetic issues, where it always
belonged. The missile gap—the prediction of an overwhelming
Soviet superiority in I.C.B.M. in the early 1960's—was the
product of partisan politics and service (primarily Air Force)
pressures. The same forces and the same Congressional and
journalistic mouthpieces who manufactured an alleged bomber
gap in the 1950's sponsored, and indeed invented, the alleged
missile gap in the 1960's. Today, judged by the hard-bitten
estimates of actual Soviet strength, to which all services apparently subscribe, the " missile gap " has vanished; the quantitative
advantage, if any, is on the side of the United States. . . . The
issue became one in part because Air Force intelligence estimates
of Soviet missile capabilities, which were always far higher than
other estimates, were used as political and propaganda footballs.
The Air Force thought it a good lever with which to pry more
money out of the administration and Congress. The Republi-
cans, needlessly on the defensive, got a bad case of foot-and-mouth
disease. The Democrats, then on the political out, used the
alleged " missile gap " as a club with which to belabour the
administration. The result was that a ghost, a shadow, became
a synthetic issue which obscured real national defense problems
and confused the voter.

In order to understand the possible motives behind Soviet
defence policy, it is necessary to consider the history of the
growth of nuclear weapon-power. During the period of

American atomic monopoly and overwhelming numerical superiority, say from 1947 to 1954, the role of the American Strategic Air Command was to attack and destroy Russian cities in case of war. This counter-city policy, like most traditional military doctrines, was an *action* policy with both an offensive and a defensive aspect. From the Western viewpoint this nuclear striking-power was seen to be both a counter to the possibility of attack by Soviet land forces, and also an offensive weapon to extract political concessions by threat of its use, and to be used if the threat failed.

During this period of seven years or so, the Soviet Union had to live with the fact that America had the capability of inflicting very great destruction on Russian cities, without the Soviet Union being able to reply in kind.

In retrospect, the military reaction of the Soviet Union to this American nuclear capability seems very understandable. First, they started a crash programme to produce their own nuclear weapons. Second, they embarked on a huge air defence programme: at one time, in about 1953, they were credited with an operational fighter strength of some 14,000 aircraft. Third, as the Western nuclear strength grew, the Soviet Union gradually built up her land forces so as to be able to invade Europe even after an American nuclear attack —this was at that time their only possible military reply to the Western nuclear striking-power. Fourth, they maintained strict geographical secrecy over their land area so as to deny target information to the S.A.C.

Fifth, at the political level, the Soviet Union consolidated its forward military line by the political coup in 1948 in Czechoslovakia, and integrated the other satellite countries more closely into the Soviet defence system. Since the main military threat then to the Soviet Union was from manned nuclear bombers, the greatest possible depth for air defence was vital. During the Second World War it was found that the efficacy of a fighter defence system increased rapidly with the depth of the defence zone.

Support for the view that the communist coup in Czechoslovakia was not solely due to the desire to spread the borders of the Soviet world, but had at least a strong military foundation, is seen by noting that the U.S.S.R. did not act similarly in Finland. The military difference is obvious. Czechoslovakia in the Western orbit would have greatly weakened Russia's military strength. Finland's geographical position made it unnecessary to stage a communist coup to keep her out of the Western military orbit. However, if Sweden had joined NATO, the Soviet military staff might have pressed for full integration of Finland.

The action, as opposed to the deterrent, value to the West of its nuclear power was most in evidence during the last years of the West's effective nuclear monopoly—say from 1950 to 1954. This was the period of the Western doctrine of "massive retaliation," though the term was not used till the end of the period, and of the political concept in influential circles of the United States of the "roll back," "liberation" and the "year of decision." In this concept the year of decision was to arrive when Western rearmament on land had gone far enough for the West to be able to repulse a Soviet counter-thrust into Europe. When the West had acquired this adequate strength on land, it would be able to use its nuclear power to force the Soviet Union to accept the Western terms or be bombed. These terms were generally held to include the freeing of the satellites and the unification of Germany within the Western military system.

Such possibilities became less and less plausible as the Soviet nuclear stockpile gradually grew; and they had finally to be abandoned after 1954 when H-bombs became available both to the East and to the West. This collapse of the "liberation" policy left unfulfilled the promise to unite Germany within the present Western military system.

With the development of Soviet hydrogen bombs and with the building up of a fleet of Soviet long-range bombers to deliver them, America became vulnerable to nuclear counter-attack, if the former counter-city strategy was ever put into action by the United States. So some form of nuclear stalemate by balance of terror seemed to have arrived. This balance seemed still further strengthened about 1957, when very rapid progress in the technology of nuclear weapons and of missiles made it possible to carry multi-megaton H-bombs in I.C.B.Ms. For, since such missiles cannot at present be destroyed in flight, as can at any rate a proportion of manned bombers, a nuclear aggressor would have to leave none of the enemy missiles undestroyed, if it wanted to avoid one of its own major cities being wiped out by retaliatory attack. So the advent of long-range nuclear missiles made the balance of terror more stable.

There were two contrasted hypothetical policies to meet this new situation: the first was to assume that a fairly stable kind of military balance had been reached, in which neither side could make use of its strategic nuclear power without ensuring its own destruction: in other words, that the balance was likely to be fairly stable against rational action, even though the actual nuclear strengths of the two sides were markedly different—as indeed they were in the middle 1950's, when the United States was vastly stronger in overall deployed nuclear strength. This view also rested on the assumption that neither side could hope to knock out all the enemy's nuclear system, as well as implicitly, on the further assumption that a rational government would be nearly, if not quite, as much deterred from some action by the expectation that it would suffer, say, 10 million deaths as it would if it expected to suffer 100 million. This view led to the practical conclusion as regards deployed nuclear strategic weapons that " enough is enough." In today's jargon, this is the policy of the minimum deterrent, that is, the possession of a nuclear force adequate only for a retaliatory attack on enemy cities but incapable of successful attack on the enemy nuclear delivery system.

On the political plane, the resulting period of relative stability would be favourable for a serious attempt to negotiate a substantial measure of disarmament, both nuclear and conventional. Such far-reaching disarmament was highly desirable if only because such a balance of terror is stable only against rational acts of responsible governments: it is by no means stable against irresponsible actions of individuals or dissident groups or against technical accidents. A few suitably placed individuals, say the aircrew of a nuclear bomber on a routine flight or a missile crew, could kill a few million of

11

the enemy city dwellers on their own initiative. For instance, if France had possessed a large stockpile of bombs for some years, some might now be in the hands of the O.A.S. The best way to reduce such dangers is drastically to reduce the number of nuclear weapons on both sides.

The second and very different doctrine was that the balance of terror was not stable even against rational acts of responsible governments. This was based on the view that a determined nuclear power might be able to launch a surprise attack on the enemy's nuclear delivery system of such strength that the enemy would not be able to retaliate. So the aggressor, without suffering unacceptable casualties, would have the enemy at his mercy. The practical consequences of this doctrine is to strive for both the maximum superiority in number of weapons, the maximum invulnerability of one's own nuclear delivery system, and for the maximum intelligence about the enemy's nuclear system. A successful nuclear attack of this nature would require first-class operational intelligence about all the enemy's nuclear missiles and air bases, and the power to despatch several weapons against each, so as to ensure that at least one reached its target. So a counter-force strategy implies the necessity for a many-fold overall nuclear superiority over the enemy. Moreover, since for such a strike to have the slightest chance of success it must come as a complete surprise to the enemy, it must be a " first strike ": that is to say, the country which makes it must be the aggressor as regards strategic nuclear war. This policy has various pseudonyms, a maximum deterrent posture, a first-counter-force-strike-capability, or, in plain English, providing the capability for nuclear aggression.

On the other hand, the first view, that of the stability of the balance against rational actions, involves planning, not to initiate nuclear war, but only to retaliate against enemy cities if attacked. It is clear that only a small nuclear delivery system is necessary for such a minimum deterrent—for one big hydrogen bomb on a big city could kill several million. However, the small delivery system must be highly invulnerable, otherwise the enemy might think it possible to bring off a successful counter-force strike. Little operational intelli-

gence is needed for such a minimum deterrent policy, since
this involves retaliating on cities whose locations are known
and does not involve surprise attack on nuclear bases, whose
locations therefore do not need to be known.

If the Washington figures for the Soviet nuclear strength
are valid, it is clear that the U.S.S.R. has planned for a purely
retaliatory nuclear role, and has definitely not planned for
a surprise attack on the American delivery system. For in
1956 the U.S.S.R. was believed to be capable of making 25
long-range bombers a month: in fact the Russians appear
today to have only some 150, compared with the 1,700 American long-range bombers able to reach Russia. Even though
Soviet medium-range bombers could reach America on one-
way flights, this is much more than counter-balanced by the
1,500 or so Western fighter-bombers, carrier-borne aircraft
and medium-range missiles able to reach Russia. Equally, it
is probable that the Russians could have made many more
than the 50 or so I.C.B.Ms. with which they are now credited,
for their outstandingly successful civil space programme
indicates substantial industrial resources for making missiles.
The U.S.S.R. has clearly based its safety against the West's
huge nuclear power on a few long-range missiles and aircraft
operating from bases whose locations are kept as secret as
possible. Their value as a deterrent is certainly enhanced by
the prestige of their space programme. If the U.S.S.R. can
photograph the back of the moon, then it is likely to be
credited with the power to destroy New York, even after an
all-out American attack on Russia.

That the Soviet Union believed that the danger of a major
war, intentionally initiated, had been reduced by the advent
of hydrogen bombs seems indicated by the fact that they
reduced the total number of men in their armed forces from
5·8 million in 1955-56 to 3·6 million in 1959, and announced
in January 1960 their intention to reduce this to 2·4 million
by the end of 1961, as a first step towards a still lower figure.[3]
They needed fewer troops as they no longer had to rely on
a retaliatory land-blow in Europe to counter a Western
nuclear attack. Their concern about the danger of accidental,

[3] See Appendix, p. 241.

irresponsible or escalated war is probably one of the reasons for the very strong espousal in 1955 of drastic measures of comprehensive and general disarmament.

During 1961 Soviet military policy underwent some drastic changes. The projected decrease of total armed forces to 2·4 million in 1961 was deferred and the arms budget was markedly increased; heavy pressure has been exerted to bring about changes in the status of Berlin and to get the division of Germany recognised; and, finally, nuclear tests have been re-started in spite of a promise in January 1960 by Khrushchev that the U.S.S.R. would not be the first to re-start them.

No doubt there were some political motives behind these drastic moves. Possibly heavy pressure was put on Khrushchev from China and from the opposition elements in the Soviet Union to abandon his policy of co-existence with the West and to admit it had not produced political gains commensurate with its possible military risks. However, such very drastic changes, with the inevitable adverse reaction of much of world opinion, would hardly have been made unless there had been some strong military reason for them. What were the most likely military reasons for this rather sudden switch of Soviet policy? To attempt to answer this question it will be necessary to trace, in more detail, the history of the military postures and policies of the Western and Soviet blocs from 1954, the year of the hydrogen bomb, to 1961, the year of rapid rearmament.

First it is to be noted that even now, in early 1962, when the Soviet rearmament programme must be well under way, their nuclear planning appears still to be for a purely retaliatory role—at least if Malinovsky's statements are correct. For he has said that the U.S.S.R. does not need to increase considerably her missile force and that it was not now a question of stockpiling but of natural renewal and perfection of weapons: their present stocks were sufficient to defeat any enemy. These statements can be true only of a purely retaliatory counter-city strategy. A counter-force strategy, in contrast, would demand a continuous build-up of nuclear strength in order to compete with the expected gradual decrease of the vulnerability of the enemy's delivery system as a result of progress in missile technology. The only circumstances in which a similar continuous build-up of an invulnerable and purely retaliatory force would be required, would be if the enemy produced an effective anti-missile missile or if its cities could be adequately protected. Neither is at present technologically possible and probably never will be. Even if it were possible, a modest increase of the small retaliatory force would restore the *status quo*. Hence, in general, the unimportance of defence measures against a retaliatory nuclear attack: the opponent can easily cancel them out.

Turning to the history of American defence policy over this period, it is to be noted that the total service manpower fell slowly from 2·9 million in 1955 to 2·6 million in 1960. The development of improved nuclear weapons, missiles and aircraft continued, but not at a very great rate, even after the Sputnik in 1957 and much boasting by the U.S.S.R. of her missile prowess. Although subjected to considerable public pressure to engage in a crash programme to close the alleged missile gap, President Eisenhower maintained that the existing programme was adequate for the safety of the nation, and he stated that " the bomber gap of several years ago was always a fiction and the missile gap shows every sign of being the same."

In 1959 the Democratic National Committee published a detailed study of defence problems and recommended a $7,000m. increase (16 per cent.) to the $43,000m. defence budget proposed by Eisenhower, partly for increased conventional forces and partly to increase both the strength and invulnerability of America's nuclear striking power. In January 1961, almost immediately after taking office, the new administration authorised an increase of $3,000m. and later in the year another $4,000m., thus carrying out the programme of rearmament demanded in 1959. The present plans include the provision by 1965 of up to 800 I.C.B.Ms. of the solid-fuel Minuteman type in underground protected bases.

The Democratic party's campaign for increased nuclear armaments was closely linked with the theoretical doctrine of the instability of the balance of terror, due to the alleged overwhelming advantage accruing to the nuclear aggressor; this was ably argued mainly at first by civilian analysts in close relation with the American Air Force. The Soviet Union was indicated as likely to have both the capability and the intention to launch a surprise nuclear attack on the United States.

In view of the very great nuclear superiority of the United States over the U.S.S.R. during all these years, which is now announced from Washington, it is clear that if there was any truth in the doctrine of the overwhelming advantage of the nuclear aggressor, it was to the United States and not to the U.S.S.R. that this advantage would accrue. In retrospect these " looking glass " strategists endowed the U.S.S.R. with a capability which it did not have and which America once had but had now lost.

Although the overall nuclear strength of the United States is now, and was then, much greater than that of the U.S.S.R., there was one vital factor in the Soviet position which would have made an American nuclear attack on the U.S.S.R. exceedingly risky: this was the secrecy as to the locations of the Soviet nuclear bases.

Now one of the main objects of the U2 flights was to locate the Soviet nuclear bases. It is said in Washington that these flights failed to find any appreciable number of operational missile sites and that it was such information which led President Eisenhower to start reducing the numbers of operational B47 nuclear bombers.

Khrushchev knew, of course, that these flights had been going on for some years before the first aircraft was brought down in the spring of 1960; presumably the Soviet Command reacted by greater dispersal and camouflage. What must have disturbed the Soviet military staff was President Eisenhower's justification for them as essential for American security. This implied that American security could be maintained only if the United States had sufficient information as to the locality of Russian nuclear sites to make possible a successful surprise, and therefore aggressive, nuclear attack on the Soviet nuclear delivery system. In other words, America appeared to be planning for the capability to make a first counter-force strike.

Some time in the latter half of 1960 or early 1961 it seems probable that the Soviet Command began to have doubts as to the adequacy of the minimum deterrent posture in relation to America's much greater nuclear strength. It must have been later than January 1960, since in that month Khrushchev announced a drastic cut-back of both long-range bombers and conventional forces. Perhaps they feared that the geographical secrecy of their nuclear bases might be compromised by further air or satellite reconnaissance, or by espionage or defections. So the Soviet military staff may have feared that the United States might in this way acquire the capability to make a successful attack on Soviet nuclear bases. They certainly noted the doctrine of some civilian analysts that it would be quite rational to make such an attack even at the cost of 10 million or so deaths to the attacking side, and the doctrine of others that America should prepare herself mentally and materially to suffer such casualties.

Probably the main fears of the Soviet Government arose from doubts about the reliability of the decision-making organisation in Washington, and about the danger of small wars escalating uncontrollably into all-out nuclear war. In an important analysis of these dangers, published recently in *Foreign Affairs,* Sir Solly Zuckerman warns of the tendency to entrust decisions involving the life and death of nations to predetermined calculations based on misleading reasoning. Such fears must have been increased by the frank but alarming valedictory address by President Eisenhower:

This conjunction of an immense military establishment and a large arms industry is new in American experience. The total influence—economic, political, even spiritual—is felt in every city, every state and every office of the federal government. . . In the councils of government we must guard against the acquisition of unwanted influence, whether sought or unsought, by the military industrial complex. The potential for disastrous use of misplaced power exists and will persist.

The full implication of this courageous statement became clearer in the autumn of 1961 when President Kennedy launched a vigorous campaign against all those in the United

States who urged " total war and total victory over communism," who sought to find an American solution for all problems—and in fact against all those who were living in the long-past era of the United States atomic monopoly. In this campaign Kennedy has been vigorously supported by Eisenhower. Very possibly the U.S.S.R. may have overestimated the potential influence of these American ultra-right-wing groups and super-patriots. However, the fact that both Kennedy and Eisenhower have felt it necessary to combat them must also imply that the Soviet military planners could not afford to ignore their existence.

On this basis it is possible to understand some of the motives behind the sudden change of Soviet policy in the spring of 1961. Fear of the loss of the security of their nuclear bases, and fear of the rise to power of groups who might try to make use of America's great nuclear superiority to attack the Soviet nuclear delivery system, were probably the most cogent. Also of considerable weight was the fear that if NATO defence policy continued as it was, the time could not be far distant when West Germany would get *de facto* control of her own nuclear weapons. Then the refusal, in Soviet eyes, of America to take disarmament seriously at the Committee of Ten in 1960 was evidently an important factor. As early as November 1960 individual Russians bluntly stated that if the West continued to stall on disarmament, the U.S.S.R. would be forced into massive rearmament.

If these then were the Soviet fears, the rejection by the U.S.S.R. of the British-American test-ban draft treaty in the spring of 1961 finds a simple military explanation. For if a detailed study of this document is made, it is clear that the process of setting up and operating the proposed international inspection system might conceivably have served to reveal the location of some, at least, of the Soviet missile sites. At any rate, it would be very hard to convince a military staff officer of any nationality that this possibility was negligible.

If the West had been content to monitor only atmospheric tests, a much less comprehensive inspection system would have sufficed and the Soviet military staff might well have accepted as worth taking the risk of their missile sites being revealed, and so a test-ban treaty might well have been signed. The obvious Soviet fear of inspection may well have been because they had so little to inspect.

The Soviet resumption of testing in September 1961 falls into the same pattern of motivation. Though its timing may have been influenced by the Berlin crisis which Khrushchev himself brought to a head, the testing of up to 50-megaton warheads, and the simultaneous and publicised success in putting seven I.C.B.Ms. on their target in the Pacific at a range of some 7,000 miles, was a very effective way of re-establishing Russian confidence in the deterrent value of the few deployed I.C.B.Ms. which formed their main retaliatory force, by emphasising to the United States their accuracy and the possible power of their warheads.

These tests have certainly reduced to some extent the relative weakness of the Soviet nuclear deployment compared with that of America, and have thus tended to make the balance more stable.

On balance, the resumption of nuclear tests by the U.S.S.R. and the explosion of a 50-megaton bomb probably strengthened Kennedy's campaign against the Ultras; for, though it doubtless increased the ardour with which many of them demanded a show-down with the U.S.S.R., that is, preventive nuclear war, it also greatly increased the general awareness of the catastrophic casualties which would result from successful retaliation by even a very few undestroyed Soviet nuclear missiles.

Support for this view is found in the London *Times* report from Bermuda on 22 December last: " It is now privately admitted at the Pentagon that the United States can no longer hope to impose its will on any nuclear battlefield. . . . This may have been apparent since the first H-bomb was exploded, but it is another thing for senior American generals to accept it and draw conclusions other than the need to build more and bigger missiles and bombers."

The recent vigorous official emphasis on America's overwhelming nuclear superiority over the U.S.S.R., and the assertion that America possesses a second strike which is as strong as Russia's first strike—thus burying officially the sedulously propagated fear of a rationally planned Soviet first strike—might perhaps be held in the U.S.S.R. to suggest a move by the U.S. administration towards a preventive war posture. Certainly the exact reverse is the case. For the U.S. administration knows quite well that preventive nuclear war against the U.S.S.R. would risk tens of millions of Americans killed. What many individual Americans fear is that at a moment of crisis, precipitated perhaps by some brutal Soviet action even on quite a local scale, a wave of indignation might sweep America and force the administration to make a nuclear attack on the U.S.S.R.

The most dangerous pressure might come from those who believe that the Soviet Union has planned for, and in fact now has, a first counter-force capability, and so at a time of crisis might use it. If this were the situation, then the argument that America must forestall the Soviet blow might seem strong. The U.S. administration evidently foresaw this danger arising and effectively removed it by denying that the Soviet Union has ever had an effective counter-force capacity; thus, there would be no reason for a forestalling blow in a crisis. Kennedy, by emphasising U.S. nuclear superiority over the Soviet Union, has forestalled the potential forestallers or, in the current jargon, has pre-empted the potential pre-empters. At the same time he has refuted many of the arguments on which the Democratic party based much of its election campaign, and indeed many of the arguments for its own present rearmament programme.

It is, for instance, hard to see the military justification for the programme of up to 800 Minutemen I.C.B.Ms. in the next few years. If these are, as claimed, reasonably invulnerable, then this number is at least 10 times higher than is necessary for an effective retaliatory force to attack Russian cities.

It cannot be seriously believed now that the U.S.S.R. has either the capability or the intention to make an all-out attack on American missile sites and bomber bases. It will be noticed that the Soviet adoption of a purely retaliatory nuclear strategy has brought two great advantages. Firstly, it has saved scarce industrial and technological resources which are valuable for their economic development and economic competition with the West. Secondly, it has avoided much the greatest single military danger—this is that America might attack Russia because of a belief that Russia was about to attack America.

Much genuine alarm might have been allayed in the West, particularly after the brutal Soviet action in Hungary in 1956, and after their technological triumph of the Sputnik in 1957, if Soviet leaders had earlier made it clearer that they disbelieved in the possibility of a counter-force strike and were not planning for such an operation. However, Khrushchev did make this quite clear in his speech in January 1960, in which he stated the view that a surprise nuclear attack could never succeed in destroying all the nuclear installations of a large country, so that a powerful counter-blow would always be possible. In the same speech he announced a big cut-back in bomber production.

If the analysis given here has some approximate truth, what are the prospects of progress towards disarmament at the meetings of the eighteen-nation forum which is due to meet in Geneva this month? Both blocs are fully committed by official pronouncements to the goal of complete and general disarmament under strict control and inspection: notably by the British Commonwealth Prime Ministers' statement in the spring of 1961, by President Kennedy's speech to the Assembly of the United Nations, and by the Soviet-American joint statement of principles, both in September. Moreover, both sides are committed to attempting to work out first steps of the disarmament process, which do not impair the present strategic balance.

No attempt will be made here to discuss all the complex details of possible first steps with the necessary phasing of disarmament and inspection. However, a sketch in broadest outline will be made of some of the essential conditions which such steps must satisfy if they are to be acceptable on military grounds to the governments of the United States and the U.S.S.R.

Clearly conventional and nuclear disarmament must go in parallel. The fear by the West of Russia's superiority in trained and deployed land forces must be met by a drastic reduction during the first stage to the low levels such as those suggested by the Anglo-French memorandum of 1954: that is, to a million, or at most 1·5 million, men for the United States, U.S.S.R., and China. When the correspondingly limited contributions to the land forces of NATO from Great Britain, France and West Germany are taken into account, then the armies of the Soviet bloc would not have the capability of over-running Europe in a surprise land attack.

The number of nuclear weapons, their explosive power and the diversity of the delivery systems on both sides, are so large that no small step of nuclear disarmament can have much decisive military significance though it might have great psychological importance. To justify the labour of negotiating any agreed reduction, and to offset the undoubted strains and disputes which will inevitably arise out of the operation of any inspection and control system, the negotiated reduction must be a major one: in fact of such a magnitude as to change qualitatively the nature of the nuclear postures of the two giant powers. On the other hand, any disarmament measures, however small, made unilaterally, would do much to promote mutual confidence.

The simplest big first step, and the one most consistent with realistic military considerations, is that the two giant powers should reduce their nuclear forces to a very low and purely retaliatory role—that is, that each should retain only sufficient invulnerable long-range vehicles to attack the other's cities if it is itself attacked; less, for instance, than 100 I.C.B.Ms. with one-megaton warheads. This is still a terrific force able to kill 100 million people or so. A reduction to a level of, say, twenty I.C.B.Ms. or less would be preferable. Such a reduction would at once prevent nuclear weapons from being used by sane governments as weapons of aggression or blackmail. It would not, of course, prevent them from being used by irresponsible groups who do not calculate the cost. It is only at a later stage in disarmament, when nuclear weapons are completely destroyed, that this danger will be excluded. It has always been clear that the ever-present danger of accidental or irresponsible war is a cogent reason for big and rapid steps in the disarmament process.

Detailed studies are needed of possible ways in which both Russia and America could make such a first big step, while maintaining the present strategic balance. A major problem is how to phase the building up of a system of general inspection, while at the same time making a drastic reduction of nuclear delivery systems by their actual destruction under international verification. Taking military considerations only into account, I believe that a procedure acceptable to both blocs could be devised.

However, the problem becomes more difficult when non-military considerations are taken into account. Since it is clear that non-military considerations have played a major role in shaping defence policies of the great powers, they must inevitably also affect their disarmament policies. For instance, since it is difficult to find legitimate military reasons for the vast number of American nuclear weapons and delivery vehicles, it is clear that military arguments alone are not likely to be dominant in American discussion of a possible drastic first step of nuclear disarmament. This is widely admitted in the United States, where the impediments to disarmament are becoming more and more seen as economic, political and emotional in origin, rather than as based on operational military considerations. The main problem facing the U.S. administration is how to overcome the political pressure of these groups, who for various political, economic and emotional reasons, believe in having lots of nuclear armaments, and are just opposed to disarmament in general, and to Kennedy's commitment to drastic disarmament in particular.

A vital aspect is the effect which drastic disarmament steps would have, not only on the economy as a whole, but on those special sections of high grade science-based and highly localised industries, which are now so overwhelmingly involved in defence work. A valuable step would be for both the American and Soviet Governments to produce and publish detailed, and politically realistic, economic plans for the transition to a low and purely retaliatory nuclear capacity.

The arguments given above lead one to conclude that a realistic military basis for an agreed drastic first step in disarmament may not be impossible to find. However, the anti-disarmament factions may intervene, to prevent action, unless great public support is forthcoming to implement the accepted policy of drastic disarmament, as eloquently expressed by President Kennedy to the United Nations in September:

Today, every inhabitant of this planet must contemplate the day when it may no longer be habitable. Every man, woman and child lives under a nuclear sword of Damocles, hanging by the slenderest of threads, capable of being cut at any moment by accident, miscalculation or madness. The weapons of war must be abolished before they abolish us. . . .
For fifteen years this organisation has sought the reduction and destruction of arms. Now that goal is no longer a dream—it is a practical matter of life and death. The risks inherent in disarmament pale in comparison to the risks inherent in an unlimited arms race.

This great goal will be achieved only if the real nature of the arguments against disarmament are clearly identified and frankly faced: they must not be allowed to be obscured, as they sometimes have been in the past, by ingenious but fallacious military doctrine, applied to false intelligence estimates.

The growing power of China provides an added reason for urgency in the drive for disarmament. It is important that Russia and America agreed to limit drastically their nuclear arms before China becomes a major nuclear power. It is to be noticed that whatever influence China may now be exerting on Russia to adopt a harder policy with the West, arises certainly in part from the failure of Khrushchev's world-wide campaign for disarmament. It is this failure which greatly weakens Khrushchev's argument for the feasibility of peaceful co-existence of the Soviet and the Western world. It is clearly urgently necessary to bring China into the disarmament negotiations.

Part II

Operational Research

One

Operational Research[1]
1948

The technique of the scientific analysis of operations of war, particularly as developed in Great Britain during the late war, has been the subject of a considerable amount of public discussion, as for instance at the recent meeting of the British Association at Dundee. The interest in these developments lies partly in the practical importance of the results achieved and partly in the feeling that similar methods might be applied with success to some of the urgent problems of the post-war world. Short accounts of some aspects of the wartime development of operational analysis have appeared in various publications,[2] but no systematic account has yet been published, though some are in preparation.[3] While awaiting these fuller accounts, permission has been obtained to publish two notes written by the author during the war, in which some of the principles of the organisation of the operational research sections, and the methods of analysis, are set out in some detail.

The first of these, entitled "Scientists at the Operational Level," was written in December 1941, in order to inform the Admiralty of some of the developments which had occurred in the Operational Research Sections already established at Fighter, Anti-Aircraft and Coastal Commands. It so happened that this hurriedly and somewhat flippantly written document received subsequently a rather wide

---

[1] *The Advancement of Science*, v, No. 17 (Apr. 1948).
[2] Charles Kittel, "The nature and development of operational research," in *Science*, cv (Feb. 1947); C. H. Waddington, in *World Review*, June 1945; P. M. S. Blackett, "Memoir of E. J. Williams, F.R.S.," in *Obituary Notices of Fellows of the Royal Society*, VOL. v, Mar. 1947 (see below, p. 935 ff.).
[3] A fairly full account has recently been published in Crowther and Widdington, *Science and War*, London 1947.

circulation in Service Departments both in this country and also in the United States, where it seems to have had some influence on the setting up of similar organisations.

The second document, under the title, "A Note on Certain Aspects of the Methodology of Operational Research," originated in 1941 as an attempt to set out, for the benefit of new scientific recruits to the operational research sections, some of the principles that had been found to underlie the work of the first two years of the war. The text as reproduced here dates from May 1943. A few notes have been added to the original documents. As the nearest existing approach to a " text book " of operational research, it also received a fairly wide circulation, and has, along with the former document, been fairly extensively quoted in various official and semi-official documents. It must be emphasised that these two papers cover only a small part of the great field of operational research as developed in Great Britain and the United States during the war and that very many important achievements are not mentioned at all. For instance, the examples given were chosen rather haphazardly and mainly with a view to illustrating points of methodology.

There are surely lessons to be learned from these war-time developments that may help us to tackle wisely some of the problems of peace. It is hoped that the publication of these documents will stimulate such application. Of more theoretical interest is the general problem of the limits of predictability in the inexact sciences. For instance, some parts of modern economics seem to use a variational technique closely analogous to that described in the second paper.[4]

The writer wishes to take this opportunity to pay tribute not only to his scientific colleagues who were engaged with him directly or indirectly in this new development, but also to those senior officers of all three fighting services, whose sympathy, understanding and encouragement were the essential basis without which the development could not have taken place. Among the latter, the writer wishes to mention particularly, General Sir Frederick Pile, Air Chief Marshal

---

[4] For instance N. Kaldor's Appendix III to Sir William Beveridge's *Full Employment*, London 1944.

Sir Philip Joubert, Air Chief Marshal Sir John Slessor, and Admiral Sir George Creasy. It is only possible to mention a few of the scientists whose influence in the formulation of the ideas expressed in the two documents have been paramount. From the earlier formative period there were Sir Henry Tizard, Sir Robert Watson Watt, A. P. Rowe and G. H. Larnder. During the latter period the names of the late Sir Ralph Fowler and E. J. Williams, L. H. Bayliss, Henry Whitehead, C. H. Waddington, H. R. Hulme, E. C. Bullard, Andrew Huxley and Charles Kittell, stand out pre-eminently.

I wish to express my gratitude to the Minister of Defence for permission to publish these two papers.

DOCUMENT I

SCIENTISTS AT THE OPERATIONAL LEVEL
(1941)

1. The object of having scientists in close touch with operations is to enable operational staffs to obtain scientific advice on those matters which are not handled by the service technical establishments.

Operational staffs provide the scientists with the operational outlook and data. The scientists apply scientific methods of analysis to these data, and are thus able to give useful advice.

The main field of their activity is clearly the analysis of actual operations, using as data the material to be found in an operation room, e.g. all signals, track charts, combat reports, meteorological information, etc.

It will be noted that these data are not, and on secrecy grounds cannot, in general, be made available to the technical establishments. Thus such scientific analysis, if done at all, must be done in or near operation rooms.

The work of an Operational Research Section should be carried out at Command, Groups, Stations or Squadrons as circumstances dictate.

2. SCIENTIFIC ANALYSIS OF OPERATIONS

To what extent is it useful to do analysis of operations in a more scientific manner than is done normally by service specialist officers?

Experience over many parts of our war effort has shown that such analysis can be of the utmost value, and the lack of such analysis can be disastrous. Probably the main reason why this is so is that very many war operations involve considerations with which scientists are specially trained to compete, and in which serving officers are in general not trained. This is especially the case with all those aspects of operations into which probability considerations and the theory of errors enter. Serving officers of the highest calibre are necessarily employed in important executive posts, and are, therefore, not available for *detailed* analytic work.

Schedule of Typical Operational Research

The records of some war operations (e.g. air attacks on U-boats for the previous six months) are taken as the data. This is analysed as quantitatively as possible, and the results achieved are " explained " in the scientific sense, i.e. brought into numerical relation with the other operational facts and the known performance of the weapons used. When this has been done, consideration is given to possible modification of the tactics to improve the operational results.

The first step—that of collecting the actual data—is by itself of enormous importance, for it is not uncommon for operational staffs to be unacquainted with what is actually being achieved. An Operational Research Section is not in general concerned with " hot news," though they should be prepared to so concern themselves if specifically requested to do so.

On the Validity of Deductions from Observations

A typical problem is as follows: —a weapon A is calculated by a service technical department to be 50 per cent. more efficient than a weapon B. Actual operations over a given period show, say, 2 successes for A and 4 for B. Does this prove that B is a better weapon than A?

Such points arise continually and require the highest scientific judgment to resolve. In particular a grasp of fluctuation phenomena (i.e. Poisson's Distribution) is required. If the average number of hits on some target in a given time is m, then (on certain assumptions) the chance that exactly x hits will be obtained in the same time is

$$\frac{e^{-m}m^x}{x!}$$

Value of Scientific Confidence and Numerical Thinking

The scientist, in considering an operational problem, very often comes to the conclusion that the common-sense view is the correct one. But he can often back the view by numerical proof, and thus give added confidence in the tactics employed.

Or when two alternative qualitative views, "A is best," " B is best," are in dispute, he can often resolve this numerically into some such statement as that "A is x per cent. better than B in January and y per cent. worse in June."

In fact, the scientist can encourage numerical thinking on operational matters, and so can help to avoid running the war by gusts of emotion.

Operational Experiments

Since new weapons and devices are inevitably put into service relatively untested, the first few months of the use of a new device must be considered as an extension of its development trials. An Operational Research Section can function usefully here in a liaison capacity between the operational staff, the technical department which produced the device, and the development unit which tested it.

Further it is often possible, by collaboration between Controllers and the staff of an Operational Research Section, to arrange operations on certain occasions so as to obtain data to clarify some doubtful point. For instance, the relative merits of different forms of anti-submarine sweeps by aircraft is a matter of (*a*) mathematical calculation, (*b*) test by actual operations, perhaps over a long period of time.

3. Distribution of Reports on Operations

One of the functions of an Operational Research Section is clearly to write periodical reports on various aspects of operations. Except when secrecy questions prevent, these should be given a wide circulation, e.g. in the Air Force to Squadrons to be read by the aircrews. In this way, the tactical education of the men on the job can be raised.

4. Operational Requirements

One of the most important duties of a Command is to state its requirements for new devices and weapons. Such requirements are passed, in general, through a department of a Ministry (which acts partly as a filter room, partly as a specialised department and partly as a post office) to a service technical establishment.

The only places in this chain where the real operational facts are known is at the Command Groups and Stations. Unless the operational requirement is considered scientifically at the Command jointly by the operational staffs and scientists, it is possible that the operational requirements decided on will not correspond (*a*) to the real need, (*b*) to the technical possibilities.

In other words, an Operational Research Section can act usefully by interpreting

(*a*) the operational facts of life to the technical establishments, and

(*b*) the technical possibilities to the operational staffs.

A considerable wastage of war effort has occurred through lack of this joint discussion.

Nothing in this section or in section 2 should be taken as implying that an Operational Research Section should be the only channel by which a Technical Establishment obtains operational experience—on the contrary, the direct contact between a Technical Establishment and operational units is generally essential.

5. ORGANISATION AND PERSONNEL

An Operational Research Section should be an integral part of a Command and should work in the closest collaboration with the various departments at the Command.

The head of the Operational Research Section should be directly responsible to the Commander-in-Chief and may with advantage be appointed as his scientific adviser.

A considerable fraction of the staff of an Operational Research Section should be of the very highest standing in science, and many of them should be drawn from those who have had experience at the Service Technical Establishments.

An Operational Research Section which contents itself with the routine production of statistical reports and narratives will be of very limited value. The atmosphere required is that of a first-class pure scientific research institution, and the calibre of the personnel should match this. All members of an Operational Research Section should spend part of their time at operational stations in close touch with the personnel actually on the job.

6. NEW DEVICES

" New weapons for old " is apt to become a very popular cry. The success of some new devices has led to a new form of escapism which runs somewhat thus: " Our present equipment doesn't work very well; training is bad, supply is poor, spare parts non-existent. Let's have an entirely new gadget!" Then comes the vision of the new gadget, springing like Aphrodite from the Ministry of Aircraft Production, in full production, complete with spares, and attended by a chorus of trained crews.

One of the tasks of an Operational Research Section is to make possible at least an approach to a numerical estimate of the merits of a change-over from one device to another, by continual investigation of the actual performance of existing weapons, and by objective analysis of the likely performance of new ones.

The actual operational effectiveness over a period of time of any weapon can usefully (even if platitudinously) be considered as the product of three factors; the first $N(t)$ is the number in use, expressed as a function of the time; the second P is the scheduled performance of the weapon; and the third $S(t)$ is the average state of serviceability and training, i.e. the actual performance expressed as a fraction of the schedule. The probable form of $N(t)$ could be obtained from the production statistics of existing weapons. Relatively little is known of the form of $S(t)$, but probably a good first approximation would be to take $S(t) \propto (1 - e^{-t/T})$ where T is of the order of 2 months to 1 year according to the type of gadget. Some operational research might usefully be directed towards elucidating this function. One could then attempt a numerical estimate of the gain or loss involved in the change-over from one device to another, and so attempt to avoid the unduly heavy overhead costs of too rapid change-over.

7. In general, one might conclude that relatively too much scientific effort has been expended hitherto in the production of new devices and too little in the proper use of what we have got. Thus, there is a strong general case for moving many of the best scientists from the technical establishments to the operational Commands, at any rate for a time. If, and when, they return to technical work, they will be often much more useful by reason of their new knowledge of real operational needs.

DOCUMENT II

A NOTE ON CERTAIN ASPECTS OF THE METHODOLOGY OF OPERATIONAL RESEARCH (1943)

1. INTRODUCTION

Now that more and more of the operations of war are being analysed by teams of operational research workers, it may be of some value to discuss certain methods of approach which have proved fruitful in practice. It is hoped that these notes may assist new operational research workers to extract rapidly from any field of work the greatest possible amount of useful information.

It is not, of course, suggested that the very obvious common sense of the variational methods discussed below is in any sense novel. On the contrary, they are in general use, implicitly at any rate, in those branches of science whose subject matter has similar characteristics. These characteristics are that a limited amount of numerical data are ascertainable about phenomena of great complexity. The problems of analysing war operations are almost all of this type and are therefore rather nearer, in general, to many problems, say, of biology or of economics, than to most problems of physics, where usually a great deal of numerical data are ascertainable about relatively simple phenomena. However, operational research, like every science, must not copy in detail the technical methods of any other science, but must work out techniques of its own, suited to its own special material and problems. These techniques must not remain rigid but must change with the nature of the problems.

One obvious characteristic of operational research, as at present practised, is that it has, or should have, a strictly practical character. Its object is to assist the finding of means to improve the efficiency of war operations in progress or planned for the future. To do this, past operations are studied to determine the facts; theories are elaborated to explain the facts; and finally the facts and theories are used to make predictions about future operations. This procedure ensures that the maximum possible use is made of all past experience.

The main fields of operational research can be classified under the following headings, the study of weapons, the study of tactics, and the study of strategy. The first consists mainly in analysing how and why existing weapons perform as they do, with the object of finding out how they could be improved. The second consists in analysing the various tactical methods in use, with the same object of finding methods of improving them. The third consists in studying the results achieved by various types of operation, and the cost in the resources of war of achieving them. The actual form of the method of variational analysis lends itself immediately to the calculation of "marginal" profits and costs—which is in general what is required.

Predictions about the future are of course always subject to much uncertainty, but experience has shown that many more useful quantitative predictions can be made than is often thought possible. This arises to a considerable extent from the relative stability over quite long periods of time of many factors involved in operations. This stability appears rather unexpected in view of the large number of chance events and individual personalities and abilities that are involved in even a small operation. But these differences in general average out for a large number of operations, and the aggregate results are often found to remain comparatively constant. (Appendix A. 4.)

The somewhat formal—even pedantic—character of some of the following discussion is chosen for the sake of brevity and generality. It will have achieved its object if, on the one hand, it encourages research workers to tackle problems which might otherwise be put aside as too complex, or, on the other hand, if it leads to apparently simple problems being recognised in their true complexity. Although the main object of operational research is to make useful predictions, it has also an important function in assessing the possibilities of prediction and in calling attention to fields in which no or little quantitative prediction is possible.

The examples given in the Appendices illustrate some of the arguments of the note. Time has not permitted the compilation of a comprehensive set of examples.

2. OPERATIONAL RESEARCH PROCEDURE

When embarking on a new problem of operational research, the first step is usually to collect as much numerical data about the operations as possible. But much data remain unavailable, either because no records exist, or because their collection is impracticable. Thus, a very incomplete numerical picture, in the form perhaps of tables or curves representing some results of the operations as a function of some few variables, is all that can usually be obtained.

This first step alone may be of the greatest importance and lead to practical conclusions of great value. For the suitable presentation of the actual facts of past operations, without any interpretation, may be so striking as alone to compel reconsideration of tactics and methods. (See Appendices B.1 and B.5.)

But to go further, it is clearly necessary to relate these observed results to (a) the actual properties of the weapons employed, and (b) the actual tactics employed. In other words, the object is to find a scientific explanation of the facts. Only when this is done can the two main objects of the operational research be attained. These are the prediction of the results of new weapons and of new tactics.

3. THE A PRIORI METHOD

One possible method of procedure is to attempt to find general solutions to certain rather arbitrarily simplified problems. In times of peace, when up-to-date numerical data on war operations are not available, this method may alone be possible. This procedure is to select, out of the numerous variables of a real operation of war, certain important variables which are particularly suitable for quantitative treatment, and to ignore the rest. Differential equations are then formed and solutions obtained.

Certain results obtained by this method are of great interest. An example is Lanchester's N^2 Law (Appendix D). But it is generally very difficult to decide whether, in any particular case, such a " law " applies or not. Thus it is often impossible to make any practical conclusions from such an a priori analysis, even though it be of theoretical interest.

Another difficulty with the a priori method is that when a solution in a certain number of variables has been obtained, and it is found necessary to introduce an additional variable, very often a completely new start must be made. In fact the method seldom lends itself to the solution of problems by successive approximations.

4. THE VARIATIONAL METHOD

The more common-sense procedure is to abandon the attempt to construct from " first principles " a complete imaginary operation *something like* the real one under investigation, and to replace it by an attempt to find, both by experimental and by analytical methods, how a real operation would be altered if certain of the variables, e.g. the tactics employed or properties of the weapons used, were varied.

Suppose the result of any operation of war is denoted by quantities Y_1 Y_2 etc., called the yields. Then these yields must be considered as functions of a large number of operational parameters or variables X_1 X_2 . . . X_n. Some of these can be given a quantitative measure but some can only be expressed qualitatively. Any attempt to find the form of such a function:

$$Y = F(X_1 \ldots X_n) \qquad (1)$$

from first principles is useless, in general, owing to the complexity of the problem and the non-quantitative nature of many of the variables (e.g. Appendix A.1).

The common-sense procedure is to use the result Y of some past operation under known conditions to predict the result Y' of a future operation under new conditions. If the new conditions differ too widely from the past conditions, the problem of calculating the yield becomes, in effect, an *a priori* one, and, as already explained, such problems are generally insoluble.

But when only relatively small changes in some only of the variables are anticipated a fairly accurate answer is often attainable by investigating the variations of the yields with the relevant variables. Such predictions can be made when it is possible to determine the partial differential coefficients:

$$\frac{dY}{dX_s}$$

of the yields with the different variables. In some cases the complete form of the partial function $Y = f(X_s)$ may be determinable, but generally this is not the case, and only the first derivative can be found.

If these differential coefficients can be determined, then the operational effect of possible changes in weapons, tactics and training can be estimated quantitatively, giving a predicted yield:

$$Y' = Y + \frac{dY}{dX_1} dX_1 + \frac{dY}{dX_2} dX_2 + \text{ etc.}$$

As is pointed out above, it is often not worth while to attempt to predict at all accurately the effect of large changes of variables, since it is usually only for small changes that the different differential coefficients can be considered as constant or as independent. In certain cases (see section 7. 1), however, a causal relation, and in other cases a tactical relation (section 7. 2) between some of the derivatives is known, and can be taken into account.

It must be remembered that some of the variables (e.g. many of those listed for a particular problem in Appendix A. 1) are not easily susceptible to numerical estimation, and so no numerical values for the differential coefficients are obtainable. But this does not invalidate the use of those derivatives which can be given a numerical value. This fact is in marked contrast to the case of the analytic (*a priori*) approach to the problem where lack of knowledge of the effect of any one non-quantitative variable (e.g. morale) can make any significant solution impossible.

The variational method under discussion must be considered as the formal treatment of the common-sense approach. It is applicable whenever operations have been in progress and tactics have been sufficiently stabilised, as they often are for months at a time, for definite experimental data on the results of past operations to be obtained. It should be remembered that the technical instruments of warfare do not usually change rapidly owing to the long duration of development and production. And even tactics cannot usually change very fast owing to the necessary duration of training. Thus the condition of relative stabilisation of operational technique is quite often fulfilled.

In the method of procedure under discussion, any new tactical situation (B) is to be treated as a *variation* of some old one (A) about which, at any rate, some facts are known.

Even though the two situations may not be very similar, and so the differentials dX_1 dX_2 etc., by which one derives the yield of B from that of A, may not be in fact small, the results may sometimes be fairly reliable, provided common sense and judgment are used (e.g. Appendix C. 1). This is particularly the case where analytical methods can be used to determine, not only the differential coefficients, but the actual form of the relevant partial functions $Y = f(X_s)$ etc.

It must not be thought that any explicit reference to the differential or variational terminology is demanded in the working out of most problems, which usually follow straightforward and common-sense lines. But the cultivation of the method of thinking differentially about operational problems and of prediction by the variational method does seem of definite value.

Thus, the first attack on any operational problem is often to estimate as many of the derivatives as possible: first the *tactical* derivatives to judge what changes of *tactics* would lead to improved yields; then the material derivatives to estimate the effect of improved *weapons*. Many mistakes have been made by inverting this order, e.g. a new weapon may be demanded which promises an improved yield over existing weapons with existing tactics, but which may prove to give a lower yield compared with existing weapons with improved tactics. Much of this type of analysis reduces to the process of fighting a past campaign in imagination with improved weapons and tactics.

Expressed in geometrical language, the first task of operational research faced with a new operation, is to investigate the shape of the multi-dimensional surface

$$Y = F (X_1 \ldots X_n)$$

surrounding the point corresponding to a past operation, and to use this knowledge to predict the properties at a neighbouring point corresponding to a future operation.

5. METHODS OF FINDING THE DERIVATIVES

5. 1. *Statistical Method.* In some cases the operational data are extensive enough and cover sufficient diversity of con-

ditions to allow the coefficients to be deduced directly. This process is one of extrapolation from known data, and is clearly reliable in principle (Appendix A. 2). In practice, however, the observed yields are often so small numerically as to make random fluctuations important, and so to prevent significant values of the coefficients being deduced. Even when the *statistical* significance of some observed differential coefficient dY/dX has been established, it is very important to recognise that dY and dX are not necessarily *causally* connected. Rather they may, in some cases, be causally deducible from the variation of some third variable, which may not have entered explicitly into the analysis.

A well-known example is the " Top Hat Fallacy." Statistical investigation of the population of many cities would show that the wearers of top hats are significantly taller than the average. The missing causally effective variable here is clearly the higher average income and so better nutrition of the top-hat-wearing group.

5. 2. *Theoretical Method.* When, as is often the case, the total amount of data available is too small to make a reliable calculation of (dY/dX) possible, it is necesary to calculate these derivatives theoretically, by analysing in detail that part of the operation in which the variable under consideration plays the chief part (e.g. Appendix A.3).

5. 3. *Mixed Methods.* A desired derivative $\dfrac{dY}{dX_1}$ may often be obtained from another operational derivative $\left(\dfrac{dY}{dX_2}\right)_{obs}$ by using (a) a theoretical or (b) an experimental relationship between the assumed causally related increments δX_1, and δX_2.

Formally one can express the above method by the relation

$$\frac{dY}{dX_1} = \left(\frac{dY}{dX_2}\right)_{obs} \times \frac{\delta X_2}{\delta X_1} \qquad (3)$$

where $\delta X_2/\delta X_1$ is determined either theoretically or by special experiment. (Appendix A. 5 and 6.)

6. The Yield as a Product of Several Probabilities

Often the yield of an operation can be usefully expressed as the product of several probabilities $P_1 P_2$ . . . etc., so that, say

$$Y = P_1 P_2 P_3 P_4$$

where the separate probabilities refer to more or less distinct phases of the operation. For instance in the simple case of air attack on a ship, the four main probabilities are (1) the chance of a sighting, (2) the chance the aircraft gets in an attack, (3) the chance of a hit on the ship, and (4) the chance that the hit causes the ship to sink.

In such cases, a comparison can be made of two past operations, or a prediction of the yield Y_B of a future operation from that Y_A of a past operation by the expression

$$Y_B = \alpha_1 \, \alpha_2 \, \alpha_3 \, \alpha_4. \; Y_A$$

Where $\alpha_1 \, \alpha_2$ etc., are the multiplying factors for the various separate probabilities.

Many important problems can be treated in this way (e.g. Appendix C).

7. Various Comments

7. 1. *Causally Related Differentials.* If the variation of some yield with some one variable is being investigated, one must remember to look for and take into account as far as possible all the resulting changes in other variables. To take a trivial example, if the geographical location of an operation is changed, the change in the average weather conditions, time of daylight, average visibilty, etc., must be taken into account.

7. 2. *Tactically Related Differentials.* If a large change in an operation is contemplated it is to be expected that the enemy will react by changing his tactics or weapons. This will not in general occur at once, so that initially the enemy tactics may sometimes be considered as constant, but are likely to change in a manner to minimise the effectiveness of the new operation in a time measured in days to months.

7. 3. *Alternative Derivations.* When a new operation differs considerably from any past one, it may be the case that there are two or more past ones about equally different from the new ones. In this case the new operation can be treated in turn as a variation of each, and the results compared.

7. 4. *The Place of* a priori *Solutions.* These are often possible for especially simple problems, or partial problems, and of course should always be obtained where possible. They arise particularly often in the analysis of weapon performance, less often in tactical problems, and very seldom in strategical questions. This follows from the increasing order of complexity of these three fields.

7. 5. *On the Use of Rough Data.* No pregnant problem should be left unattempted for lack of *exact* numerical data, for often it is found on doing the analysis that *some* significant conclusions recommending concrete action can be drawn even with very rough data. In other cases, this is, of course, not so. But till the problem is worked out, one cannot tell.

It often happens that when the problem has been worked through in a very rough form, it is found that data which were thought to be important are actually unimportant, and vice versa; in fact, the rough value of the various derivatives must be assessed before the relevance of the accuracy of any data can be judged. (Appendix B. 6.) It must always be remembered that the object of the analysis is practical—that is, that it should lead to action. Attempts at undue and unnecessary precision are to be avoided.

7. 6. *On the Use of Inequalities.* Sometimes upper or lower limits of the value of certain yields or variables are known more accurately than the actual values. In this case it is often convenient to work throughout with inequalities rather than with equations.

Whether useful conclusions are obtained by this method depends on the result of the calculations, and the nature of the practical action that can be taken. Very often practical action can be legitimately taken after proof that some quan-

13

tity is larger than another, even though how much larger is not known.

To compare a proposed new tactic B with an existing tactic A, of which the actual Yield Y_A is known, assume upper limits (i.e. most favourable to B) for the relevant variables. Then if the calculated upper limit Y'_B of the yield of the new tactic is less than Y_A, tactic B is *certainly* inferior and so the relevant decision can be taken. On the other hand if $Y'_B > Y_A$, no useful conclusion is obtained without further calculation. Now assume lower limits (i.e. most unfavourable to B). If now $Y''_B > Y_A$, tactic B is certainly superior, etc.

8. SOME PROPERTIES OF OPERATIONS

8. 1. *An Equilibrium Theorem.* It is clear that an intelligently controlled operation of war, if repeated often enough with reasonable tactical latitude allowed to the participants, will tend to a state where the yield of the operation is a maximum, or the negative yields (losses) a minimum. Exceptions will, of course, occur for various reasons. For instance, if the tactics of the operation are restricted by too rigid orders, or if the yield of the operation is not known to the participants.

This result clearly follows from the fact that in the course of repeated operations by many different participants, most of the possible variations of tactics will be effectively explored, so that any large derivatives will eventually be discovered, and given intelligent control, improved tactics will become generally adopted. The result will be a gradual approach to a tactical state with certain maximum properties, that is, one in which what may be called the *free* tactical derivatives are nearly zero.

This theorem may be of use in attempting to detect in some complicated operation those tactical derivatives which have large values and so repay close study. These large tactical derivatives are most likely to be found under circumstances where their large value would not easily have been detected by the participants because, for instance, control has been too rigid, or because the yields have not been observable, or because the yields, though observed, have not been subject to the necessary analysis. (Appendix B. 5.) Such derivatives can be called *locked* derivatives to distinguish from *free* derivatives.

When some condition of maximum *net* yield has been attained, it must be due to some balance having been attained between counterbalancing factors, such as increasing absolute yields and increasing absolute losses. The interpretation of certain operational situations may be considerably facilitated by such considerations. Provided a real equilibrium condition can be established, one can make useful deductions in a way that is analogous to the use of the "virtual work" theorem in mechanics.

8. 2. *Operational Constants and Operational Functions.* Closely related to the above considerations is the observation that often the numerical characteristics of some type of repeated operation retain a surprising constancy over a long period of time.

An example of such an approximate operational constant is the fraction of U-boats sighted by aircraft in daylight which are attacked while still visible. More general and significant, however, than this fraction, is the distribution of times of submergence of U-boats at the moment of attack. This operational function is also found to remain surprisingly the same over wide periods of time and place. (Appendix A. 4.)

Very often such functions are of a type that are completely incalculable from first principles, depending as they do on numerous and complicated factors such as the average fatigue of look-outs, etc.

The determination of such nearly invariant functions and constants may be a step of great importance in the analysis of certain types of operations.

The following examples are given to illustrate some of the special points discussed in the text. The figures and results quoted are not to be taken as necessarily accurate or authoritative.

APPENDIX A (DOCUMENT II)

EXAMPLES FROM THE AIR CAMPAIGN AGAINST U-BOATS

A. 1. Consider the case of anti-U-boat operations by aircraft. The yield of the operations may be taken as the number of U-boats damaged by aircraft in a given time; it will depend at least on the following variables:

U-boats :
Number operating
Tactics
Defensive strength
Offensive armament
Geographical distribution
State of training and morale of crews
Efficiency of look-outs

Aircraft :
Number and duration of sorties
Search tactics
Height of patrol
Attack tactics
Bomb load
Accuracy of bombing
Geographical and temporal distribution
Performance
Camouflage of aircraft
Performance of radar
State of training and fatigue of crews

Weather Conditions :
State of the sea
Cloud, height and amount
Visibility.

To attempt an *a priori* solution of this problem is clearly absurd. But if past operations are studied to give actual values of the yield, reasonably accurate predictions of future operations may be possible by the variational method. Many calculations of this type are to be found in Coastal Command Operational Research Reports.

A. 2. Suppose one wishes to estimate the probable gain in numbers of sightings by the introduction of a new type of radar. Suppose that there are already in use two different types characterised by different ranges R_1 and R_2 of detection. Then given sufficient numbers of sightings by the two equipments, the ratio (dY/dR) can be obtained and so the effectiveness of the new equipment predicted.

A. 3. When insufficient experimental data to give a statistically significant answer are available, one must use a theoretical argument. For instance, for the above problem, one would assume the number of sightings to be proportional to the radar range when this is larger than the visual range, and independent of the radar range when this is less than the visual range. Thus, using the relevant statistics of the actual frequency of occurrence of different visibilities, one can calculate the required predicted gain.

A. 4. *Conditions of U-boats at Moment of Attack*

An analysis of a large number of day attacks in 1941 in the North Atlantic give the following statistics for the number of U-boats visible and having submerged for different times at the moment of attack.

TABLE I

Condition of U-boats	P = *Percentage of all attacks.*
U-boats visible	34%
Submerged 15 secs.	27%
„ 15-30 secs.	15%
„ 30-60 secs.	12%
„ 60 secs.	11%

This observed operational function $P = f(t)$ where t is time of submergence at the moment of attack, was found to remain nearly unchanged throughout 1942 and was approximately the same on the eastern seaboard of the U.S.A. as in the Atlantic.

The form of this function depends on extremely complicated factors such as the distribution of the state of fatigue of the U-boat and aircrew look-outs etc. It is clear that if U-boat look-outs were always as efficient as they can be and sometimes are, then no U-boats would ever be caught on the surface except in low visibility. Thus the actual effectiveness of much of the air campaign against U-boats depends essentially on the failure of the U-boat look-outs to be uniformly efficient.

This provides a good illustration on the one hand of the essential unpredictability from first principles of many of the most important aspects of war operations, and, on the other, of the wide field for exact calculation, opened up once the essential operational functions have been experimentally determined. For by using the figures of the above table a number of precise deductions can be made.

A. 5. *Effect of Speed of Aircraft on the Fraction of Sightings that Lead to Attack on a Visible U-boat*

Assuming as a first approximation that the mutual sightings of aircraft by U-boat, and vice versa, depend only on their mutual distance, then the increased number of attacks on visible U-boats due to the reduced time from sighting to attack due to increased aircraft speed can be deduced directly from Table I.

As a second approximation, the variation of average *distance* of reciprocal sightings with speed of aircraft, due to the finite speed of visual scanning, can be taken into account by making use of suitable laboratory or field observations.

A. 6. *Effect of Aircraft Colour on Fraction of Sightings that Lead to Attacks on Visible U-boats*

The first step is to make an *experimental* determination of the effect of change of colour on the distance at which an aircraft is likely to be picked up. Then from the figures of Table I and a knowledge of the average aircraft speed to which they referred, the required effect of camouflage can be calculated.

The detailed calculation, as made by the late E. J. Williams, is as follows:

"Let us suppose that painting a black Whitley white reduces the distance at which it will be seen by a U-boat by 20 per cent. (which is roughly the estimated effect of the change). We shall assume that it takes a U-boat 45 seconds to dive. Then a U-boat which is submerged t seconds when attacked by a black Whitley will have seen the aircraft when it was at a distance of about $(t + 45) v$ away, v being the speed of the aircraft (assuming a roughly straight approach). If now the Whitley had been white, it would have been seen at a distance of 20 per cent. less, i.e. $0 \cdot 8 (t + 45) v$. Therefore the time the U-boat would have available for diving would be $0 \cdot 8 (t + 45)$. Therefore, if this expression were equal to 45 seconds, the U-boat would be caught just at the end of its dive. Actually $0 \cdot 8 (t + 45)$ is equal to 45 when $t = 12$ seconds. The answer, therefore, is that a white Whitley will catch as many U-boats on the surface as a black Whitley, plus those which, with the black Whitley, will have been submerged 12 seconds. Reference to Table I shows that this would correspond to an increase of the order of 30 per cent. in the number of U-boats caught while still partly visible. The improved camouflage would also increase the total number of sightings."

A. 7. *Quantitative Estimate of the Value of a Good Visual Look-out from A/S Aircraft*

For certain aircraft on A/S operations, it was found unexpectedly that the number of U-boats seen on the port side was just double the number seen to starboard. This is undoubedly due to the fact that the pilot normally scans his own side (the port side), and that he has little else to do, since the aircraft is flown by automatic pilot. On the other hand, the second pilot responsible for the starboard side has various duties and distractions.

It can thus be deduced that if the look-out to starboard had been as good as that to port the number of U-boats sighted would have been increased by 33 per cent. By this simple analysis, based on an unexpected statistical result, a quantitative estimate can be given of the probable gain by improved look-out organisation.

This example shows the value of exploratory investigations even in seemingly unprofitable fields. Any such discovery, say, of an unexpected asymmetry as above, may serve to give a value of some desired differential coefficient.

A. 8. *Asymmetry of Sinkings in Convoy*

Another example of the value of exploratory investigation is the discovery that, over a certain period, half again as many ships were sunk on the starboard side of the North Atlantic convoys in 1942 as on the port side. This quite unexpected, and previously undetected asymmetry, could be used to give immediate operational advantage by the adoption of suitable escort tactics. (Since no explanation was ever found of this effect, it was finally concluded that it might be due to a statistical fluctuation and so no action was recommended.)

APPENDIX B (DOCUMENT II)

EXAMPLES FROM THE CONVOY BATTLE

B. 1. *Variation of Loss of Ships with Various Parameters*

The first step in the analysis is to break down the statistics of loss in such a way as to give their variation with the main variables of immediate interest. These variables are:

> Number of escorts
> Size of convoy
> Speed of convoy
> Amount of air cover.

For instance, in the North Atlantic convoys in 1941 and 1942, such a breakdown gave the following results:

Number of Escorts

An increase of number of escort vessels from 6 to 9 led to a reduction of losses by about 25 per cent.

Size of Convoy

An increase of size from an average of 32 to 54, was associated with a decrease of fractional losses (i.e. ships sunk ÷ ships sailed) from 2·5 per cent. to 1·1 per cent., i.e. a reduction of losses by 56 per cent.

Speed of Convoy

An increase of speed from 7 to 9 knots was associated with a decrease of fractional losses from 2·1 per cent. to 1·2 per cent., i.e. a reduction of losses by 43 per cent. The analysis also showed that this effect of speed was dependent on the existence of the air cover.

Air Cover

Air cover of 8 hours per day in the last half of 1942 was associated with a reduction of losses by 64 per cent.

B. 2. Derivative Form of these Results

Since in each of these derivations it was verified that the average value of the other variables was about constant, the four results represent in effect four partial derivatives.

Making the reasonable assumption that these derivatives are causally significant, one can use them to calculate the relative value in saving shipping in 1941-1942 of the four factors, numbers of escorts, size of convoy, speed, and air cover.

B. 3. Comparison of Derivatives

Thus it follows immediately that the number of escorts would have to be increased from 6 to 14 to make a convoy without the above amount of air cover as safe as one with air cover. Such an extrapolation, from 6 to 14 escorts, must be considered a rather large extrapolation, and so be subject to a large probable error. The same consideration applies to the following comparisons.

Similarly the number of escorts would have to be increased from 6 to 10 to make the average slow convoy as safe as the average fast convoy.

Again the number of escorts would have to be increased from 6 to 11 to reduce the percentage loss of ships in small convoys of average size 32 to the losses in larger convoys of average size 54.

The above calculations enable the rough profitability of various possible changes to be compared, and so a basis can be laid for costing such operations of war. It will be noticed that it is the *marginal* profitability, i.e. the gain resulting from small increases in some factor, that is given directly by such analysis.

B. 5. *Comments on the Above Results*

Though the value of escorts, speed and air cover has always been appreciated, till this analysis was made there appears to have been little *quantitative* knowledge of their value. The very high value of speed and air cover, under at any rate the special condition of the North Atlantic convoys, was somewhat of a surprise.

It is interesting to note that, previous to this analysis, even the qualitative advantage of large convoys (i.e. a few large convoys in comparison with more small convoys) had not been generally recognised. In fact the general view had been that large convoys were more dangerous than small.

B. 6. *Marginal Value of Very Long Range Aircraft for Convoy Protection*

For the case quoted in B. 1, it can be deduced that every three sorties of a very long range aircraft employed on these duties saved one merchant vessel. Allowing 40 sorties per aircraft expended, this gives 13 merchant vessels saved for each aircraft expended on this type of operation. Even if this estimate were, say, over ten times too high, so that each aircraft expended saved only one ship, the operation of giving an escort to convoys in mid-Atlantic would be extremely profitable. This illustrates the moral of the section on the use of rough data.

This example also illustrates the danger of undue extrapolation. For it would be clearly rash to assume that the relation between aircraft losses on the convoys and ships saved is a linear function, i.e. that the differential coefficient d (ships saved) $/d$ (aircraft hours) is constant. To estimate what would be the saving of ships by a doubled air effort, i.e. 16 hours per day, would clearly need a theoretical investigation of the mechanism of the saving so as to establish the *form* of the function relating the protection afforded to the amount of the air cover.

B. 7. A *Quantitative Estimate of the Importance of Training, Leadership and Efficiency of Escort Groups in the Convoy Battle*

An order of merit for the efficiency of Convoy Escort Groups was obtained by evaluating for each group the total number of ships lost in convoys escorted by the group together with the number of days in which U-boats were in contact with the convoys. By division the number of ships lost per U-boat day was obtained for each group, and so the groups were arranged in an order of merit of efficiency. The groups in the upper and lower half of the list were designated the first and second class groups respectively, and the average losses calculated for the two classes, with the following results:

	Ships lost	U-boat days	Ships lost per U-boat day
1st class	20	181	0·11
2nd class	78	175	0·45
Total	98	356	0·27

If the second-class groups had been on the average as efficient as the first-class groups, the total number of ships which would have been lost is $356 \times 0.11 = 38$ instead of the actual 98, that is a saving of 60 ships, i.e. a saving of 61 per cent. of the actual losses.

This estimate is conservative, since the more efficient groups undoubtedly succeed in reducing by tactical evasion the number of days U-boats are in contact with a convoy.

This example shows how it is possible to deal quantitatively with differentials with regard to such "non-quantitative" variables as training, etc. Some of the observed variations between the different groups may, of course, have been statistical in origin, and so further data and analysis would be needed to establish the real difference in efficiency.

APPENDIX C (DOCUMENT II)

EXAMPLES FROM BOMBING OFFENSIVE

In early 1942, it was important to attempt to estimate the effects of the British bombing campaign on German war production. To do this it was necessary to use the data about the German attacks on Britain in 1940-41 as a basis. These showed that, roughly speaking, the loss of industrial production, material damage to buildings and civilian casualties, were all, on the average, about proportional to the weight of explosives dropped. As a first step, therefore, to calculating the effect on production, it was useful to calculate the probable civilian casualties in Germany due to our bombing effects. This calculation is a useful exercise, as it gives a simple numerical answer which should be compared, after the war, with the actual figures.

C. 1. To estimate from first principles, say, the number of civilian casualties likely to be produced by a given bombing effort, it would be necessary to make numerical assumptions of at least the following factors.

Lethal efficacy of different types of bombs and fusing.

Distribution of bombs about the target.

Types of housing attacked and vulnerability to different types of bombs.

Habits of population, i.e. how many in streets, houses and shelters.

Such an investigation, even if possible, would be laborious and the result would be uncertain.

A quicker and, in general, more reliable method is to use the known results of one bombing offensive where the casualties are known to predict the effect of another offensive where the casualties are not known. In the calculation allowance is made for the differences between the two cases of as many factors as possible.

C. 2. As an example, an estimate can be made of the effects of the British bombing offensive against Germany in 1941, using the known results of the German bombing offensive against Great Britain in 1940.

In the ten months from August 1940 to June 1941, the total weight of bombs dropped on the United Kingdom by the enemy was about 50,000 tons, that is, at the average rate of 5,000 tons per month. The number of persons killed was 40,000, or an average of 4,000 per month, giving 0·8 killed per ton of bombs.

Static detonation trials showed that the British G.P. bombs then in use were about half as effective as the German light-cased bombs of the same weight. Hence, these bombs should produce only 0·4 killed per ton, when dropped under the same conditions. Our bombers had further to go to their targets, the enemy towns are less easy to find, and are smaller, and no radio aids were then available. One must therefore assume that the fraction of bombs falling in built-up areas in Germany was not more than half of the fraction of German bombs falling on built-up areas of Great Britain. Hence, we should expect about 0·2 killed per ton of bombs dropped. During 1941 an average of about 2,000 tons of bombs were dropped on Germany per month. The expected number of killed is therefore $2,000 \times 0·2 = 400$ per month.

The calculation above consists essentially in estimating $d(\text{casualties})/d(\text{type of bomb})$ and $d(\text{navigational error})/d(\text{type of operation})$.

When the actual figures become available through intelligence sources or at the end of the war, it will be interesting to see how far this estimate is in error; and, if it is seriously in error, to find which other differential coefficients should have been taken into account.

The calculation above could be refined to take any other derivatives into account, e.g. $d(\text{navigational errors})/d(\text{meteorological information})$. In a similar way the difference in building technique and shelter policy could be taken into account, given sufficient information.

The above problem illustrates how any answer obtained by the variational method can be considered as an approximation to be improved successively as more information about other derivatives becomes available. It also illustrates the method of the derivation of the yield of one operation from that of another, by estimation of a number of multiplying factors appropriate to the various variables under consideration.

Note (1948)

From the United States Strategic Bombing Survey we find that the average monthly numbers of German civilians killed by bombers were roughly 200 in 1941 and 400 in 1942.

APPENDIX D (DOCUMENT II)

AIRCRAFT IN WARFARE (1916)

BY F. W. LANCHESTER

A simplified treatment of Lanchester's Theorem is given below. Suppose A units of one force of hitting power α are engaged with B units of an enemy of hitting power β. Suppose further that the engagement is of such a kind that the fire power of force A is directed equally against all units of B and vice versa; then the rate of loss of the two forces is given by

$$\frac{dA}{dt} = -k\,\beta\,B \text{ and } \frac{dA}{dt} = -k\,\alpha\,A$$

where k is a constant.

The strength of the two forces is defined as equal when their fractional losses are equal, i.e. when

$$\frac{1}{A}\frac{dA}{dt} = \frac{1}{B}\frac{dB}{dt}$$

Using the above relation we get

$$\alpha\,A^2 = \beta\,B^2$$

Thus the *strength* of a force, on these assumptions, is proportional to the fire power of a unit multiplied by the *square* of the number of units.

Lanchester develops this interesting theorem with great ingenuity and shows clearly its limitations. Its possible application to historic battles, in particular to Trafalgar, is discussed in a very interesting manner.

Such *a priori* investigations as this are of very little use for handling a complicated event like, say, a mass U-boat battle against a convoy. They are of some use sometimes in handling selected parts of such battles, for instance, to calculate the chance of a U-boat penetrating undetected an escort screen of a given number of escort vessels under given weather conditions. Such *a priori* calculations are nearly always useful and necessary to study the performance of the actual weapons, for example, to calculate the chance of killing a U-boat with, say, a 14 pattern depth charge attack, under certain assumed conditions of plan and depth errors.

The Scope of Operational Research[1]
1950

The main outlines of the growth of operational research in the armed services during the Second World War have been described in numerous articles and books and are certainly sufficiently well known not to need repetition here. As to the actual practical results attained since the war by application of these methods to the great task of increasing the efficiency of our social system and the well-being of our population, many readers of the timely new venture, *Operational Research Quarterly*, will know more than I, for the readers will include, I hope, all those in Great Britain who are actually engaged in this work as well as those abroad. Leaving aside, therefore, both its history and its present achievements, I wish to touch on some points relating to its methodology and its organisation.

It will be convenient to begin with three questions which could be asked, and certainly often have been asked, about operational research. Is it new? If so, in what way? Is it scientific?

Referring to the last question first, many attempts have been made to define operational research and nearly all include some such phrase as "the application of scientific method." The answer to the last question must therefore be "yes" by definition. It is as well, however, to consider briefly what is meant by scientific method. A broad but eminently reasonable view is that scientific method consists of a systematic method of learning by experience (Jeffreys). In more detail, scientific method may be defined as that combination of observation, experiment and reasoning (both deductive and inductive) which scientists are in the

[1] *Operational Research Quarterly*, 1, No. 1 (Mar. 1950).

habit of using in their scientific investigations (Yates). It may be noted that it is the use of appropriate and precise methods of observation and reasoning which make an investigation scientific. The fact that the initial material is scanty, as may sometimes be the case in operational research, does not of itself render an investigation unscientific, although no amount of scientific method can get more out of data than there is in them. One of the initial approaches to any problem must be to examine the material, consider what conclusions can be drawn from it and decide what further information is required and how it can be obtained.

Now there can be no doubt that scientific method has often in the past been applied to the complex phenomena of human life and organisation. The abundant literature of applied economics and the social services generally, is evidence enough of this.

Most larger firms and many industrial consultants have special staffs which are concerned with many kinds of statistical analysis. Costing analysis, market research and various kinds of efficiency surveys are examples of work commonly undertaken. Similar activities are carried out by research associations, by other co-operative organisations and by independent institutes such as the National Institute of Economic and Social Research, P.E.P., and the research organisations of the political parties. Particularly during the war, government departments were forced to bring into being teams of specialised analysts, not only to advise on policy relating to particular aspects of the national economy, food, fuel, manpower, raw materials, etc., but also to plan in some measure the overall economic policies of the country. Then again, university schools of social science, particularly at the London School of Economics, have studied scientifically many aspects of our society.

If, therefore, operational research is merely the scientific method applied to the complex data of human society, then, however useful it might be, it certainly is not new.

I believe this conclusion to be over-simplified and that operational research, as developed during the war, and subsequently, has an appreciable degree of novelty. In my view, the element of relative novelty lies not so much in the material to which the scientific method is applied as in the level at which the work is done, in the comparative freedom of the investigators to seek out their own problems, and in the direct relation of the work to the possibilities of executive action. Dr Kittell's well-known definition of operational research as "a scientific method for providing executives with a quantitative basis for decisions," expressed this clearly, or, as another writer has put it, operational research is social science done in collaboration with and on behalf of executives.

In this sense Sir John Boyd Orr's brilliant study, *Food, Health and Income,* was not operational research, as it was not done on behalf of any executive. However, like many other social studies, it was intended to lead to political action, and certainly did so, by its effect on the policy of the Ministry of Food during the war.

Let us consider what might actually happen if, for instance, some firm, research organisation or public body set up an operational research group, consisting of perhaps two or three operational researchers. Possibly the firm's executives might have initially some specific problems in mind, on which profitable work could be started at once. It is, however, one of the clearest lessons of our war experience that the really big successes of operational research groups are often achieved by the discovery of problems which had not hitherto been recognised as significant. In fact the most fertile tasks are often found by the groups themselves rather than given to them. That this is so, is only to be expected, since any problem which is clearly recognised by the executives is likely, in an efficient organisation, to be already a matter of study.

How should an operational research group set about looking for pregnant problems? One method they must not adopt is blindly to make statistical analyses of all that is going on, in the hope that some of the statistics may somehow and sometime prove useful. Collection of statistics for the sake of statistics is no more operational research than collecting beetles is biology.

14

Since the groups must generally, and even preferably, be small, it is essential that their work is canalised into those fields where results of interest to the executives are likely. Drawing again on war experience, one of the best methods of achieving this is to put the group in close personal contact with the executives and let them watch them at work—that is, let them watch the decisions being made and give them the right to ask such questions as, " Why did you decide to do A rather than B?" or to intervene with the executives thus, " Next month, you will have to decide between course of action D, E or F. You will probably have no firm data on which to choose and you will, in all probability, have to guess which course is best. We think that possibly we may be able to help you by analysing quantitatively the effects of these possible actions. But we must have access to all the available facts and have authority to go and collect those that are not available."

During the war operational research workers attended the regular staff meetings at many operational headquarters and so learned the type of problem facing the executive officers and the normal methods by which decisions were arrived at. In this way they were enabled to spot problems capable of being tackled scientifically, which had either not been considered as relevant problems, or had been held to be too complex for scientific analysis.

One example of this from the anti-submarine war may be quoted. The proof that large convoys were safer than small ones arose from an investigation into the protective value of convoy escorts. This analysis was undertaken as a result of an operational research worker being present at a meeting of the Anti-U-boat Committee at 10 Downing Street, when the problem arose as to how best to divide our limited ship-building resources between merchant ships and escort vessels.

Though it is, in my view, essential for the greatest efficiency that senior operational research workers should be admitted to the executive levels as observers and potential critics, and, whenever possible, should have close personal relationships with the executives—the situation during the war when they often shared the same mess was ideal—they should never, in general, have executive authority. If they had, they would soon get so involved in detail as to cease to be useful as research workers.

Conversely, though the research workers should not have executive authority, they will certainly achieve more success if they act in relation to the conclusions of their analysis as if they had it. I mean by this that when an operational research worker comes to some conclusion that affects executive action, he should only recommend to the executives that the action should be taken if he himself is convinced that he would take the action, were he the executive authority. It is useless to bother a busy executive with a learned résumé of all possible courses of action leading to the conclusion that it is not possible to decide between them. Silence here is better than academic doubt. Research workers must also guard against the temptation to expect the executive machine to stop while they think. War, manufacture, trade, government business—all must go on, whether the research worker is there or not.

It is not possible to lay down rigid rules about the qualifications required in an operational research worker. As has been said, operational research is scientific, and training in some scientific discipline may be regarded as essential, although it need not necessarily be in the exact sciences. The most important qualification is ability to take a broad view of a problem, so that important factors will not be missed. Some knowledge of statistical methods will be required, at least within an operational research group, even if not in every worker in the group. Specialist knowledge (technical, industrial, economic, or social) appropriate to the field of application is desirable, but is usually acquired on the job. A high degree of general intelligence and enthusiasm for the work are important. Above all, the right personality is vital, so that during an investigation the operational research worker can obtain the confidence of the men on the job, and at the end can put his conclusions across to the executive. I want here to state specifically that I entirely repudiate the notion that operational research scientists are necessarily in any sense more intelligent or clever than the executives. They are usually not, but they are differently trained and are doing a different job.

The last point I want to touch on concerns the form and presentation of operational research reports. Since these are essentially meant to achieve executive action, they must appear convincing to the executive personnel. It is unlikely that this will be achieved unless the writer of such a report is intimately familiar with the methods of thought of executives. To convince an executive that some new course of action is to be preferred to some old one, it is essential to understand why the old one was adopted. Often this can only be found out through close contact between the scientists and the executives.

Three

Recollections of Problems Studied, 1940-45[1]
1953

The Armed Services have for many decades made use of civilian scientists for the production of new weapons and vehicles of war, whereas the tactical and strategical use of these weapons and vehicles has been until recently almost exclusively a matter for the uniformed Service personnel. During the first years of the Second World War circumstances arose in which it was found that civilian scientists could sometimes play an important role in the study of tactics and strategy. The essential feature of these new circumstances was the very rapid introduction of new weapons and devices, pre-eminently radar, into the Services at a time both of great military difficulty and of such rapid expansion that the specialist officers of the Armed Services, who in less strenuous times can and do adequately compete with the problems raised, found themselves often quite unable to do so. I will attempt to describe below how it was that civilian scientists, with initially little or no detailed knowledge of tactics or strategy, came to play a sometimes vital role in these affairs, and how there grew up a virtually new branch of military science—later to be dignified in the United Kingdom by the name " Operational Research," or " Operations Analysis " in the United States. By the end of the war, all three Services had operational research groups of mainly civilian scientists either at headquarters or attached to the major independent Commands. These groups were, in varying degrees, in close touch with all the main activities of the Service operational staffs and were thus in a position to study the facts of operations in progress, to analyse them scientifically, and, when opportunities arose, to advise the

[1] *Brassey's Annual*, 1953.

staffs on how to improve the operational direction of the war. Rather than attempt a systematic history of the origin and growth of all the various operational research groups, which attempt would need access to many reports and files not now accessible to me, I will draw mainly on my own personal experiences, which, of course, only cover a small part of the developments of these interesting years.

In August 1940, during the early phase of the Battle of Britain, I was invited by Sir Frederick Pile to become his scientific adviser at the Headquarters of Anti-Aircraft Command at Stanmore. My immediate assignment was to assist the Service staff to make the best use of the gun-laying radar sets (GL.1 and later GL.2) which were then being delivered to the A.A. batteries around London. These fine sets, only just out of the laboratory stage of development, were initially liable to many technical defects, and civilian scientists both from the firms who manufactured them and from the research establishments (T.R.E. and A.D.R.D.E.) which designed them, were already actively employed on the gun sites, helping the Service personnel to get them to work satisfactorily. As this technical servicing aspect was being well looked after, the small group of young scientists whom I hurriedly collected to work with me and which included physiologists, an astronomer, and a mathematician, as well as physicists, soon found themselves studying, both at H.Q. and on the gun sites, a variety of problems connected with the operational use of radar sets, guns and predictors.

This group was not the first such group of civilian scientists studying operations, but it was certainly one of the first groups to be given both the facilities for the study of a *wide range of operational problems,* the freedom to seek out these problems on their own initiative, and sufficiently close personal contact with the Service operational staffs to enable them to do this.

Already in 1937-38 a civilian scientist, B. G. Dickins, had been posted to Biggin Hill to assist the operational staffs of the fighter group in the use of radar for intercepting enemy bombers. Sir Henry Tizard and Mr A. P. Rowe, then Superintendent of the Bawdsey Research Station, were the initiators in this development. The great value of the scientific study of the tactics of interception by radar was amply proved by the work of Mr Dickins, and the trials led to important changes in the organisation of Fighter Command. Many high Service officers realised that scientists had something to teach the Services as well as providing them with new equipment. At the outbreak of the war Mr Rowe and Wing-Commander R. Hart were mainly responsible for sending a small group of scientists from Bawdsey to R.A.F. Fighter Command at Stanmore. This group played a very important part in working out the tactics of interception which played such a decisive part in the Battle of Britain.

One of the first important problems tackled by the A.A. Command group was how best to make use of the radar data to direct the guns. As the radar data came from the operators in the form of range, bearing, and, later, height, it was far too crude, in the sense of being subject to much too large errors, to be fed directly into the mechanical predictors then in use, which were, of course, designed for the reception of accurate direct visual observations. Very simple plotting methods were already in use in which the position of the enemy aircraft, as determined from the radar set, was plotted on a large sheet of paper, and from the plot estimates were made of the future position of the target. Then using range tables for the gun in use, the required elevation, bearing and fuse setting were passed to the battery verbally together with the moment to fire. This fire control system amounted to a system of predicted barrage rather than continuous prediction. Thus for a time predictors were not used at all in the battle against the night bombers, and it was necessary to return to the old pre-predictor age of manual plotting. This situation illustrates very clearly one of the gaps which operational research groups can help to close: the gap between the new instrument or weapon as developed in the research and development establishments, and its use in the actual conditions of war. Immense scientific and technical brilliance had gone into the rapid design and manufacture of the GL sets; likewise at a more leisurely pace into the design and construction of the guns and predictors. Understandably, but unfortunately, partly through shortage of scientific and technical personnel but also partly through a certain lack of imaginative insight into operational realities, hardly any detailed attention had been paid to how actually to use the GL data to direct the guns until the Battle of Britain was in progress. Thus the first months of the A.A. battle against the night bomber were fought with highly developed radar sets and guns, but with the crudest and most improvised links between them, belonging technically to the level of the First rather than the Second World War.

One of the first important tasks of the A.A. Operational Research Group was to help to work out in a week or two the best method of plotting the GL data and of predicting the future enemy position for the use of the guns, on the basis only of pencil and paper, range and fuse tables. The second task was to assist in the design of simple forms of plotting machines which could be manufactured in a few weeks. The third stage was to find means of bringing the existing predictors into use in conjunction with the radar sets. This was found to be possible if, by intensive training of the predictor crews, the inaccurate radar data could be *smoothed* manually. A special school was set up by A.A. Command to work out the best methods of doing this and to give the necessary training. The fourth stage was to attempt to modify the predictors to make them handle the rough GL data more effectively. This proved possible with the Sperry predictor, leading to what came to be known as the *amputated* Sperry, which played a useful though limited role as an alternative to the use of plotting methods.

The problem of marrying successfully the radar data with a predictor was not solved satisfactorily until much later in the war. Only when in 1944 the much more accurate American 10 cm. set came into operation and was linked with the new American electronic predictor, was a really adequate radar A.A. system attained. This combination, together with the proximity fuse, came just in time to compete brilliantly with the V1 menace in the summer of 1944.

Soon after the formation of the A.A. Operational Research Group in August 1940, a problem of a quite different char-

acter came up in the following way. In the night defence
of London only those A.A. batteries which had radar sets
could play any useful part, but there were not enough GL
sets to supply more than one half of the four-gun batteries in
the London area, so reducing the effective defensive power
of the A.A. to one half of its nominal strength. The Operational Research Group attempted to weigh up the advantages
and disadvantages of the existing deployment of the available
120 or so guns in 30 four-gun batteries compared with their
possible deployment in 15 eight-gun batteries. The then
existing location of 30 four-gun batteries had been based on
the requirement to cover the whole of the London area by
the field of fire of some battery. The batteries were therefore
so located that circles on the map drawn round each battery
with a radius equal to the maximum effective range of the
guns effectively covered the whole area. If, however, in the
interests of giving each battery a radar set, the number of
batteries were reduced to one half, clearly a considerable
area, in fact about one half of London, would no longer be
covered by the fire of any gun. The problem was to assess
the penalty resulting from halving the area of London
covered. Investigation showed that the penalty was so small
as to be quite unimportant compared with the calculated
gain by the adoption of fewer eight-gun sites, so giving every
gun access to radar information. For, when looked into in
more detail, the " complete cover " provided by the 30 four-
gun sites turned out to be illusory. The conception of
complete cover must have originated in the days when slow
aircraft were engaged visually in daylight, and just did not
apply to the conditions of 1940 when fast aircraft were being
engaged at night by means of radar. In the latter condition
a battery could only usefully engage an enemy bomber
coming more or less towards the battery, and while the
bomber was in a rather narrow crescent-shaped zone limited
on the one hand by the maximum effective range of the guns
and on the other by a minimum distance from the guns set
by the maximum rate of change of bearing and elevation
which could be handled by the radar sets and the plotting
methods used. So, even with the 30 four-gun batteries, there

were large areas of London over which enemy aircraft could not be fired at at night. The concentration of the available guns into fewer eight-gun batteries certainly increased this blind area, but also greatly increased the chances of a successful engagement in the area still covered, since all the guns now would be fed with radar information. If the enemy bombers had done precision bombing runs, a case could be made for keeping them continually under fire, however ineffectively, in order to disturb their aim. However, this was not the case; the night bombing at that time was area bombing of London; precise aiming had no relevance. What remained legitimate in the demand for complete cover of the area of London was the demand that the periphery of London should be completely covered so that no enemy aircraft could get through without coming within the range of some battery, and further that the blind areas inside the periphery should not be so large as to become known to the enemy pilots. Since these two conditions could be satisfied with the 15 eight-gun sites, the theoretical case for a re-deployment was complete. A number of eight-gun batteries were formed in accordance with these ideas, but practical considerations and a speeding up of the arrival of new GL sets made a full re-deployment unnecessary.

This example of operational analysis, though not perhaps leading to spectacular operational gains, is given in some detail as an example of the value often attending the critical analysis by operational research groups of the established doctrines and objectives of a Service command, with a view to seeing if they are related to the existing circumstances. Sometimes it is found that they were once quite correct, but that they have become out of date by changing external circumstances. Later it became established practice to subject as many as possible of the rules and dogmas of a fighting Service or Command to critical but sympathetic analysis. In nine cases out of ten, the rules or dogmas were found to be soundly based; in the tenth, sometimes, changed circumstances had made the rules out of date. Further cases of this will be described in connection with operational research at Coastal Command and at the Admiralty.

My last example from the work at A.A. Command during my period of work there, August 1940 to March 1941, is of still another character, being concerned with the statistical checking of intelligence reports. Incidentally, it contains an element of discovery of the unexpected in the sense in which the words are used by natural scientists.

A.A. Command were clearly greatly interested in the effectiveness of their A.A. gunfire, and to measure this calculated the average number of A.A. shells which were fired by each battery to destroy one enemy night bomber. At the start of the blitz, when control methods were poor, the "rounds per bird," as we called this number, was about 20,000. As methods and instruments improved this gradually fell to some 4,000 the following summer.

On looking into the rounds per bird achieved by the different regional defences, it was noticed with surprise that the coastal batteries appeared to be shooting twice as well as those inland; their rounds per bird were only about one half. All kinds of far-fetched hypotheses were considered as possible explanations of this strange result. Were the coastal guns better sited, or did the radar work better over the sea? Perhaps the enemy aircraft flew lower and straighter than over the land. Then suddenly the true explanation flashed into mind. Over the land a battery, say, in the Birmingham area, which claimed an enemy aircraft destroyed, would have this claim checked by the search for and identification of the crashed machine. If no machine were found, the claim was disallowed. But, in general, no such check could be made of the claims of the coastal batteries, since an aircraft coming down at sea would not be traceable. The explanation of the apparent better shooting of the coastal batteries turned out to be due, therefore, to an overestimate by the coastal batteries (as by almost all other batteries) of their claims of enemy aircraft destroyed, by a factor of about two. This explanation should have been thought of at once, as there is plenty of experience to show that unchecked combat claims, made in absolute good faith, are generally much too high.

The same over-optimistic and multiple reporting might be expected in any complex battle such as, for instance, the daylight phase of the air battle over southern England in August and September 1940. A careful check was therefore made of the number of enemy aircraft crashing on land during this time. If my memory serves me right, the number amounted to less than 20 per cent. of the Air Force claims of aircraft destroyed. Even making a generous allowance for the many aircraft which must have crashed in the English Channel, it was very difficult to believe that the true number of enemy aircraft destroyed was more than about one half of those claimed. It was therefore no surprise when the capture of the archives of the German Air Force in 1945 revealed that their combat losses in the Battle of Britain were less than half the British claims. This easily explicable exaggeration of claims in no way detracts from the brilliant and gallant fight of Fighter Command against heavy odds throughout the late summer of 1940. The fight was decisively won, and with it Hitler's Germany met her first defeat. From this sprang the actions which led to Hitler's final overthrow. So in this case the misreporting of enemy losses had no serious adverse consequences, and some favourable ones to the sorely tried British national morale; but under somewhat other circumstances it might have had serious consequences. This tale has a moral—even if a very obvious one. All intelligence reports must be checked, wherever possible, by statistical and other scientific methods. A case where failure to do this, or rather a failure to act on the conclusions reached, did have serious consequences will be described later.

The three examples quoted here of operational research work carried out at A.A. Command during my time there— the study of the best methods of conveying radar information to the guns, the problem of the best deployment of guns and radar sets in the London area, and the checking of claims of enemy aircraft destroyed—are alike in one respect: the work could not easily have been done at the time except by the existence of groups of scientists in close contact with the Service staffs directing the operations. Scientists in the research and development establishments could not, in general, have known enough about the operational facts; the Service personnel at Headquarters were too busy with immediate operational duties to undertake such analytical work, which anyway was better done by scientists trained in the techniques of original investigation.

When, in March 1941, I was posted to Coastal Command, on the initiative of Air Marshal Sir Philip Joubert, to advise on problems arising in the air war against the U-boats, I had a fairly clear idea of how I thought an operational research group at an Air Force Command should be organised and what sort of work it was competent to do and what it should not attempt. Amongst the things to avoid were: not to take on any responsibility for technical trouble-shooting in the new Service equipment—this must be left entirely to the technical branches of the Service in collaboration with the research and development establishments and to the manufacturing firms; not, in general, to take on any daily routine responsibilities in relation to the staff work of the headquarters, but rather to keep the group free for non-routine investigations and researches. On one organisational point I was most insistent. The operational research group must be an integral part of the Commander-in-Chief's staff and all the reports or recommendations must be to the C.-in-C. of the Command and not to the Air Ministry direct. The importance of this lies in the fact that a considerable part of the work of an operational research group at a Command must inevitably involve criticisms of the work of the Command coupled with suggestions for improvement. For any part of the Command's work in which no improvement seems possible is not likely to be subject of a report by the group. When, however, the group find, say, that some tactics in use are faulty and could be improved, their report would necessarily have a critical character. If these reports were sent (as at one time was the suggestion) direct to the Air Ministry, then the staffs at Command would rightly feel aggrieved and the intimate collaboration between operational Service staffs and operational research workers, which is the essential basis of fertile operational research, would become impossible. If, however, the report went to the C.-in-C., and if the recommendations were adopted successfully, the Air Ministry would hear of it first as a successful achievement of the Command itself.

Within a few months I had collected together a group of young scientists at H.Q. Coastal Command. I was both director of the group and, at the same time, personal scientific adviser to the C.-in-C., Air Marshal Sir Philip Joubert, who had by then succeeded Air Marshal Sir Frederick Bowhill. Amongst the many problems investigated by the group during the time, from March 1941 to January 1942, when I was at Coastal Command, a few stand out especially vividly in my memory, some because of the importance of the results achieved and some because of the points of method which they illustrate.

One of the most striking from both points of view was the case of the depth setting of the depth charges dropped by Coastal Command aircraft against U-boats. As soon as I arrived at Coastal Command, I remember studying the inevitably fragmentary reports from air crews of the attacks made on U-boats in the previous few months and wondering why it was that they had proved relatively unsuccessful, as judged by the number of U-boats reported sunk. Enlightenment came from a stimulus from another quarter. In the spring of 1941, the late Professor E. J. Williams was attached to the Instrument Department at the R.A.E. Farnborough and had been asked to consider the possibility of designing a depth charge with a proximity fuse, which would explode, as it fell through the water past the U-boat, at whatever depth the U-boat happened to be. It was reasonably thought that such a weapon would be much more effective than the conventional depth charge which had to be set to some predetermined depth. A few months later Williams joined the Coastal Command group and, with the requirement for the proximity depth charge in mind, started to analyse the reports of air attacks on U-boats with the idea of estimating the actual depth of the submarines at the instant of attack. As soon as a U-boat sighted the attacking aircraft, it dived so as to get as deep as possible before the depth charge reached it. So the earlier the aircraft was sighted the deeper was the U-boat at the time of attack. On the assumption that a U-boat would, on the average, sight the attacking aircraft some two minutes before the instant of the attack, and that in this time it could dive to about 100 feet depth, the Coastal Command and Admiralty orders were that depth charges were to be set to explode at 100 feet depth.

Williams spotted a fallacy in the argument leading to the 100-foot depth setting. It might be true that *on the average* a U-boat might sight the aircraft a long way off and so manage to get to 100 feet depth before the attack. However, just in these cases the U-boat had disappeared out of sight of the aircraft for so long that the air crew could not know where to drop the depth charges, so that the effective accuracy in plan of the attack was inevitably very low. Williams drew attention to the few cases when the U-boat failed to see the aircraft in time and so was on the surface when attacked. In these cases the bombing accuracy in plan was high, as the U-boat was visible at the time of attack. However, Williams pointed out that just in these cases the explosion of the depth charges at 100 feet would fail to damage seriously the U-boat, as the radius of lethal damage of the depth charges was only about 20 feet. Thus the existing method of attack failed to sink deep U-boats owing to the low bombing accuracy and failed to sink surfaced U-boats due to the deep depth setting. Williams calculated that if the depth setting were reduced from 100 feet to 25 feet, one would expect the average number of U-boats sunk for a given number of attacks to be increased by two and a half times. After some time spent in convincing the relevant departments that the argument was correct, and after some minor technical difficulties had been overcome, the shallow depth setting was introduced into Coastal Command in early 1942 with spectacular results. Captured German U-boat crews thought that we had introduced a new and much more powerful explosive. Actually we had only turned a depth-setting adjuster from the 100-foot to the 25-foot mark. There can be few cases where such a great operational gain had been obtained by such a small and simple change of tactics.

In the light of this result, Williams showed that the proximity depth charge pistol, on which he had previously been working, was not needed. For, though perhaps better than the standard depth charges with 100-foot setting, it was little better and much more complicated than the standard depth charge with the 25-foot setting. This story has several morals. It may be considered as an example of the old military precept to concentrate offensive effort on the good targets and ignore the poor targets. Then, too, it teaches that it is generally wise to understand fully the possibilities of better use of existing weapons before asking for new ones. Finally, the importance of keeping operational orders under critical but sympathetic analysis is evident.

My next story begins one night in April 1941 in the operations room of the C.-in-C. Western Approaches in Derby House, Liverpool. On a large wall map were displayed the guessed positions of U-boats in the Atlantic. From the recorded number of hours flown by Coastal Command aircraft over the relevant area, I calculated in a few lines of arithmetic on the back of an envelope the number of U-boats which should have been sighted by the aircraft. This number came out about four times the actual sightings. This discrepancy could be explained either by assuming the U-boats cruised submerged or by assuming that they cruised on the surface and in about four cases out of five saw the aircraft and dived before being seen by the aircraft. Since U-boat prisoners asserted that U-boats seldom submerged except when aircraft were sighted, the second explanation was probably correct. How then could one raise the chance of the aircraft sighting the U-boat first other than by the use of radar? All the obvious courses of action were considered and recommended where necessary—better lookout drill for the air crews, better binoculars, etc. Then the best direction of aircraft course in relation to the sun was considered. If the aircraft flew down sun, the U-boat crew might have more difficulty in seeing it. Discussing these questions one day in Coastal Command, a Wing Commander said casually: "What colour are Coastal aircraft?" Of course, I knew they were mainly black as they were mostly night bombers such as Whitleys. But before the question was asked me, I had missed the significance of the fact. Night bombers are painted black so as to reflect as little light as possible from enemy searchlights. When there is no artificial illumination by searchlights, an aircraft of any colour flying at moderate or low height, both by day and night, is normally seen at a great distance as a dark object against a lighter sky and only seldom as a light object against a darker sky. The only exceptions to this are, in general, when the sun or moon is reflected off some part of the surface of the aircraft as off a mirror. But common experience shows that this happens but rarely and never when the sun or moon are not shining. The lighter the colour of an aircraft, the less dark in general will it appear against the lighter sky, and so the less easy will it be to see. It would seem, therefore, that the best colour for a Coastal Command aircraft, particularly in the North Atlantic where there is much overcast weather, would be white. Model and full-scale tests were made of the average sighting distances of white aircraft compared with black, and it was found that the average distance at which a white aircraft was sighted was about 20 per cent. less than the distance at which a black aircraft was sighted. Using this numerical result, Williams calculated that a white aircraft would catch the submarine on the surface on 30 per cent. more occasions than a black one would, and so should sink 30 per cent. more submarines for the same number of sightings. Within a few months, all Coastal Command anti-submarine aircraft were painted white. No direct statistical check on the accuracy of the calculated gain could be made, since the number of U-boats sunk was rising so rapidly month by month due to a variety of causes, but it is possible to be confident that this admittedly belated recognition of the importance of the colour of anti-submarine aircraft was a contributing factor.

It may seem strange, in retrospect, that such a simple matter as the best colour for a Coastal Command aircraft, a matter which after all is only a special case of the much publicised and investigated subject of camouflage, could have been overlooked. The scientific effort in choosing the right

15

colour for the aircraft was negligible compared with the effort then being put into many other aspects of the anti-submarine war. This example emphasises the importance of applying a scientific method to *all* aspects of a given tactical problem— even to the simplest and most obvious ones.

I have already pointed out, for instance in connexion with the problem of the siting of anti-aircraft guns, the importance of keeping a clear grasp of the numerical magnitude of essential average values of the numerical probabilities of achieving given results. One finds nearly always that any conception of 100 per cent. cover, 100 per cent. defence, or 100 per cent. search efficiency, is completely unattainable and that, in fact, most wars are won (or lost) by the addition of large numbers of small successes (or failures) for each of which the probability at any given operation is small. I remember well a discussion at Coastal Command in the spring of 1941 which illustrated this point.

The long-range German aircraft, the Focke-Wolf 200, were taking a heavy toll of our shipping west of Ireland. To meet this there were available only a few Beaufighters. The problem was how best to use these fighters. A strong case was argued by the operations staff for the following procedure. Suppose the FW200s were known to be operating mainly in an area west of Ireland 200 by 200 miles. Suppose further that a single Beaufighter could " sweep " a lane 20 miles wide, that is, that an enemy aircraft could be expected to be sighted at a distance of 10 miles. It was argued that the best tactics would be to wait until all the available ten Beaufighters were serviceable and then to fly them equally spaced over the area, so that the ten swept lanes, each 20 miles wide, would cover the whole area of supposed operations of the FW200s. In this way it was hoped the area would be " swept clean," that is, any enemy aircraft operating that day would certainly be sighted.

The disadvantage of only flying when all ten fighters were serviceable was clearly that on most days no fighters would be out at all; moreover perhaps the day the fighters flew the enemy would not. The alternative was, of course, every day to fly any fighter when serviceable, even if only one, so as to have a chance, even though a small one, of sighting an enemy aircraft every day. The controversy between the exponents of the two tactics resolved itself into how to compare the theoretical certainty of sighting any enemy aircraft flying on the few days when all ten fighters were flown, with the sum of all the small chances of sighting the enemy on all the days when any aircraft were flown. The view of the Operations Research Section was that the two tactics gave about the same overall chances of sighting the enemy, assuming that the enemy flew every day and that the same amount of flying was done, but that in practice for many reasons there was a very strong case for flying every day with all available aircraft, however few. In the course of long arguments on this controversy, a view was expressed which revealed a not uncommon misconception about a problem in the theory of probability. The fallacious argument was as follows. When ten aircraft were flown, the whole area was swept clean and the chance of sighting the enemy was 100 per cent.; *that meant that it was certain he would be sighted.* When, however, any fewer number of fighters were flown, then the chance of sighting the enemy was less than 100 per cent.; *in that case he might not be sighted at all.* The last statement is, of course, correct; the misconception lay in an exaggerated estimate of the actual probability of his " not being sighted at all." This probability can be calculated mathematically by the application of what is known as " Poisson's Distribution "—which I refrain from quoting out of consideration for my non-mathematical readers—to the actual case of the problem of search; and it turns out to be much smaller than the crude statement above would seem to suggest. I remember having a table of the values of this probability circulated round the staff of A.A. Headquarters during the blitz, as a warning against neglecting the factor of statistical error when analysing combat results, and thereby drawing false deductions and adopting measures which the facts did not actually justify.

At a more everyday level the controversy centred on the obvious truism, already brought out by the case of the A.A. defence of London, that success in most operations of war

in general and almost all operations of air war, is due to the
sum of a number of small victories, for each of which the
chance of success in a given operation is small. These simple,
but not unsubtle, points of probability theory, a practical
understanding of which is of the utmost importance for the
correct control of air operations, were the subject of many
lively discussions between the Operational Research group
and the operational Service staff at Coastal Command.
Finally the Operations Research view prevailed and the
Beaufighters were thereafter flown whenever serviceable.
The arguments for success by summing small probabilities
seemed won against the arguments for gambling on an occa-
sional certainty.

A few days later, I was met with the pleased tribute from
the Controller of Operations: " I say, Blackett, I am so glad
you explained to me all about probability. As soon as the
war is over I am going straight to Monte Carlo and then I
really will win."

In January 1942 I moved from Coastal Command to the
Admiralty and started building up an operational research
group to deal with naval matters. Much of the initiative in
bringing this group into being lay with the Director of Anti-
U-boat Operations, Captain, now Admiral, Sir George
Creasy. The group, which later was named the " Department of Naval Operational Research " (D.N.O.R.), was
placed directly under the Vice-Chief of the Naval Staff, but
worked not so much as an independent department but as
an aid to, and in close collaboration with, the various operational departments in the Admiralty.

The group was most active in problems of the anti-U-boat
war and worked in close contact with the group at Coastal
Command, then under the direction of the late Professor
E. J. Williams, F.R.S., and later of Professor C. H. Waddington, F.R.S. Of particular importance was the continuation
of the scientific study of the tactics of the air war against the
U-boats which had been started the previous year at Coastal
Command. Since Coastal Command was under the operational control of the Admiralty the air war was a joint
responsibility of the two Services. From the summer of 1941

until the virtual defeat of the U-boat campaign in the summer of 1943, a battle of technical and tactical wits was waged over the Atlantic between aircraft and enemy submarines.

In 1941 some Coastal Command aircraft began to be fitted with airborne radar sets by which it was possible to detect a surfaced submarine even though it could not be seen visually because of darkness or bad visibility. These sets were known as ASV (air-surface-vessel) and worked on $1\frac{1}{2}$ metres wavelength. Owing, however, to the relatively low performance of these sets, not very many sightings were made with them by day, and they were not accurate enough to make possible actual attacks by night. Later in the year Coastal Command aircraft began to be fitted with special search-lights (Leigh Lights) with which to illuminate a surfaced submarine located by ASV at night. A few night attacks of this kind so frightened the U-boats that they began to submerge by night and remain surfaced by day, and so exposed themselves to the attacks by all Coastal Command aircraft whether fitted with ASV or not. After some months they found this too dangerous, so they reverted to surfacing to charge their batteries mainly by night, and attempted to counter the night attacks by fitting radio sets which could listen for and so give warning of the approach of an aircraft fitted with $1\frac{1}{2}$ metre radar. This success for the U-boats was short-lived, for in 1942 a new radar set working on 10 centimetre wavelength was introduced into Coastal Command.

The invention in the Physics Department of Birmingham University of the magnetron which made centimetric radar possible was, of course, one of the most decisive technical developments made during the war. Brilliant technical developments at the Telecommunications Research Establishment (T.R.E.) of the Ministry of Aircraft Production produced the 10 cm. ASV set for Coastal Command, the AI set for Fighter Command, and the H_2S set for Bomber Command. At the corresponding Air Defence Research and Development Establishment (A.D.R.D.E.) under the Ministry of Supply the GL.3 set was produced for A.A. Command. All these sets, in their respective fields, played a decisive part in the last years of the war.

As soon as the 10 cm. ASV was introduced into Coastal Command, U-boat sightings by radar rose rapidly and a very satisfactory monthly toll of U-boats were sunk. The German U-boat Command were very slow in tumbling to what had happened, and even later on, when a captured 10 cm. equipment told them the wavelength of our new radar sets, they were very slow to fit adequate listening sets.

The U-boats seemed at first more frightened of the night attacks than the day attacks, for they began again to surface by day and attempted to fight off the air attacks by gunfire. In this they had little success and they exposed themselves to very heavy and continuous air attack. Later they were forced to spend much of both day and night submerged, so enormously reducing their freedom and range of action. During these months the number and efficiency of the naval anti-submarine escort vessels was steadily increasing, and this combined with the rapid increase of the air effort led to almost complete victory in the U-boat war by the summer of 1943.

All these tactical developments were studied and analysed by the Operational Research Groups at Coastal Command and at the Admiralty. Careful statistical studies were made of the number of hours flown by Coastal aircraft, of the number of U-boats believed to be at sea. From these figures and the known range of detection of a U-boat by radar and visual means, the expected number of U-boats contacted could be calculated—assuming, as was the case at first, that the U-boats spent nearly all their time on the surface. These expected numbers of sightings were then checked up against the actual numbers of sightings. So long as the numbers agreed statistically, then it was concluded that the U-boats were still operating on the surface. When the day sightings fell below the expected number, it was deduced that the U-boats were submerged by day. When the night sightings fell off too, then the U-boats were deduced to be submerging also at night. When a U-boat, contacted by radar, dived before the aircraft got close enough to be seen visually by the

U-boat, it was deduced that the U-boat must be fitted with a radar listening device.

In this way a very close statistical check was made of all phases of this decisive air campaign against the U-boats. All the tactical resorts to which the enemy were driven could be followed, and the best tactics could be devised to meet them. The results of operational research, reports of hours flown, U-boat densities, search rates, calculated sightings, statistical uncertainties and the like, became a normal part of the discussions of the fortnightly Anti-U-boat Committee meetings at No. 10 Downing Street under the chairmanship of the Prime Minister.

Here I intend to break the narrative of the scientific analysis of the anti-U-boat war to describe some simultaneous investigations on quite a different subject, but one which later became intimately linked with the air war against U-boats.

In March 1942, I became involved in the study of the theory and practice of the bombing offensive. This arose in the following way. The Prime Minister had asked the Air Staff to write an appreciation of the possibility of assisting our sorely tried Russian allies in their great land battle by extending the British bombing offensive against Germany. The basis of such an appreciation was to be an analysis of what had been achieved by the British bombing offensive in the previous eighteen months. The Air Staff report to the Prime Minister was also sent for information to the Admiralty and I was asked to comment on it. I found that estimates of the probable future efficiency of the bombing offensive were based on intelligence reports on the results of past raids on Germany. These intelligence reports, some of which seemed to be unduly optimistic both as regards destructive effects and effects on morale and production, seemed mainly to be derived from reports emanating from neutral capitals, and there seemed no direct way of checking their reliability. I therefore set about the task of checking these reports statistically, by using as a basis the known results of the German bombing offensive on Great Britain. The relevant calculations were, in themselves, extremely simple, though a considerable background of knowledge of other matters not appearing directly in the calculations was needed to be confident of their accuracy.

In the ten months from August 1940 to June 1941, the total weight of bombs dropped on the United Kingdom by the enemy was about 50,000 tons, that is, at the average rate of 5,000 tons per month. The number of persons killed was 40,000, or an average of 4,000 per month, giving 0.8 killed per ton of bombs. Static detonation trials showed that the British G.P. bombs then in use were about half as effective as the German light-cased bombs of the same weight. Hence, these bombs should produce only 0.4 killed per ton, when dropped under the same conditions. Our bombers had further to go to their targets, the enemy towns were less easy to find and were smaller, and no radio aids were then available. One must therefore assume that the fraction of bombs falling in built-up areas in Germany was not more than half of the fraction of German bombs falling on built-up areas in Great Britain. Hence we should expect 0.2 killed per ton of bombs dropped. During 1941 an average of about 2,000 tons of bombs were dropped on Germany per month. The expected number of killed is therefore $2,000 \times 0.2 = 400$ per month.[2]

Since the normal civilian road casualties in Germany amounted to some 700 killed per month, one would not expect the casualty aspect of our bombing offensive on morale or production in 1941 to have been of much significance.

The accuracy of this estimate of civilian casualties, which was an order of magnitude lower than that deduced by the Air Ministry from intelligence reports, could not finally be checked until after the war. The actual number of German civilians killed in 1941 was 200 per month, just one half of my estimate.

Since by 1942 it was clear that the war would be a long one and that resources in manpower, especially skilled manpower, might well prove decisive, it seemed useful to draw up a balance sheet of manpower losses to the enemy and to ourselves resulting from the 1941 bombing offensive.

The average number of bomber sorties per month, then mainly by Wellingtons, was 1,000, and of these some 40 were lost with their crews of five men, giving a loss of airmen, all highly skilled men, at the rate of 200 per month. Comparing

[2] See above, p. 195.

this with the estimated number of enemy killed, that is, 400 *men, women and children* (now known to be twice too large), it was concluded that in the matter of personnel casualties the 1941 bombing offensive had been nearly a dead loss.

A similar analysis of the probable effects of our bombing offensive on German production, based on the known effects of German bombing on British production, led to the conclusion that the reduction in German production was almost certainly less than 1 per cent.

Probably the only way the British bombing offensive in 1941 had brought appreciable help to the Russian armies was through the diversion to defensive use of enemy military resources in fighters and A.A. guns, and civilian resources in civil defence and repair personnel. The numerical assessment of this indirect effect was difficult. If it had then been recognised realistically that this secondary function of drawing fighters from the eastern zone to defend Germany, rather than the damage done to German industry, was the main way in which the bombing offensive could help Russia, the bombing offensive would have been planned rather differently. For instance, there would have been much more diversity of target and less expensive repeated hammering at a few highly defended targets. The operation would have been planned to divert the maximum possible number of fighters rather than to inflict the maximum damage.

Later in the war, particularly in 1944, the bomber offensive became incomparably more effective, due to the introduction of very large numbers of four-engine aircraft and of radio navigational aids and the development of path-finding tactics. The results of this campaign have been told with a wealth of statistical detail in the United States Bombing Survey Reports. From the analysis in these reports it is deduced that German production was reduced by 9 per cent. in 1943 and 17 per cent. in 1944.

The Admiralty[3] passed on to the Air Ministry a paper by me setting out these arguments and figures in detail. If my memory is right, it was in April 1942 that a Cabinet Office paper was issued on the probable effect of the bombing

[3] See also Part I, Chapter 8.

offensive in the subsequent eighteen months. This paper implicitly accepted the method I had employed of using the data from the German bombing offensive against Britain as a basis for calculating the expected effect of a given weight of bombs on Germany. But now the emphasis was on the destruction of housing rather than of people or factories. Data on the house area destroyed in the Midland industrial cities of England in 1940-41 for a given weight of bombs dropped was used to calculate the fraction of German housing which could be destroyed in the next eighteen months, that is, by the autumn of 1943. The claims were high—something, I think, of the order of 50 per cent. of all working-class houses (middle-class housing is usually too diffuse to be a good target) in all towns of over 50,000 population in Germany should be destroyed if the United Kingdom concentrated its effort on the production of bombers and on their use for this purpose. The Cabinet Office paper concluded that this strategy was the best one available to give the maximum help to the sorely tried Russian armies.

This paper came to the Admiralty and was passed on to me for comment. My reply was that the *method* of calculation used was correct in principle, but that the actual numerical answer, that of number of houses which could be destroyed within eighteen months, was six times too high. The main mistake in the calculation was that it was assumed that all bombers which would be delivered from the factories in the next eighteen months would *in the same* period have dropped all their bombs over Germany. It was forgotten that not only does at least six months, if not a year, elapse between the *production* of a bomber and the *completion* of the average 20 bombing missions which it makes during its active life; but also that to absorb into operational squadrons all the planned output of bombers in this period would need an increase of number of operational squadrons by a factor so large as to be quite unattainable owing to limited training facilities, etc. Sir Henry Tizard, to whom the Cabinet Office paper was also sent, came to roughly the same conclusions as I had, that is, that the paper exaggerated the probable effect of the bombing offensive between April 1942 and

October 1943 by a factor of about 5 to 1. Subsequent history showed that we were both wrong. The actual factor of error was 10 to 1. The Air Ministry agreed with the Cabinet Office paper and the policy of making a major contribution to the Allied war effort, until the autumn of 1943, the dehousing by bombing of the German working-class population, with the object of lowering her morale and will to fight, became official British policy.

While this analysis and planning of the bombing offensive was in train the war at sea was going very badly. In the autumn of 1942 the U-boat war on our shipping was exceedingly menacing; the huge toll of shipping losses, up to 800,000 tons a month, unless rapidly checked, might make the invasion of Europe in 1943 or even 1944 impossible through lack of shipping. Since the high efficacy of long-range aircraft in escorting convoys and in patrolling the Bay of Biscay had been proved, and since a very large number of long-range bomber aircraft existed, the obvious course was to divert some of the bombers from bomber operations to anti-submarine operations. To be sure that the diversion would be a net gain to the Allied cause demanded a quantitative estimate of the comparative effectiveness of long-range aircraft when employed in the two alternative roles. Now the techniques of operational analysis were just what was required to furnish such a quantitative comparison: the analysis of the bombing offensive outlined above was clearly highly germane. Operational research memoranda from the Admiralty and from Coastal Command provided much of the ammunition for the stiff inter-departmental engagement during the winter months of 1942-43 and which led eventually to the temporary transfer of some squadrons from Bomber Command to Coastal Command and their rapid and brilliantly successful re-training in a matter of weeks in an anti-U-boat role. Further, a large number of American Liberators (the finest long-range anti-submarine aircraft of the Second World War) were specifically and by special Presidential edict allocated to Coastal Command. The results were startling. By July 1943 the U-boat menace was virtually over and a large part of the decisive victory was due to the air campaign. The U-boats mastered, the necessary shipping was accumulated for the invasion of Europe in 1944. Some further details of the analysis of the air-sea war which led to the increase of air effort are given below in connexion with the analysis of convoy size.

During the heat of the controversy over the proposal to transfer some bombers from Bomber to Coastal Command, a leading airman was goaded by the welter of statistics and calculations produced by the Operational Research Groups to remind scientists " that wars are won by weapons and not by slide rules." But in fact " slide rule strategy " had arrived to stay, and the name, given perhaps originally with some derision, remained to mark a record of appreciable achievement in the application of scientific method to war.

The critical shipping losses during the autumn of 1942, which led to the belated but decisive diversion of more long-range aircraft to Coastal Command, also stimulated a very important development of quite a different kind: this was the adoption by the Admiralty of the policy of sailing large convoys instead of small ones.

Looking back, I think we operational research workers at the Admiralty made a bad mistake in not realising as soon as the group was formed in the spring of 1942 the vital importance of working out a theory of the best size for a convoy. However, it was not until the late autumn that the problem became focused in our minds, largely through discussions that took place at the Prime Minister's fortnightly U-boat meetings. The problem arose as to what was the best division of our limited shipbuilding resources between merchant ships and the anti-U-boat escort vessels. Every merchant vessel completed brought into the United Kingdom additional much needed goods; every escort vessel completed added to the protection of the convoys and so reduced their losses by U-boat attacks and so *saved* more ships and cargoes.

To make a quantitative comparison of the relative advantages of building escort vessels or merchant ships, one needed to know how many merchant vessels would be *saved*, that is not sunk, by each extra escort vessel protecting the convoys.

A detailed statistical analysis was begun of the losses of merchant vessels in convoy during the previous two years, with a view to making numerical estimates of the degree of protection afforded to a convoy by a given number of escort vessels under the conditions of U-boat attack then in progress. The analysis indicated that a convoy with nine escort vessels suffered, on the average, 25 per cent. less losses than one with only six escorts. From this result, taking into account the number of convoys run a year, the average size of the convoys and the number of escort vessels in use, it was possible to calculate that each additional escort vessel put into service could be expected to *save* between two and three merchant ships a year. The practical conclusion was definite. Provided the war was expected to last a year or more, it paid to build more escort vessels at the expense of less merchant ships. This was an important result, but had not a decisive practical importance owing to the practical difficulty of changing the shipyards rapidly over from the building of merchant vessels to the building of escort vessels. As so often occurs also with the predictions of economic theory, the theoretically optimum production programme cannot be realised quickly in practice.

The next points analysed were the effect of the speed of convoys and the effect of air escort either by long-range aircraft from land bases or by carrier-borne aircraft. It was found from Admiralty statistics that a *fast* convoy with a speed of nine knots suffered, on the average, only half the losses of a *slow* convoy of seven knots, provided both had air escort. Further, air escort amounting to eight hours a day decreased the losses of ships by one third. The explanation of these startling gains by speed and air cover lay clearly in the fact that the U-boats could only keep up with a fast convoy by cruising most of the 24 hours on the surface. But when they did this, they were liable to be spotted by aircraft and, even if not successfully attacked, were forced to submerge; their speed was then so low that they could not keep up with the convoy.

Nothing practical could be done quickly to increase the speed of Atlantic convoys, since the ships in them comprised all the available ships, gathered together from all seas of the world, and could not be replaced by faster ships in years. But a great deal could be done and done quickly by increasing the amount of air cover. For by the winter of 1942 the Allied output of long-range aircraft suitable for convoy escort was rising rapidly and but a very small fraction was allocated for this role; the vast majority were designed for and were then allocated to the bombing of Germany. From the figures on the effectiveness of air cover to the Atlantic convoys given above, it could be calculated that a long-range aircraft, such as a Liberator I, operating from Iceland and escorting the convoys in the middle of the Atlantic, *saved* at least half a dozen merchant ships in its service lifetime of some thirty flying sorties. If used for bombing Berlin, the same aircraft in its service life would drop less than 100 tons of bombs and kill not more than a couple of dozen enemy men, women, and children, and destroy a number of houses. No one would dispute that the saving of six merchant vessels and their crews and cargoes was of incomparably more value to the Allied war effort than the killing of some two dozen enemy civilians, the destruction of a number of houses, and a certain very small effect on production.

The difficulty was to get the figures believed. But believed they eventually were—something of the Whitehall battle has already been described—and more long-range aircraft were made available to Coastal Command, with the already mentioned startling results.

Since it was by no means safe to rely on the increase of air support to stop the crippling shipping losses of the autumn of 1942, an energetic search was made for some other measures which could be put into operation quickly. Detailed attention was given, therefore, to the organisational aspects of the Atlantic convoy system. Perhaps some alteration in the organisation of the convoys might conceivably improve the situation.

At that time, under the exigencies of a very critical situation, the organisation of convoys and their escort vessels was inevitably, to a considerable extent, a matter of chance. But certain broad principles to govern their organisation had been laid down by the Admiralty. Generally speaking, large convoys were thought to be relatively dangerous and small convoys relatively safe. A convoy of 40 merchant vessels was considered about the best size and convoys of more than 60 ships were prohibited. As regards the required number of escort vessels for a convoy of given size, a rough and ready guide was provided by the long-standing $3 + N/10$ rule. This laid down a minimum of 3 escort vessels for a very small convoy, and one additional escort vessel for every 10 ships in the convoy. Thus a convoy of 20 ships ($N = 20$) would have 5 escorts and a convoy of 60 ships have 9 escorts. The implication of this rule, whose origin was never traced, was that this number of escort vessels would make convoys of different size equally safe, that is, that the same average percentage losses would be expected.

However, the Admiralty $3 + N/10$ rule could be shown to be not consistent with the view that small convoys were safer than large. For consider the alternative of running (a) three convoys of 20 ships, each with five escorts given by the rule, and (b) one convoy of 60 ships with all the available 15 escorts. Clearly the large convoy, according to the rule, would be much safer. For the rule for a 60-ship convoy gave only nine escorts as necessary for equal safety with the small convoys, whereas 15 would be available by pooling the three separate escort groups of five each.

When the actual records of ships lost in convoys of different size were looked into, it was found surprisingly that in the previous two years large convoys had suffered much smaller relative losses than small convoys. The figures were startling. Dividing convoys into those smaller and larger than 40 ships, it was found that the smaller convoys, with an average size of 32 ships, had suffered an average loss of 2·5 per cent., whereas the large convoys with an average size of 54 ships had suffered only a loss of 1·1 per cent. Thus large convoys appeared to be in fact over twice as safe as small convoys.

Though the statistics seemed quite reliable, the scientists in D.N.O.R. felt it necessary to make as sure as was humanly possible that large convoys were in fact safer than small ones before attempting to convince the Admiralty that their long-founded preference for small convoys was mistaken. After all, statistics can be in error—particularly through chance fluctuations of the relatively small numbers involved in such calculations. Perhaps the lower losses of the large convoys in the previous two years had been due to chance. We felt that if we could find a rational explanation of why large convoys should be safer than small ones, it would strengthen the case for a change of policy. So an intensive study of all available facts about the U-boat campaign against the convoys was undertaken. Of great use were the accounts of prisoners of war from sunken U-boats of the detailed tactics pursued by the U-boats in their " wolf-pack " attacks on the convoys. After several weeks of intensive research, analysis, and discussion, the following facts emerged. The chance that a given merchant ship would be sunk in any voyage depended on three factors: (a) the chance that the convoy in which it sailed would be sighted; (b) the chance that, having sighted the convoy, a U-boat would penetrate the screen of escort vessels around it; and (c) the chance that, when a U-boat had penetrated the screen the merchant ship would be sunk. It was found: (a) that the chance of a convoy being sighted was nearly the same for large and small convoys; (b) that the chance that a U-boat would penetrate the screen depended only on the linear density of escorts, that is, on the number of escort vessels for each mile of perimeter to be defended; and (c) that when a U-boat did penetrate the screen, the number of merchant ships sunk was the same for both large and small convoys—simply because there were always more than enough targets. These facts taken together indicated that one would expect the same *absolute number* of ships to be sunk whatever the size of convoy, given the same linear escort strength, and thus the *percentage* of ships sunk to be inversely proportional to the size of the convoys. Hence the objective should be to reduce the number of convoys sighted by reducing the number of convoys run, the size of the convoys being increased so as to sail the same total number of ships.

This analysis convinced us that the Admiralty orders about the size of convoys should be altered. After some weeks of earnest argument the alterations to this order were made in the spring of 1943 and the average size of the Atlantic convoys gradually grew.

No detailed claims of results achieved could be made as so many other factors were changing in the Atlantic battle at the same time; in particular, the air effort was stepped up greatly. Since the battle was virtually won by the summer of 1943 the advantage of the change to large convoys could not be directly tested. But the policy of running large convoys with the resulting economy in escort vessels played an important part in facilitating the transfer of numbers of anti-submarine escort vessels from the Atlantic to support the invasion of Normandy in June 1944. Without the theory of the greater safety of large convoys, perhaps the risk of diversion of so many escort vessels would not have been taken. During the summer of 1944, the Admiralty gave publicity to the successful arrival of a convoy of 187 ships!

It was most unfortunate that we did not appreciate the advantage of large convoys much earlier. It is quite easy to calculate that had the policy of large convoys been adopted, say, in the spring of 1942 instead of the spring of 1943, the loss of merchant ship tonnage during this period would have been reduced by at least 20 per cent., that is, from the actual loss of about five million tons to about four million tons, giving a saving of a million tons of shipping or about two hundred ships in the period of a year. The problem of the optimum size of convoy was, in fact, one of considerable scientific difficulty and could only be tackled by a strong operational research group with access to all the relevant facts.

By the early summer of 1942 the operational research group at the Admiralty (D.N.O.R.) had grown to sufficient strength to tackle this complex problem successfully. However it did not occur to us till later in the year—there were many other problems demanding study—and then the

16

problem forced itself on our notice through the study of the effectiveness of escort vessels. In this case, as in most of the important cases with which I had personal contact, the really vital problems were found by the operational research groups themselves rather than given to them to solve by the Service operational staffs.

Four

Evan James Williams, 1903-45 [1]
1947

In March 1941 Williams joined the writer as a member of
the newly formed Operational Research Section at Coastal
Command. His first work there was concerned with the
methods of attack by Coastal Command aircraft on U-boats.
By collecting and analysing the statistics of past air attacks
on U-boats, Williams deduced that a complete change of
the tactics of attack was required. At that time the depth
setting of the depth charges dropped by the aircraft had
been chosen to be most effective against U-boats at a depth
of some 100 feet. Williams showed the arguments used to
justify such a setting, though very plausible, were in fact
false, and that much better results should be attained by
concentrating attention on those occasions when the U-boat
was still visible and ignoring those cases when the U-boat
had submerged for more than a few seconds at the moment
of attack. He deduced that a quite shallow setting for the
depth charge should lead to an increase by a factor of about
three in the number of kills. These changes as they took
effect revolutionised the attacking power of Coastal Command aircraft and constituted a decisive element in the
growing effectiveness of the air warfare against U-boats. So
striking was the effect on the U-boats that some prisoners
of war from among the captured U-boat crews were convinced that the increase in the lethality of the attacks was
due to the use by us of a new and much more powerful
explosive.

This work of Williams constitutes perhaps one of the most
striking major achievements of the methods of operational

[1] Extract from *Obituary Notices of Fellows of the Royal Society*, VOL. V,
Mar. 1947.

analysis. This method is simply that of the scientific study of
the actual operations of war, using all the statistical material
that can be collected combined with a detailed knowledge of
the physical properties of the weapons used and of the actual
tactical situation. Such work can only be achieved by the
closest collaboration between scientists of great analytical
ability and the Service operational staffs.

Many other problems of a similar type were analysed by
Williams during his time at Coastal Command. An important contribution was an analysis with W. R. Merton and
E. C. Baughan of the errors of the low-level bombing of
U-boats. By study both of practice trials and of photographs
taken by the operational aircraft during the actual attacks
on enemy submarines, it proved possible to both improve
and simplify the instuctions to the crews and so eventually
to achieve a marked increase in the lethality of the attacks.

Of rather a different character was the study initiated by
Williams in the spring of 1942 of the controlling factors
limiting the amount of flying by Coastal Command aircraft.
Ably and energetically pursued by C. E. Gordon, this led
to the conception of Planned Flying and Maintenance, which
was designed to achieve the maximum possible use of existing
resources in men and aircraft. These ideas were put into
practice gradually throughout Coastal Command and led to
something near a doubling of the flying hours a month from
a given number of aircraft and personnel. These methods
for the organisation of planned flying and maintenance,
worked out by Gordon, were eventually adopted throughout
the R.A.F. and the Naval Air Division. This work, which
bore a character resembling some types of efficiency study in
industry, was of very great importance in making available
increased flying resources during the critical period of 1943
when Coastal aircraft contributed so much to the final defeat
of the U-boat campaign.

In December 1941, when the writer moved to the Admiralty, Williams became Director of Operational Research at
Coastal Command and continued his studies of the U-boat

campaign, in particular initiating the analysis of the operations in the Bay of Biscay. In January 1943 Williams also transferred to the Admiralty where he became scientific adviser to the Assistant Chief of the Naval Staff dealing with the U-boat war. In 1944 he became Assistant Director of Naval Operational Research.

Of special importance for the war effort and of special interest in showing Williams's powers to the full was his work in connexion with what came to be called the Bay Offensive. As early as 1941 Williams, in collaboration with the writer, had started the quantitative analysis of the strategic value of different anti-submarine operations by aircraft, such as escort duty on convoys, general sweeps over the Atlantic, and patrolling the Bay of Biscay through which the German U-boats had to pass on passage from their operational bases on the Biscay coast to their operational areas in the Atlantic, etc. These Bay patrols, although not then in great force, had already by December 1941 interfered appreciably with the U-boats, forcing them to submerge by day to avoid attack by aircraft. Williams saw at once the possibility of making this air offensive against the Bay transit area one of the decisive operations of the sea war. During the winter of 1942-43 he worked out in great detail the best methods of conducting such an offensive by a balanced force of day and night aircraft equipped with the latest forms of 10 cm. radar. It was largely due to Williams's keen analysis and powerful advocacy that the requisite aircraft and equipment were made available to Coastal Command to mount a heavy and concentrated Bay offensive. By February 1943 the campaign was well under way and the results in terms of U-boats sunk for a given flying effort were in striking agreement with Williams's predictions, and represented an increasingly decisive victory over the U-boats. By June 1943 the U-boat menace was mastered; the Bay offensive had played a large part in this victory.

These decisive successes put operational analysis " on the map "; the operations of Coastal Command, now under Air

Marshal Slessor, became increasingly statistically and scientifically controlled; statistics on U-boat densities, sighting probabilities, rates of search, lethality of attacks, flying hours per aircraft per month, became the standard agenda for the periodical joint Admiralty and Coastal Anti-submarine meetings and of the regular fortnightly meetings of the Cabinet Anti-U-boat Committee at 10 Downing Street under the chairmanship of the Prime Minister, at some of which Williams was present. Probably the anti-submarine campaign in 1943 was waged under closer scientific control than any other campaign in the history of the British Armed Forces, though it may have been equalled later by the scientific control of the later stages of the bombing offensive conducted by SHAEF against enemy communications in Europe in 1944.

It took some four years of war and hard work for operational research scientists to educate themselves to the point at which their judgment on major military matters constituted a valuable adjunct to the more traditional and intuitive methods of the professional serving officers. Many of the latter were quick to respond both in encouraging the analytical approach and in taking executive action on the conclusions. The era of " slide rule strategy " had arrived. This phrase, coined no doubt in a half-mocking sense by one of the ablest (and most sympathetic to the scientist) of our Service chiefs, well represented what had been achieved. E. J. Williams was certainly one of the foremost of the creators of " slide rule strategy." It is interesting to note that during the last months of his long and painful illness, when Williams began to work again at his favourite subject of the quantum theory of atomic collision, he confessed that he still found the subtle intricacies of the U-boat war of comparable intellectual interest. And those who have had the occasion to study some of his papers, particularly those on the Bay offensive, would probably agree with him. The intense attraction of the investigation into the nature of the physical world is derived partly from the delight in the actual technique of investigation and partly from the sense of the universality of any results achieved. The analysis of warfare lacks the attraction of universality but possesses instead a sense of intensity due to the possible immediate practical effect of any conclusions. With shipping losses at 800,000 tons in a month, the study of the U-boat war was an exciting study.

Of the short twenty-one years of Williams's research career, five were devoted to the study of warfare.

Appendix

I. *Change in Soviet total military manpower since the Civil War*

In his speech to the Supreme Soviet on 14-15 January 1960, Mr Khrushchev gave the following figures for the total manpower in the Soviet Armed Forces.

1927	586,000
1937	1,433,000
1941	4,207,000
May 1945	11,365,000
1948	2,874,000
1955	5,763,000
Jan. 1960	3,623,000
(1962	2,430,000 planned)

Mr Khrushchev explained the rise from 1927 to 1937 as due to Japanese action in the Far East and to the rise of Hitler. The rise from 1937 to 1941 was attributed to the danger of attack on the U.S.S.R. by Germany. The rise from 1948 to 1955 was attributed to America's atomic weapons and to the formation of NATO.

No independent check on these figures appears to be available, but, on the other hand, no evidence seems to have appeared in the West to throw doubt on their approximate correctness.

II. *Comparison of Soviet and U.S. total manpower
figures since 1945*

In the figure are shown plotted Mr Khrushchev's figures
for total armed forces in the U.S.S.R. since 1945 together with
the corresponding figures for the U.S.A.

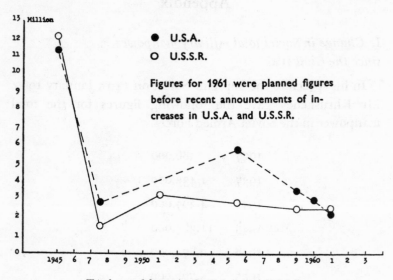

Total armed forces in the U.S.A. and U.S.S.R.

Contrary to what is often believed in the West, the U.S.S.R.
made a very big reduction of the armed forces after the war,
in fact reducing them to 25 per cent. of the 1945 figure,
compared with the U.S. reduction to 13 per cent.

Considering that the U.S.S.R. had long and potentially
hostile frontiers, in Europe, the Middle and the Far East,
whereas the U.S.A. had atomic bombs and no potentially
hostile frontiers bordering on the U.S.A. itself, the 1948 total
Soviet manpower figures of 2·9 millions would hardly seem
excessive from a purely military standpoint, when compared
with the American 1·5 million.